W9-DGS-940

LIGHTS ALONG THE SHORE

BOOKS BY FULTON OURSLER

Lights Along the Shore
The Greatest Faith Ever Known (*With April Oursler Armstrong*)
The Greatest Book Ever Written · The Greatest Story Ever Told
Why I Know There Is a God · The Precious Secret
A Child's Life of Jesus · Modern Parables
Father Flanagan of Boys Town (*With Will Oursler*)
Three Things We Can Believe In · A Sceptic in the Holy Land
Behold This Dreamer · Sandalwood · Stepchild of the Moon
Poor Little Fool · The World's Delight · The Great Jasper
Joshua Todd · The True Story of Bernarr Macfadden
A History of Protestant Missions · The Reader's Digest Murder Case
The House at Fernwood

AS ANTHONY ABBOT:

About the Murder of Geraldine Foster
About the Murder of the Choir Singer
About the Murder of the Circus Queen
About the Murder of the Man Afraid of Women
About the Murder of the Frightened Lady
The Shudders · The Creeps · These Are Strange Tales

WITH ACHMED ABDULLAH:

The Shadow of the Master · Emerald Annie
Paradise Kate · The Flower of the Gods

PLAYS

Sandalwood (*With Owen Davis*)
The Spider (*With Lowell Brentano*)
All the Kings' Men · Behold This Dreamer
The Walking Gentleman (*With Grace Perkins Oursler*)

FULTON OURSLER

Lights Along the Shore

HANOVER HOUSE
GARDEN CITY, NEW YORK

LIBRARY OF CONGRESS CATALOG CARD NUMBER: 54–9848

FIRST EDITION

DEDICATED

TO

LILA AND DEWITT WALLACE

BY

FULTON OURSLER'S FAMILY

The comments on these collected pieces have been added by those who were close to Fulton Oursler during their preparation.

CONTENTS

ACKNOWLEDGMENTS

Grateful acknowledgment to the following organizations is herewith recorded for swift and generous permission to republish many of the articles and stories in this volume:

THE READER'S DIGEST ASSOCIATION, INC.

A DEPENDABLE TRAIT OF HUMAN NATURE
ENGLAND IN SUN AND SHADOW
THE UNEXPECTED VOICE
A FORMULA FOR PRESENCE OF MIND
THE LOST 15 MINUTES
WHY THE SUN STOOD STILL
YOU FIND UNDERSTANDING AT THE TOP
WHAT MAKES A JUVENILE DELINQUENT?
THE MOST UNFORGETTABLE CHARACTER I'VE MET
THE SHADOW OF A DOUBT
THE ONE WAY OUT
A STRING OF BLUE BEADS
THE STAR IN THE DESERT
THE WOMAN WHO CHANGED HER MIND
THERE IS MAGIC IN A WORD OF PRAISE
THE HARDEST LESSON
SOMEBODY IN THE CORNER

COWLES MAGAZINES, INC. (*LOOK MAGAZINE*)

IN EVERY LIFE—THE RESURRECTION
THE REAL MEANING OF EASTER

HEARST PUBLISHING COMPANY, INC. (THE AMERICAN WEEKLY)

THE STAR IN THE DESERT

THE GREATEST MOTHER OF ALL

THE HEARST CORPORATION (COSMOPOLITAN MAGAZINE)

DO WE NEED THE TEN COMMANDMENTS TODAY?

THE HARDEST LESSON

THE BOOK WITH ALL THE ANSWERS

ATLANTIC MONTHLY COMPANY

SWINGTIME AND CHERRY BLOSSOMS

THE ROTARY INTERNATIONAL (THE ROTARIAN)

SPEAKER OF THE EVENING (ON THE PLATFORM, ANYTHING CAN HAPPEN)

UNITED NEWSPAPERS MAGAZINES CORP. (THIS WEEK)

THE SONG YOU CAN'T FORGET

HELP, INC.

THIS I BELIEVE

GUIDEPOSTS ASSOCIATES, INC.

SOMEBODY IN THE CORNER

ESQUIRE, INC. (CORONET MAGAZINE)

ONE HEAVEN OF A FELLOW!

MACFADDEN PUBLICATIONS, INC. (TRUE DETECTIVE MAGAZINE)

THE SHADOW OF A DOUBT

POPULAR PUBLICATIONS, INC. (ARGOSY MAGAZINE)

THE LOST 15 MINUTES (Published under title: WHEN MURDER HAD A THIRD WITNESS

A special word of thanks must be added to those who gave personal permissions with such joyous concurrence with the idea of this compilation as to have a tone of almost tender co-operation.

Rev. Dr. Charles H. Heimsath
for–THE UNEXPECTED VOICE

Mr. and Mrs. Sheldon Glueck
for–WHAT MAKES A JUVENILE DELINQUENT?

Mr. Gardner Cowles
for–THE REAL MEANING OF EASTER

Rev. Dr. Harry Emerson Fosdick
for–ONE HEAVEN OF A FELLOW!

Rev. Dr. John Sutherland Bonnell
for–SOMEBODY IN THE CORNER

Dr. Immanuel Velikovsky
for–WHY THE SUN STOOD STILL

Mr. Edward R. Murrow
for–THIS I BELIEVE

Brightly beams our Father's mercy
From His lighthouse evermore
But to us He gives the keeping
Of the lights along the shore.

—"Let The Lower Lights Be Burning"
by Philip Paul Bliss

A STRING OF BLUE BEADS

NEW YORK, 1951

NO one concerned with this matter likes to talk about it. They are all embarrassed. That is why I have changed the names, and altered the locality. But nothing can disguise the fact that Pete Wakefield was the most friendless man in town, on the day Barbara May opened his door.

Pete's shop had come down to him from his grandfather. The little front window was strewn with a disarray of old-fashioned things: bracelets and lockets worn in days before the Civil War; gold rings and silver boxes, images of jade and ivory, and porcelain figurines.

On this winter's afternoon a child was standing there, her forehead against the glass, earnest and enormous eyes studying each discarded treasure, as if she were looking for something quite special. Now and then she stamped her feet, for the day was bitter cold. Finally, she straightened up with a satisfied air and entered the store.

The shadowy interior of Pete Wakefield's establishment was even more cluttered than his show window.

Shelves were stacked with jewel caskets, dueling pistols, clocks and lamps, and the floor was heaped with andirons and mandolins and things hard to find a name for.

Behind the counter stood Pete himself, a man not more than 30 but with hair already turning gray. His eyelids were lowered and there was a bleak air about him as he looked at the small customer who flattened her ungloved hands on the counter.

"Mister," she began, "would you please let me look at that string of blue beads in the window?"

Pete Wakefield parted the draperies with his left hand —the right hung, helpless from a Normandy fusillade —and lifted out a necklace. The turquoise stones gleamed brightly against the pallor of his palm, as he spread the ornament before her.

"They're just perfect," said the child, entirely to herself. "Will you wrap them up pretty for me, please?"

Pete Wakefield studied her with a stony air.

"Are you buying these for someone?"

"They're for my big sister. She takes care of me. You see, we haven't Mother any more. I've been looking for the most wonderful Christmas present for Sis—and this sure is it, mister."

"How much money do you have?" asked Pete warily.

She had been busily untying the knots in a handkerchief and now she poured out eleven pennies on the counter.

"I emptied my bank," she explained simply.

Pete Wakefield's good hand drew back the necklace. The price tag was clearly visible to him but not to her. How could he explain the difficulty? The trusting look of her blue eyes smote him like the pain of an old wound.

"Just a minute," he said and turned his back. Over his

shoulder he called: "What's your name?" He was very busy about something.

"Barbara May."

When Pete faced Barbara May again, a package lay in his hand, wrapped in bright scarlet paper and tied with a bow of green ribbon.

"There you are," he said shortly. "Don't lose it on the way home."

"Don't worry about that!"

And she smiled over her shoulder as she ran out the door. Through the window he watched her go, while desolation flooded his thoughts. Something about Barbara May and her string of beads had stirred him to the depths of a grief that would not stay buried. The child's hair was wheat yellow, her eyes sea-blue, and once upon a time, not so many years before, Pete had been in love with a girl with hair of that same yellow and with large eyes just as blue.

They had chosen a little house on the eastern edge of town, and named the wedding day. But there had come a rainy night, and a truck skidding on a slippery road, and the life was crushed out of his dream.

Ever since then, Pete Wakefield had lived in solitude. He was politely attentive to customers, but after business hours he preferred his own silent society. Noontimes, in the back of the shop, he ate lunch out of a boarding-house bundle; evenings he dined by himself in a restaurant. Until late at night he sat up in his furnished room, reading tales of Dumas and other romances of a world utterly different from the empty one he knew. He was trying to forget in a haze that deepened day by day.

But the blue gaze of Barbara May had jolted him back to reality, to living remembrance of what he had lost. The pain of it made him recoil from the casual exuberance of holiday shoppers. Trade was brisk during the next ten days; chattering women swarming unto him, fingering trinkets, trying to bargain. When the last customer had gone on Christmas Eve, he sighed with relief. It was over for another year. But for Pete Wakefield, the night was not quite over.

The door opened and a young woman hurried in. With an inexplicable start, he realized that she looked familiar to him, yet he could not remember when or where he had seen her before. Her hair was golden yellow and her large eyes were blue. Without speaking, she drew from her purse a package loosely unwrapped in its red paper, a bow of green ribbon with it. Presently the string of blue beads lay gleaming again before him.

"Did this come from your shop?" she asked.

Pete Wakefield raised his eyes to hers and answered softly:

"Yes, it did."

"Are the stones real?"

"Yes. Not the finest quality—but real."

"Can you remember who it was you sold them to?"

"Of course. To your little sister, Barbara May. She bought them for your Christmas present."

"How much are they worth?"

"The price," he told her solemnly, "was $37."

"But Barbara May has never had $37! How could she pay for them?"

With amazing skill for a man who had only one hand to use, Pete Wakefield was folding the gay paper back into its creases, rewrapping the little package just as neatly as before.

"She paid the biggest price anyone can ever pay," he said. "She gave all she had."

There was a silence then that filled the little curio shop. In some faraway steeple, a bell began to ring. The sound of the distant chiming, the little package lying on the counter, the question in the eyes of the girl and the strange feeling of renewal struggling unreasonably in the heart of the man, all had come to be because of the love of a child.

"But why did you do it?"

He held out the gift in his hand.

"It's already Christmas morning," he said. "And it's my misfortune that I have no one to give anything to. Now all of a sudden I'm unbearably lonely. Would you let me see you home and let me wish you a Merry Christmas at your door?"

And so, to the sound of many bells and in the midst of many happy people, Pete Wakefield and a girl whose name he had yet to learn, walked out into the beginning of the great day that brings hope into the world for us all.

Of all Fulton Oursler's shorter pieces, requests for reprint of this are the most numerous, from all over the globe: they still roll in some 5–6 times a year.

THE ONE WAY OUT

CAPE COD, 1951

MY friend Hamblin was a jumpy fellow, moody and easily discouraged. Generally you can size up a man by the kind of thing that bothers him, but everything bothered Hamblin, from dread of possible bombings to the fear that a scratch on his little finger would bring on lock-jaw.

"Courage can be acquired," the Greeks declared, "as a child learns to speak." But not Hamblin, I would have sworn—until one day when I met him accidentally in the street.

Hamblin had become a different man.

What experience, I asked myself, had brought a sparkle to his eyes, and how had he acquired his easy air of confidence? It was as if he had found a medicine for anxiety.

Part of the mystery he explained to me himself, and the rest of it came from the man that Hamblin once had feared more than any other.

For years Hamblin had worked in a leather-goods

factory as secretary to the chief partner, a mild-faced epicure with ulcers who considered himself a student of human nature. The employees called him "Mr. Leo." One busy midsummer day when Mr. Leo was out of the office, Hamblin took a message from the buyer of a large department store.

"Ask your boss to call me just as soon as he gets back," the buyer instructed. But no sooner had Hamblin hung up than his telephone rang again. This time it was his wife with perturbing news: their older boy had come down with mumps. To avoid contagion, Hamblin promised his wife he would stay away from the house during the next week, and this upset in his routine drove everything else out of his mind.

During the sultry evenings of that week Hamblin remained in a tiny hotel room, worrying about his ailing boy, about doctor's bills and his hotel bill. Not until the middle of the week did he remember the undelivered message, and then only because the chief partner came striding to his desk flushed with anger.

That buyer had intended to place a trial order, but since Mr. Leo had not called back, he had taken his business to another firm.

"I just want to know one thing," said Mr. Leo. "Did or did you not receive such a call?"

And Hamblin, reeling with panic, fearful that his forgetfulness might cost him his job, swallowed hard and said:

"No, Mr. Leo—I never did."

"Do you suppose that buyer can be lying?" asked Mr. Leo. "Maybe he was told to give us a trial and then cooked up a story just to throw the business to one of his friends. The crook! I'll get to the bottom of this thing—you wait and see!"

There was no sleep for Hamblin that night. Between irksome sheets, he wrestled with that greatest of all inventors, fear. Fear that he would be found out, and discharged—with no other job likely because Mr. Leo would never say a good word for him. As a nearby town clock doled out the hours, Hamblin in mind conjured up an endless parade of phantom disasters—imaginings that, as night wore on, assumed a malignant reality.

Suppose the innocent buyer should learn that Mr. Leo was accusing him of collusion and skulduggery, defaming his veracity, slandering his motives, libeling his ancestry and disparaging his posterity? He might bring a suit for damages. If the case went to court, Hamblin would certainly be called as a witness. What had begun as a defensive fib would then become a crime, if he persisted in it—and if he did not stick to his story, he would be finished.

Yet, what if the buyer kept a tape-recorder on his telephone, as some executives were known to do, embalming all conversations in wax? What if the record were to be played, his own voice resounding in the crowded courtroom—"Yes, sir, I'll surely tell Mr. Leo the minute he returns"—convicting him of perjury?

Now and then almost every man knows a bad night, but to Hamblin this was the worst of all nights in his life. In the black of early morning he sprang out of bed, hastily dressed and tiptoed past the dozing desk clerk and out the front door.

Not even a milk wagon broke the stillness of the deserted streets; it was as if Hamblin walked alone through the world. Presently he was sitting on a park bench amid the dark shapes of bushes and trees, his listless eyes turned upward to the pale, retreating stars. But neither the stars nor the cool breeze on his forehead, nor the green fragrance of the park could ease his heartache. Once he had heard that in silence and meditation a man could find strength and wisdom to meet all his problems. If only he could find strength and wisdom now; his inner yearning was like a prayer.

Already the first gleam of morning was shimmering in the eastern sky, and Hamblin with despondent eyes watched the oncoming glow. Presently, without realizing that he was coming under a spell, he began to lose all sense of time, as the solemn majesty of growing light, the mystery and power of that vast gathering of color and warmth began to steal away the sharpness of his thoughts from their great burden.

How long had it been since he had last watched a sunrise? Years and years! But far back in childhood he often got up long before the rest of the family was awake, and walked barefoot into the new day.

The sky was a sea of fire. As if from some shore across that sea there came to him the memory of his third-grade teacher, Miss Emma Henderson, her old eyes squinting down at the classroom Bible, opened at the Psalms:

"The heavens declare the glory of God
And the firmament showeth His Handiwork."

What would a blind man not give to see this glory and this handiwork! And what a sight for indifferent men with two good eyes to sleep through! If there were but one sunrise in every century, no one would miss it; all beds would be empty while people waited out-of-doors to behold the flaming wonder.

Poor, nearsighted Miss Emma had never supposed that her voice would one day reach to Hamblin across the abyss of years, reminding him of her sturdy faith in right and wrong. The sun was like life itself, she had told the third-graders, in its quick passage across the sky, and its inevitable rising again was like a promise of the resurrection:

"For yesterday is but a dream
And tomorrow is only a vision
But today, well-lived, makes every
Yesterday a Dream of Happiness
And every tomorrow a Vision of Hope."

Now Hamblin felt enthralled by the glory of God and of His handiwork, and by the sudden overmastering of his youth. He had not been born afraid. When he was a boy he had played at being General Custer and Richard the Lion-Hearted; he had even risked his neck climbing a mountain and he had fought a bully and taken a thrashing and fought him again and lost a second time. Nor, as a young man, had he wanted courage; he and Agnes had married on a small salary, sure of the strength of their love.

Could it have been love that turned him into a coward? Was it not fear for his wife and boys that had given him his ridiculous, exaggerated desire to please everybody, goading him to kowtow and truckle and placate and stifle every thought of his own? Fear, born of love, making him ignoble until he hated himself—that was too deep a mystery for Hamblin. He closed his eyes and, in a muddle of agony, asked what on earth a man was expected to do.

The answer came in a very chorus of tongues. Perhaps it was just the recognition of an idea to which he had been blind and deaf too long, but to Hamblin in his distracted mood, it seemed as if the truth were being chirped at him by the awakening sparrows and shouted in the rising hubbub of the streets. All the sounds seemed to be chanting old phrases first heard in the Bible-reading voice of his teacher:

"Fear not . . . perfect love casteth

out fear. . . . The Lord is my shepherd:
I shall not want——"

It had been a long time since he had given any thought to those ancient promises. But now, with a light from immeasurable vistas coloring his ravaged face, Hamblin remembered a simpler and happier time when he had felt differently about everything. Then he had trusted the universe, knowing that he belonged to it, gathering dignity and self-respect and courage from his faith in fair play and wisdom, and dreading to trespass against the rules in which decent men everywhere took pride. Such feelings were not altogether lost to him even now for something deep inside could not stomach his life; he had indigestion of the soul.

"Play the game according to the rules, no matter how it hurts and God will back you up. . . ." That was what Miss Emma had taught. Could it be that having forgotten his faith in God he had also lost faith in himself?

Hamblin lifted his hands from his knees, as if to cast out evil spirits. He heaved himself erect from the bench, and breathed in deeply, as one who sees at last the thing he must do. He started walking toward the river.

There was a look of painful wonder on Mrs. Leo's face under her diadem of bobby-pins, as she stood at the open door of the river-view penthouse. Her husband's secretary looked as if he had had a wild night out.

"I have to see Mr. Leo," said Hamblin.

"Well, come right in, and wait a minute."

There was a whiff of fresh coffee and hot bacon, distant and mocking, as Mrs. Leo beckoned Hamblin into the dining room. At the head of a long table sat Mr. Leo. Never had he looked more stern and forbidding; he stared at his secretary with unbelieving eyes.

"Mr. Leo," began Hamblin, "I did get that telephone call from the buyer. I forgot to tell you about it. Then I was scared and said I hadn't. I'm ashamed and I'm sorry." With a sickening effort, he disgorged the words.

Mr. Leo stared into a tumbler of water as if it were a crystal ball. His face was a grim mask, hiding some inner convulsion; he was using all his powers to master himself. The silence was almost unendurable.

"I felt it in my bones," the chief partner muttered at last, with a shake of his head. "Hamblin, did it ever occur to you to wonder why you've never had a promotion? You knew as much about our business as anybody in our shop. But you never had any guts—that's what was wrong. And nobody can help a guy like that. That was why you told that miserable little lie. I was sure all along about it."

Mr. Leo sighed deeply and stood up. Almost ceremoniously he held out a tight, hard hand.

"But it damn well took guts to come here and do what you just did," he said. "Something great has happened to you, Hamblin—God only knows what—but I never felt so good about anything in all my life. Today is a new start for you and me. Annie, bring some ham and eggs for Mr. Hamblin."

What kind of coward are you? Almost every human has a besetting fear. There is only one admirable coward, the one who fears hurting others. (J. S. who overcame that.)

—FROM FULTON OURSLER'S NOTEBOOKS

A STRANGER GOES UPSTAIRS

NEW YORK, 1952

TRUSTY was born in prison. His bassinet was an old felt hat, stuffed with rags and straw, and he was one of a crop of young birds mothered by a flibbertigibbet female canary. His sister was green and gold, and he had two brothers, grayish blue warblers with a few small black spots on their wings.

But Trusty was a white canary. His master was a prisoner for life in a Western penitentiary and, as a hobby, he was allowed by the warden to raise and breed household birds. This "lifer" took his pets very seriously and practiced line-breeding and in-breeding and, like many fanciers, hoped to turn out some rare specimens of real beauty. Trusty, the white singer, was the prisoner's masterpiece.

There was not a golden pinfeather in all his pure white plumage, although, as bird breeders say, his father "had green blood in his strain." But from the first he was a problem. He showed none of the affection for his keeper that the other birds displayed; he was an individualist, remote and undemonstrative.

"He just don't seem to care a damn for me," the convict remarked. But Trusty was strong-winged, blessed with stamina and speed and his ecstatic warbling voice went straight to the heart; his master loved him in spite of his indifference.

And yet the prisoner gave his white bird away, and that was an act of gratitude and sacrifice. For some years, he had been receiving letters from my friend, Lita, a lady whose correspondence with prisoners is only a part of the good she does every day. Lita had urged the imprisoned man to find beauty in his cell, just as birds sing in their cages. She had encouraged him to read and study and try to make himself useful to his fellow inmates and he was a lot happier for taking her advice. So he decided to give her his dearest treasure and one day, nicely protected in a traveling cage, Trusty was delivered to Lita's home.

At first sight, she fell in love with the beautiful white bird. She thought him the loveliest of all creatures, bought him a large and handsome white cage, and proudly showed him off to her friends. But, as the days passed into weeks and months, Lita began to feel sad about Trusty. The little white bird would not make friends with her, and he would not sing.

She had other birds in other cages and they were intimate and sociable, eating from her fingers and singing on her shoulder. But never Trusty. Not a chirp, not a turn of the pert little head in her direction. When she stood nearby, he would hop to the farthest corner. Only when she was away would he go to his feeding box, or flutter his whiteness in the tiny bath.

Every day she would open the cage and let him out

and he would fly silently from table to chair, to the top of the open door, and on into the next room. He never ventured farther than that second room, and after a while, without coaxing, he would return to the cage.

But the day came when Lita had to leave the care of her birds to the family help. Late one night, when she was driving home, there was a collision. Lita was painfully hurt and for a while she was in the hospital. When they brought her home she was told she must remain upstairs in her bedroom for many weeks. Now she was a prisoner, very much in need herself of encouragement.

What was her surprise one sad morning to hear outside the bedroom door the flutter of little wings, and then into her room the white canary came flying. He had found his way, beyond the frontier of the second room, out into the hallway, up the curving stairs, and down a maze of corridors to the place where Lita was. Around the bedroom he darted in long, swift forays, uttering chirps, and then, finally perching on the rail of her bed, he burst into song. At the sweetness of his joyous notes, her sadness passed away and her heart, too, began to sing.

In this fragile incident my friend reads a fragment of wisdom. We never know when we have reached the heart of another, whether it be the heart of man or woman, or only a bird in a cage. We have only to keep on loving—"let me not ask so much to be loved as to love," the good St. Francis said. He was a friend of birds himself, and perhaps they had taught him some of their wisdom.

THE STAR IN THE DESERT

NEW YORK, 1951

HIS windows look out on a snowy range of Nevada mountains and the sky-blue water of Pyramid Lake. Midway in the purple sage two Piper Cubs make ready to fly above herds of galloping wild horses and corral them for dog meat. Nearer is a jumble of little houses with Indian women trudging by, carrying wood and water.

He lives in the midst of a wilderness, yet the tenant of the house in which I wait must be a man of taste and wisdom. For all around his living room are relics of a golden age of enlightenment. Within reach, on an old-fashioned round dining table, reposes a fourth folio of Shakespeare's plays. Nearby is a priceless first edition of the King James Bible, and a scattering of hand-colored leaves from twelfth-century missals; a silver chalice and a Middle Ages cross—treasures to glitter the eye of any collector.

But my gaze is drawn away to a picture lying on the bed: an old photograph of a young man. His head is thrown back in a self-conscious pose; his poet's eyes are on the stars. The youth of long ago is now the man who lives in this mysterious room; once a favorite of Broadway and Hollywood, with a prince's income and a name in lights.

Suddenly I hear sounds and alarums off stage.

"My faith looks up to Thee" resounds through the tiny house in confident baritone, and still singing he appears in the doorway. Between the arrogant young dreamer whose picture is still in my hand and this priestlike man with the long silver hair, there must lie some earthquake of the soul. The missioner wears a blue worsted cap with waggish tassel, and a haggard pea jacket, held together with safety pins; his black cassock flaps about clumsy army shoes. He is the Protestant Episcopal missioner to the Indians of the Nixon Reservation; the former actor, Gareth Hughes, now called Brother David.

Can this servant of the Lord be he who was the friend of Sir James Barrie, picked by him to play the title part in *Sentimental Tommy?* The same impetuous fellow whom Ibañez chose for *Enemies of Women?* Companion of Isadora Duncan and Anatole France; Nazimova's stage lover and Valentino's foil?

"Two things I want to know," I told him. "What changed your life? And what can you do that the government doesn't do for the people in this Godforsaken place?"

Over coffee and toast, he reminded me:

"Man does not live by bread alone. These depressed Americans need a teacher for their hearts; they must come to believe in their own capacities; to look upward and take courage; bringing hope to the hopeless is the greatest adventure of the soul."

A strain of Celtic mysticism has always dominated this Welshman. He was born in Llabalby, son of a pious steel worker and amateur elocutionist who, in an oratorical tournament, won the Silver Cross of Wales. At 13, Gareth

Hughes was allowed to travel alone to London, and join a provincial band of Shakespearean players.

"Dear God, make me a good actor," the boy entreated on his knees the night before his first opening. For the next 30 years, the theater was the holy of holies to Gareth Hughes; acting his only form of worship. He could manage almost any role; once, when a provincial leading lady fell ill, he played Desdemona, and well deceived the audience.

When he came to New York in a play that failed, he remained to become an American citizen and a favorite of critics as well as the public. The famous Mrs. Fiske told Alexander Woollcott that she could believe acting was an immortal art when watching "the glow of a performance by Gareth Hughes." And David Belasco called one of his portrayals "among the most magnificent that I have ever seen on the English-speaking stage."

In Hollywood, more triumphs awaited. Vine Street and Broadway remember Gareth Hughes in those days as "the charm boy to end all charm boys"; a petted darling of a precious set, living in a rarefied atmosphere, far from the hopes and fears of obscure people.

"Yet with star billing and $2000 a week, I was not satisfied," he says, "and I didn't guess why."

In the depression, his margins were wiped out; his home sold, savings lost. He kept on working and playing, but as time passed, the vague unease in his mind began to deepen. He prayed for help, feeling a desperate need, but no help came. At last, he admitted to himself that he had never really known one minute's happiness. He had won the prizes of life, in an atmosphere of pleasure and selfishness, but nothing had ever satisfied him. What was the use of more acclaim, larger salary, greater crowds and brighter lights, when always there remained an unreachable craving for some mystery, some happy secret that others seemed to possess and that eluded him; a hidden source of strength in friends like Maeterlinck and Rupert Brooke; a treasure they had found in the field of life, finer than anything he knew?

That night, dismayed by the remembrance of the faith of his father, he said to himself: "Why should I go on asking God to help me? My father knew a better way." And falling on his knees, he burst out: "Dear God, is there anything I can do to help You?"

In his mind, he seemed to hear a voice like that which spoke to Samuel, and the message was "Why don't you give yourself to Me?"

All the goods that he had left he sold and gave to the poor. And on the altar of humility, he performed an actor's greatest sacrifice; he burned his press notices.

Within a few weeks, the doors closed behind him in a Massachusetts monastery. Shutting out the world, he became a postulant, or novice, in the Protestant Episcopal Society of St. John the Evangelist, an order of men who spend much time in meditation and prayer. Gareth Hughes' year in the Mother House on the River Charles was full of needed discipline for a headstrong soul.

Wiser for such discipline, the candidate for holy orders realized that he must look elsewhere to find his true place; the actor recognized his own necessity for action, aching to get back into the world and to preach the rebirth possible for the spirit of every man. No doubt Broadway needed such a message, and Hollywood, but Brother David wound up instead with Indians.

By chance, one day, he had heard that a missioner was needed on a Nevada reservation; a region of sub-zero winters and oven-baking summers; of poverty and loneliness. That first post was in St. Anne's Chapel at Fort McDermitt, on the remote Oregon Border, with 350 Paiutes and almost no conveniences of civilization; not even an outhouse. Through an apprentice year of violent extremes of weather, Brother David experienced a new satisfaction, a growing joy of discovery—he was beginning to feel kin to all people, at home with any man.

What difference was there between these tribal folk and the Welsh families of his childhood; the people of London, New York or Hollywood? No basic difference anywhere, except that the Indians complained less, no matter how bitter their woes. All knew birth and hunger, sleep and love and death.

There were high I.Q.'s in this Indian parish; the tensions of civilization had not distorted the simple thought ways of the people. And the passions of all living tormented them. They grew jealous and hated and sought to get even; they were ridden by fears and desires; they gossiped like Mayfair and Park Avenue, mixing truth and fairy tale, and making mischief.

And they were well aware of the world's contempt; with inexorable logic they forswore hope or aspiration; they felt certain they could never amount to anything, firmly skeptical when the missioner told them no one except themselves could ever deprive them of self-respect. But their somber eyes brightened when he recounted, not only the gospels, but also Aesop's tales of the Dog and the Shadow, the Wolf and the Lamb—animals they knew and could follow straight to the point of the fable. And Brother David prayed:

"Oh, Lord, help me to help these children of yours; You made them; You must love them. Let me teach them it is worth-while for them to be in earnest; let me encourage them to hope for the time when they can take a grown-up place in the world."

He learned their history and legend and folklore and encouraged their arts and crafts, especially their beadwork; they were his students and he a dean to counsel them. His first job was to make them trust him; they must believe in a white man if they were to believe in the white man's God. Better to die than break a promise made to the least of them; better to share their labors and never talk down to them:

"You know a man who believes in devils? All right—where do devils make their homes? In human hearts—and only love can drive them out."

Two Indian half brothers were killed while he was there—Francis Shawe, infantryman, who fell at Salerno, and Art James, a tail gunner shot down in the South Pacific.

"Let us be glad!" he tells the grieving relatives. "We have heroes now, who died to make others free."

"Can Indians be heroes? They die for free people who despise them."

Brother David hugs the objector to his heart. He argues, tells them of rich men and women who pay large fees just to prove that they belong to old American families.

"But you are the oldest of old families. You are the original aristocrats. And you must live up to your part. Show yourselves to be model citizens—no matter whether you can vote or not. More than anything else, the white people need models of good citizenship."

Two Indian boys ask if it is true that if they love God and keep the Commandments, their skin will turn white like other Americans. Brother David opens a pocketknife and plunges the point into his palm until the blood spurts.

He drips the blood on tissue paper; then he stabs the right hand of each boy, so that the blood of all three is mingled in one scarlet stain.

"No difference!" he cries. "Our blood is the same. We all have the same Father in heaven. Treat every man like your brother, every woman like your sister."

The Paiute Indians approve that beautiful doctrine. They are waiting for American citizens to treat them like brothers and sisters. And they are aware that they must wait a while yet; they teach patience to their teacher. The new happiness of Brother David that first winter came as much from learning as from teaching. He tells them so:

"Far away in the east by the ocean the people are very proud of their works of charity. They build big houses just for orphan boys and girls. But you have no need for such houses. If an Indian child has no home, the people next door open their arms. 'Come in,' you say. 'Come right in.' This is just the way Christ wants everybody to act."

Soon the Bishop of Nevada added to Brother David's charge the Chapels of St. Mary at Nixon, and others at Wadleigh, and Fernley—hamlets more than 200 miles from Fort McDermitt. For years he commuted, traveling, when necessary, 500 miles a day. Now, he has given up Fort McDermitt. Proudly, he showed me his gospel jeep.

"Marion Davies, my long-time friend, gave it to me," he explains, not quite literally. What the former screen beauty gave Brother David was a shiny new sedan. But it was not roomy enough for use as bridal coach or hearse, or for taking two dozen boys and girls on a ride to the state capital at Carson City. So the stylish equipage was traded in for a secondhand station wagon, and by now its mileage is astronomical.

Old playfellows of stage and screen send clothes and

candy to Brother David; there is a room in his "God man house" as the children call it, where warming clothes are piled high, with a seasoning of Schiaparelli ballroom gowns, John Fredericks hats, and English riding breeches. A good use is found for everything.

At five A.M., when Brother David awakens, he repeats six words he has taught to all the Paiute children. Ask any of them what they say on waking, and they will answer: "Good morning, God, and thank You."

If it is Monday, Wednesday, or Friday, Brother David joins the entire population at Crosby's Trading Post to wait for the mail bus. Letters from soldiers in Korea he reads to illiterate mothers and wives. The rest of his day is spent in visiting schools and homes in his three towns. As rewards for study, he gives the children autographed pictures of friendly stars. He encourages the youngsters to write him about their daily lives; a typical letter from a nine-year-old reads:

"My father is a council member. He goes hunting for deer and he hunts rabbits and also hunts ducks and geese. Also he goes fishing for trout. The council talks about the cattle. Also they talk about the lake, they also talk about the new policeman. They have a round-up every spring and summer and after that they have a cattle sale. Most of our Indian men raise cattle to sell. . . . Your friend, Ruth Tobey."

He talks over family problems in an astonishing blend of modern English, Paiute, Shakespeare and the Gospels. Down the road totters T-Bone Liz, 93 years old, but carrying a sack of pine nuts, which she will grind into flour, one stone over another.

"Ah, Elizabeth, my dear," he will say. "You grunt and

sweat under a weary load. But my yoke is easy, my burden light. Let Brother David help. Me catch 'um."

He confers with another Indian lady who carries herself like a tragedy queen. Tales are being spread about her by a woman of the village; lies! Brother David must get her punished.

"Hate lying, not the liar," Brother David pleads. "We all need forgiveness. Let us try what love can do."

Love is a difficult remedy for the daughter of a once warlike tribe. But someone, says Brother David, must teach her; must stay close and prove love to her, until she and all the others are convinced of its miraculous power to solve human problems. So he will help her in some welcome favors to her enemy—why not return good for evil with a gay new hat out of his storeroom? By tomorrow sundown the feud is over.

Why does he give things away? His generosity confounds them. He explains that he trusts a never-failing God. And the awed Paiutes tell, with wry wonderment, a story of his faith. One arctic day Brother David meets old Eva Crutchener carrying an armful of firewood. All she has for a coat is a shawl of worn-out rabbit skins. With the gallantry of Sir Walter Raleigh, the missioner of St. Mary's Chapel rips off his sweater and helps it over her head.

"But now you will die from the cold," she mutters.

"God will keep me warm. You wait and see."

The same day the mail bus brings a package to Brother David from Mother Arnold of Trinity Cathedral in Cleveland. Inside is a wonderful new sweater.

"I just had a strong feeling," Mother Arnold wrote, "you would be needing something to keep you warm." To the Indians—as to Brother David—this was a miracle of grace.

One Saturday afternoon he crams 18 squirming Indian boys into the station wagon, their destination the finest hotel in the state. He seats the lads at a gay luncheon table, then leads forth his guest of honor. The boys whoop with pride. For here, actually shaking hands with them, is a hero to thrill every Reservation boy—William Buffalo Cory Cano; most decorated of all American Indian soldiers, he who holds the world's record of 583 parachute jumps with the United States Army.

Often, in the evening, boys and girls play games on the floor of Brother David's living room. They sing together, and finally they gather at his round table, to learn the stories of King Arthur and his brave knights. This is Brother David's happiest hour; "eventide," he quotes, "that brings all things home."

Early Sunday morning he turns on a record player, and in the crisp out-of-doors, stately hymns of the Protestant Episcopal Church sound forth from a loudspeaker. Gradually, groups of Indians begin to congregate near the oblong wooden chapel and the tall white cross before the open door. Old men sit silently together in the warm sunshine and stare at nothingness. Wives in colorful long dresses and brightly quilted shawls huddle and chatter, while girls of quite surpassing sleekness walk hand in hand, up and down, tossing long black hair, and giggling as they pass the boys, their beaded earrings shaking in their mirth. Wrinkled grandmothers, meanwhile, keep watch on babies crawling too near the older boys, playing handball around the cross.

In black cassock, his unruly crop of silver dressed neatly for the Sabbath, Brother David appears on his screened porch, and small boys rush stomping to grab the steeple ropes and set the bell to ringing. Into the church the councilmen come shuffling, leading braves and squaws and their papooses. Through windowpanes stained with vivid dyes, the morning sun spills red and golden pools of light that are like leaves from old missals spread over the wooden benches.

Girls and mothers sit on the left, males on the right. The air of the narrow church is heavy with a mixture of incense and chewing gum, and the doggy smell of a hound dozing near a crucifix. From the vestry room, Brother David marches in, very ecclesiastical in surplice and black tippet scarf. He lights the candles at the altar, then sits before a cottage organ; his mellow voice leading in the sumptuous rhythms of "Holy, Holy, Holy."

Timidly at first, the congregation joins in, conning proper Episcopalian hymnals racked behind the pews. But soon they will put aside the books and turn to mimeographed sheets of old dissenter tunes; thin voices deepen in rousing revival choruses.

Standing beside a service flag, Brother David names the 15 lads in Korea. Confidential and neighborly, he imports good news from the battlefront. One Nixon Paiute has been made a first-class private; another a corporal, no less! But there is worry, too. Florrie's husband, Danny Wayne, has not written home for six weeks. Overwhelmed with premonition, Florrie in a middle pew sobs aloud; she totters down the aisle and out of the church. Who was it told me Indians were stolid and never showed emotion?

Before this Sunday's nightfall, the bell in Nixon's sole telephone booth is going to ring. The booth is on the road, just outside Crosby's Trading Post. The twilight call will come from the nearest telegraph office; condolences from the Secretary of Defense because Danny Wayne is dead, killed in the service of his country. Brother David will be up all night praying with Florrie.

But at the moment he is ready for pulpit discourse. Undeniably, his sermons are among the most remarkable in the history of homiletics. A born actor, superb alike in pantomime and elocution, he uses all his capacity for vivid expression to make Bible truths clear to his flock.

Perhaps he will tell them the parable of the widow who lost a coin. To prepare, Brother David disappears into the vestry. When he comes back, he is wearing a gingham apron, tied around his middle. In his right hand is a broom; the left holds a lighted candle. But an even greater transformation is upon the man himself; an inner change, which is the actor's art; a conviction that he is not Brother David any longer; he is now a frightened old woman in a dark house.

"Where is my money?" the senile voice laments.

And down the aisle creeps the ex-star of Broadway and Hollywood, poking under the benches, causing small boys to stand aside, peering over window sills and into the baptismal font. When the coin is found, the old crone's joy electrifies everybody.

This is a more absorbed audience than any other Gareth Hughes ever played to. Though all the papooses cry at once, he is not chagrined; his voice tops the infant chorus, for his congregation is hanging spellbound on his story, and the show must go on.

He tells—and acts out—the Good Samaritan. Having made the action vivid, he drives its meaning home:

"John is young and strong. He lives next door to Freddie, who is a blind old man. No one to saw Freddie's wood. And he is nearly 90! No one to fetch his water. And he is too feeble to get it for himself! But John comes to saw Freddie's wood. John goes to fetch Freddie's water. John is a Good Samaritan. And if Freddie has no shoes or underwear, Johnnie tells Brother David. Good people give clothes and shoes to Brother David for people like Freddie. They are Good Samaritans. We all can be Good Samaritans."

The doctrine he teaches is simple and strong. They have disappointments and sorrows? So has everybody else. Our troubles may not be our own fault; but it *is* our fault if sorrow and disappointment do not teach us their lessons. To trust in God, no matter how badly we are off—that is the way to turn our water to wine.

Life will never end for them; he tells them there is no death; we go from one place of living to another; we are living immortally now. If there are prizes in death, they surely will go to those who live life bravely and decently.

A little final prayer, and then this announcement:

"Popsicles and ice cream for everybody right outside."

Such a dramatic and tempestuously energetic candidate for holy orders is bound to be a problem to a Bishop of a Church traditionally discreet and reserved. Fortunately for Brother David, he is under the governance of a wise and discerning superior, a scholar not only of Greek but of human nature, the Right Reverend William F. Lewis, Bishop of Nevada.

From the start, Bishop Lewis must have suspected that in Brother David he was inviting a problem to the Diocese. With such a past the man was bound to seem, and to be, theatrical. But with patience and encouragement, and now and then, a whispered bit of godly counsel, Bishop Lewis is bringing out the best from an actor, who left all that he had, including his press notices, to help out God in a lonely place. The worst anyone seems to find to say about him is that, in theatrical parlance, he is still a "ham."

"I am a ham," smiles Brother David sadly. "I do my own soul more good than I do to the Indians, maybe." My last sight of him is as he stands at the edge of the desert, in the shadow of one of his white crosses, the Sierras ringing him round in a vast snowy circle.

"I am a ham for Christ's sake," he says. "And oh, my God, how happy I am."

The most generous of people, Americans give largely the world over. Often our own needy are woefully forgotten. Old friends who love Brother David have been helpful to him and his American *Indians. But the winters are not easy, the distances great, the old, very young and the sick numerous. Brother David needs many, many things—he had been without a watch, for example, six years!*

THE SONG YOU CAN'T FORGET

NEW YORK, 1943

THE RUNAWAY choir boy wrote the message painfully with the stub of a pencil:

"Dad, please forgive me. Wire me money to come home."

And he signed his full name, Albert Hay Malotte.

"Say," grinned the telegraph clerk, "ain't you the extra special attraction I saw last night at Lubin's Picture Parlor —standing on your head while you played the piano? I hope your old man don't turn you over to the police!"

Two hours later, Albert Malotte was on a train, homeward bound. And it was on that long-ago journey that he began to compose music that now is being sung in concert by notable artists and by the American people with deepening and rich affection—the musical setting of The Lord's Prayer.

Not that Al realized he was beginning its composition, back there in the day coach. But his thoughts had taken an odd turn. Perhaps because he had been a choir boy and had studied music in a Philadelphia church, he found himself repeating in rhythm with the train wheels the words of the prayer.

"Our Father!" Yes, it was wonderful to think of the Boss of the universe like that. A father from whom you might run away, leaving without a word; yet when you turned to him again, he sent you a loving message and money to come home. One who understood and forgave.

Ever since then, the prayer has been, for Malotte, a spiritual tonic. Once he recited it while roped to the loading mast of a liner in the midst of an Atlantic storm. Another time was when he touched gloves with Jack Dempsey, as an amateur light-heavy in a Memphis arena, and a moment later fell a'dreaming on his back. Most fervently of all, perhaps, when he made his first solo flight in an old-fashioned two-seater Boeing. That was in 1921 when he received his flying license.

The prayer was with him through ups and downs. It was not many years ago that he was earning a lean stipend as pipe organist and in his leisure did what seemed an impractical thing: he wrote the music for two ballets. By a streak of good fortune, the choreographs were staged in the Hollywood bowl and the audience yelled for the composer. He sat in the back row, unmoving; because, as he told me, there were big holes in his shoes.

Nevertheless, it was his ballet, *Little Red Riding Hood,* which induced Walt Disney to engage him. Malotte created the music for eighteen *Silly Symphonies,* including *Ferdinand the Bull* and *The Ugly Duckling.* And right after that, Malotte's piece, the "Song of the Open Road" became a national favorite.

Now the wanderer was being told that he was a success; the information made him humble. One day he called his actor friend, Conway Tearle, on the telephone:

"What would you think if I wrote music for The Lord's Prayer?"

Tearle was cautious. But Malotte wanted to do it. "I feel so grateful to God," he said.

In the deeps of the composer's mind the chords and harmonies for the prayer had long ago taken deep root. Now from the roots the melody began to grow. Presently, from his workroom, he called to his mother and father, who had taught him the deathless words.

"Listen, Mom. Listen, Pop!"

And the composer sang for them the prayer which Christ had one day given to the world from a hilltop in Galilee. When he finished, there was a long silence. He looked up. Father and mother were crying. They threw their arms around him and sobbed, but they could not speak.

There was the same silence when, a month or so later, John Charles Thomas sang it for the first time over the radio. The studio audience sat still for a long moment; then, tumult! It is almost invariably like that with audiences. The first time I heard the music was at a luncheon of the New York Dutch Treat Club. The members are writers, painters, musicians; most of them suburbanite, many creak in the joints, but like to consider themselves rakehells and scalawags. John Charles Thomas had sung many pieces, and they were asking for more. He asked for suggestions and some wag called out:

"Sing anything at all. Even The Lord's Prayer."

"All right," said Thomas. "I'll sing The Lord's Prayer."

It was new to those sophisticated ears. As the soaring, impetuous crescendo of the kingdom and the power and the glory forever broke into the great amen, there was a hush—a stillness in which you might have heard a cigar ash crash on a rug. And then, again—tumult!

I have seen many audiences behave like that, but I have also watched one man alone, hearing it for the first time. At the risk of being misunderstood and traduced by my Democratic friends, I shall name him as Thomas E. Dewey. It was a night in Autumn and he was stretched on the floor in front of my Cape Cod fire. I put the record on the phonograph without ballyhoo. As Dewey listened, he kept dark eyes fixed on the sound box as if he could see into it. Four times I played the record and when he went home, he carried the record with him.

But I think my finest memory of this composition goes back to a Spring when I was invited to speak in a Brooklyn synagogue. Before I was introduced, the cantor of the temple, a massive, handsome man, walked to the edge of the platform and suddenly announced:

"I shall sing The Lord's Prayer."

Well, I thought to myself, our Jewish friends must have a prayer of their own which is also called The Lord's Prayer.

But I was mistaken. The moment the accompanist struck the first chords, I knew them. And the mighty voice of the tenor—"Our Father——"

Mentally, I chucked away the speech I had come there to deliver. I was filled up with the sweetness and kindness of that gracious welcome. Through the words and music of the prayer they had shown me how men of varying faiths can love each other.

Of course, there is nothing new about the union of sacred words and noble music. I was astonished to learn that the house of G. Schirmer, Inc., which published the Malotte setting, had previously issued eighteen other versions, not one of which reached popularity. But the custom is ancient. When Jesus and His disciples trudged the dusty roads of Judea and Samaria they sang at the top of their voices. The lyrics were the Psalms of David and the music had been plucked from his lyre by the Shepherd King. They were the popular songs of that day. Now, with the increasing sale of sheet music and phonograph records—even a Hollywood picture included the composition—it would not be surprising if the great prayer reached the Hit Parade some day. But that gaudy incidental will be meaningless; what is more important is that the hearts of the people are touched by it. The other day I heard a Third Avenue bootblack whistling the music. The prayer of the people is becoming the people's song.

Fulton Oursler's voice was better than ordinary, his singing full of emotion. His memory for lyrics in many languages was phenomenal, whether operas, nursery ditties, hymns, barbershop, Victorian ballads or the hit numbers throughout his lifetime. He loved to know the stories behind a song, and ferreted out many of them. It enchanted him that The Lord's Prayer, one of his favorites, was by a Walt Disney composer: he considered Disney a true genius of our time and the kind of man who attracted great souls to him.

In daily life Mr. Oursler sang a great deal, always when he was very sad, or hurt and determined not to be, almost always as he shaved because he hated to shave, and if a small son or daughter were not visiting with him at shaving time, only singing made it bearable. As editor of Musical America and Music Trades (his first job in New York), he knew many of the Metropolitan and con-

cert clique, and a sound old disciplinarian coach had taught him the proper fundamentals of singing.

From him he learned that a resonant speaking voice could be developed by singing or humming as he walked. This he did, first as self-assignment, later as a joy. To him singing was not only a great outlet but the silver of human exchange. He loved nothing more than to have you sing with him for long miles of driving. He felt families and other groups of today were robbed in the passing of "parlor song fests." He was sure unison singing would return: the companionship is too basic and moving a joy: but he sorrowed for the generation it had skipped.

Ruth and Norman Vincent Peale once gave a dinner party to prove a challenge as to whether Fulton or Homer Rodeheaver would first run out of the lyrics to the old hymns stanza by stanza. Talk was so rich that night that by high moon a future date was made to hold the contest, but it was frequently postponed. Dr. Peale vowed each man feared the other's prowess.

THE GIRL WHO WORKED FOR NOTHING

CAPE COD, 1948

There is an old English song which runs:

"What's amiss, I'll strive to end,
and endure what can't be mended."

IN those simple lines there lives a recipe for peace of heart. It is the key to happy adjustment; difficult but potent. One of its best examples is a girl whom I shall call Frances, because that is really her name.

I first met Frances when she asked me for a job. She exhibited three letters from important New York firms, praising her abilities as a secretary in such ecstatic terms that I told her I would give her a two weeks' trial. On the second Friday night, she asked if I intended to keep her permanently. When I told her I was more than satisfied, she burst into tears. Then she told me her story:

Frances was the daughter of an attorney in a city in Iowa. Her father gave her a sound musical education. Before she was 18, Frances made a concert appearance as a violinist; later she organized her own chamber music quartette.

Suddenly her widower father was paralyzed. Without hesitation, Frances gave up her tours to stay at home with him, nurse and comfort him. By the time he died, two years later, the family savings were almost used up; with what was left, Frances took a train for New York. A good violinist, she felt sure, would soon find work on the radio. Only after months did she begin to realize how many thousands of other young musicians had the same idea, and what few chances there were. That was when Frances shut herself up in a hall bedroom and had a heart-to-heart talk with memories of her father:

"You always told me never to dodge facts, Daddy, but to look them straight in the eye."

Well, the facts in her case were clear enough, so, with her remaining $200 Frances put aside her musical ambitions and entered business college. But even when she was graduated near the top of her class, her problem remained unsolved, for she still could not find work.

Then one Sunday an ad appeared in that source of miracles for many puzzled folk, a newspaper classified advertising column:

> *I am an expert secretary and stenographer, but I can't get a job without experience, and I can't get experience without a job. That is why I will work four weeks for you without pay—and then leave you. All I want is to earn a reference. You have no obligation whatever. And remember, I'm good!*

Out of more than 1000 replies, Frances picked three of the best. At the end of the first week in her first job, she was handed an envelope containing $35. They paid her, anyhow, because they were so pleased with her work. After four weeks, they offered her a permanent job but she refused it; she wanted only a letter of recommendation. At the end of three months, she had worked for three reputable firms; she had been paid a full salary every week by every one of her employers, and when, right afterward, she applied to me for a permanent job, she was able to dazzle me with those iridescent testimonials.

There is an odd sequel to her story. Col. Louis McHenry Howe, confidential aide to President Roosevelt, was so much impressed when I told him about it that one day, poking me in the ribs, he asked if I would not sacrifice my comfort for the welfare of the country. So Frances left me for an office in the White House and there she remained until one enchanted evening, across a crowded room, romance struck her like a bolt of lightning.

Then Frances, as wife and mother, went back to her violin, but only to play lullabies for her baby, and sometimes solos for her friends. Refusing to be discouraged, she had ended what was amiss, endured what could not be mended, and so found happiness.

THE WOMAN WHO CHANGED HER MIND

NEW YORK, 1952

Although I have changed the names of persons and places and altered certain details, this history, strange as it sounds, is true. Philosophers have always known the truth about the possibilities of human nature; it was Prof. William James who said:

". . . . Compared with what we ought to be, we are only half awake. We are making use of only a small part of our physical and mental resources. Stating the thing broadly, the human individual thus lives far within his limits. He possesses powers of various sorts which he habitually fails to use."

THE AUTHOR

I WAS sitting beside Warren Bellman the first time he saw her.

Spear in hand, she was treading a pearl and black velvet staircase that seemed to slant from hanging stars down to the Follies stage. Her silver helmet could not altogether smother the bonfire of her hair. Like a sleepwalker she came down in a slow and stately prance; eyes staring across the footlights, as if she did not know that an audience was there.

"What is the mystery of those great green eyes?" I asked romantically.

"Astigmatism," Warren answered.

He was an incorrigible skeptic and regarded himself as the shrewdest as well as the best-educated man in show business.

"The nearsighted hussy needs glasses," he insisted. "And how I would like to be the one to buy her what she needs!"

Many men had been drawn to Jou-jou. That was the name the program gave her, and Mr. Ziegfeld had told her it meant "plaything." In Jou-jou's young life there had already been many a playful amourette but she had never been seriously in love. Youth roved through her veins in a troublesome abundance. After show-time she was squired to the fashionable night spots by laughing gentlemen who rejoiced to send her presents. Yet, Jou-jou dressed simply. Backstage the legend was that she sold all gifts and turned over the money to a puritanical and domineering Mamma.

Warren Bellman said that such tales were pipe dreams. He despised all sentimentalism; he hailed from Harvard and Newport and was determined to accept with good humor a sense of final futility, which was all he had yet found in life.

"A really intelligent man," he once told me, "can play everything so that he will never get hurt, no matter what happens. That's why I study all the angles."

For two months he besought her for dates, lunches, tea, dinner or supper after the show. He had her address —a flat in Brooklyn—but when he drove there in his Cadillac, he found the rooms empty. The Schultz family had moved away (the name was quite like Schultz), leaving no forwarding address. But Jou-jou finally did answer one of his notes, pinned to a nosegay on the dressing room table. In over-large, childish script, she wrote that at present all her time was taken up; later in the spring, he might, maybe, ask her again?

"Playing hard to get," chuckled Warren. "But I am playing hard to get rid of. Watch who wins."

On a May midnight at a roof-top club they first sat down together.

"Why did you have to keep me panting for two months?" he asked her.

"My mother was sick."

"What was wrong?"

"Cancer."

He winced at the word, spoken so matter-of-factly.

"Well—is mother better now?"

"She died last week," said Jou-jou.

There had been only the two of them. The father had died before Jou-jou was born. Even then the mother had been ailing; when Jou-jou was thirteen, without finishing eighth grade, she had gone to work, selling tickets in a Fourteenth Street movie theater. By degrees she had found her way to the musical comedy stage.

"She knows nothing," Warren told me, exulting, "except what she needs to know: steps to dance, songs to sing in the show of the moment—and how to make a man happy. She hasn't read *any*thing; she doesn't care a hang about what is going on in the world, and doesn't know a single capital of the 48 states. She just fixes those marvelous, enormous green eyes on your face, and she seems to hang on your every word—even when she doesn't understand a single thing you are talking about, which is most of the time. The whole effect of her is incendiary. She was born to please and what more can any man ask for?"

I suppose it never occurred to Warren to wonder whether Jou-jou might some day ask for something more for herself.

Among the guests at the wedding breakfast in the Crystal Room of the Ritz were perhaps a dozen former admirers of Jou-jou; Warren called them "the old battalion." Just for their benefit, the bridegroom made a toast: he lifted Jou-jou to the top of the head table, then sprang up beside her, one arm around her lacy waist. His foxlike face glowed with the pride of possession, as with a grandiose gesture he lifted a cup of champagne:

"Attention, everybody! I know what some of you are thinking, and you are wrong. I am marrying an artist; a woman born with the knowledge of pleasure, the one courtesan left in a sickly world. We understand each other, my wife and I; we enter into marriage in perfect accord; a wedding of beauty and, if I may say so, brains. I intend to let my bride do just as she pleases—no jealousy! And she —she is my beautiful biological necessity who will deny me nothing. Believe me, we have figured all the angles! So drink to our happiness!"

There was something humble and defenseless in the way Jou-jou watched Warren during that outrageous speech; it was as if he had made her feel like a barefoot beggar girl before the throne of his wisdom. And she accepted the role, as something in the nature of things.

Friends who sailed with them on the ship to England reported that they were the most energetic and tireless of passengers; always busy, at skeet shooting or walking miles around the promenade, playing shuffleboard or deck tennis, swimming in the ship's pool, dancing long after midnight. It was as if both were afraid of what would happen if they sat down and just talked. From sheer weariness, Jou-jou would sometimes fall asleep in a deck chair; then Warren would read his books, or tiptoe away to chat with friends.

A month later, I, too, was in London and had dinner with Jou-jou. Warren, she explained, was off for the evening with a famous novelist, a horsy woman who smoked little black cigars. The bride's comment jolted me:

"I've got nothing against all these intelligentsia, as Warren calls them," she said. "Only I do think, honest to God, they waste one hell of a lot of time. They stay up all night long, just talking. They talk about everything. But as far as I can see they never do *any*thing about *any*thing they talk about."

But it was in Paris, as I learned later, that trouble really started. In a sumptuous bedroom at the Hotel Crillon, Warren was awakened in the middle of the night by sobbing. He found Jou-jou standing on a small balcony, looking down on the soft yellow lamps of the Place de la Concorde, and weeping.

"This place! This Paris! Half the time I don't understand what people are saying."

"But Jou-jou, dearest—all our crowd speak English!"

He put his arm around her and talked as to an afflicted child, trying hard, no doubt, not to sound supercilious to himself.

"You do know there are many different languages in many different countries, don't you, Jou-jou?"

"Of course, I know that."

"And that some French people still speak French in France?"

"But I never had to put up with it before," stormed Jou-jou. "I can't endure going to a show and not understanding one word that I hear."

"I will get you a French teacher tomorrow morning—the handsomest in Paris."

To Armand, the young instructor, Warren tactfully explained:

"All that my wife really wants is a few phrases to use—sort of holding up her own, you know. She has not had much time for schooling, but——"

"I have talked with Madame," said the young man, and exclaimed: "She is magnificent! What wit! What observation! What soul!"

So Warren should have known from the first that Armand was a sentimentalist. A graduate medical student at the *Université,* he was glad to earn a few extra francs by giving lessons while working for a postgraduate degree in tropical diseases. Some fine day before long he would go to the Cameroons and work among African natives.

From Armand, Jou-jou was soon learning far more than a few French words and phrases. For example, her teacher grew lyrical about the great French heroines from Joan to Madame Curie. He had an ardent respect for women simply as women. They created life! They were, at one and the same time, he proclaimed, thinkers and doers and inspirers, a blessed trinity indeed.

"Armand!" cried Jou-jou. "Do you know what? A lot of these French words—I don't even know the meaning of the American words that mean the same thing. There's so awful damn much I don't know."

"I have observed," Armand said, in his precise and

elegant English, "that you are actually learning two languages at once—your own and mine. And that is going to make you a much wiser and more wonderful person."

"Can words make anyone wiser?"

"Of course! How can we think except with words? The more words we know, the better we think."

There was a certain covert gaiety about Jou-jou in those days; color back in her cheeks and a new sparkle to her eye, as one who, faced with a challenge, rises to meet it. Over flavored water ices on the terrace of a Champs Elysées café she would conjugate the irregular verbs and, like a litany, she would recite vocabulary lists, la's and le's, while Henri, friseur at the Crillon, waved and set her sleek and glossy hair. Before the summer was over, she had begun to speak French as if she had been born on a boulevard.

One night, to Warren's stupefaction, he heard her discuss in elegant Parisian, better far than his own, the dinner sauces and vintages with captain and wine waiter, and she carried it all off in such éclat, such showiness of achievement, that the husband had to clap hands and shout: "Bravo!"

But he noticed a light shade of difference in the way Jou-jou smiled at him. It was as if she were thinking to herself: "It's not so hard to learn this as he thinks. It's really easy." And her contemplative stare bothered Warren. Could it be that she was losing her head over this Armand? Next day, and with no warning, Warren advanced the date of their return sailing by two weeks.

"I want to pay you off," he said brusquely to Armand. "Too bad, but Madame is losing interest——"

The teacher took his long, deliberate time in writing

out a receipt for Warren's money; actually he was adding these lines above his signature:

"Do not be jealous of me, Monsieur. Realize the great fact—your wife has discovered her mind. Therefore she has fallen in love with the universe—a formidable rival, even for you!"

Coming home on the *Queen Mary*, Warren did not know how to talk to Jou-jou, so altered she seemed. To treat her as he had treated her at the start of the honeymoon would be like trying to rock a grown woman in a cradle.

"Now that she can talk French," he lamented, "she thinks she can do anything."

Yet Jou-jou was still the perfectly submissive wife, willing to walk, to play shuffleboard, to swim and to dance. Only she also insisted on taking time out for her reading.

"What's your book?" Warren would ask.

It might be the *Odyssey* of Homer, Armand's going-away present.

"I won't have you putting yourself through skull-breaking books like that."

"Don't forget our bargain, Warren. I can do what I please——"

"But why have an affair with a book?"

"To keep me quiet," was Jou-jou's unexpected answer. And seeing that Warren was flabbergasted, she explained:

"I've just begun to realize that I've been very restless ever since mother died. It's a queer thing but those last months, when she was suffering so much, now seem to me to be the happiest of my life. Armand said——"

"Damn it," snarled Warren. "I'm sick and tired of hearing what Armand said."

But later he did listen. Armand's idea was only that

she should read the ideas of great minds. Not all their thoughts would remain with her, but some would. From them she would learn why it was that assisting the helpless could be a great happiness—greater than being the prettiest girl on Broadway, with silver helmet, shining spear and velvet staircase.

Warren nodded amiably. Yes! We all need to help worthy causes. Jou-jou must go right ahead and send checks to any charities she favored. Meanwhile, darling—what about the new show?

"Warren," said Jou-jou, "I want to go to high school."

Under her old name of Lucille Schultz, Jou-jou finished her high-school work, through a correspondence course, and with a tutor to help her. During those two years, she lived up scrupulously to all that Warren asked of her. For his sake, she wore ermine and rubies and walked proudly with him into his gilded haunts. She chattered banalities with stars, ex-stars, would-be-stars and never-would-be-stars; with newspaper scribes and café society pharisees. She gave perfect dinner parties for his friends at the East River front apartment. When she and Warren were alone together, she listened to his prattle about casting, mounting, staging.

There also persists a rumor that at this time Jou-jou told Warren she would like to have a child. But Warren laughed, and pinched her bottom and the subject was never mentioned again.

Presently Jou-jou started taking some courses at a Brooklyn college.

"What are you studying now?" Warren asked one night.

"Biology."

Perhaps because that answer of hers had made him

look at her more closely he noticed that a physical change was also coming over his wife. She was wearing a blue and white checked blouse and brown corduroy pants; her fiery hair was done up in a businesslike knot. She was no longer pretty. But all dreaminess, or astigmatism, or whatever it was, had fled from her eyes. In those green depths now there was an unwavering light, full of purpose.

"Have you any idea what you are studying for?" Warren demanded.

"I'm hoping to be a laboratory assistant," she told him with a sudden, small eagerness. "I've been working with Professor Royle and his wife, and I think that one of these fine days I'm going to be a microscopist for a cellular pathologist."

"Say all that again!" gasped Warren.

His lips continued to shape the words soundlessly, after she had left the apartment. Standing alone, Warren had to face the fact that Jou-jou had changed in spirit, mind and body. By a mysterious process, quite unperceived by him, his wife had passed through some experience that tests, purifies and transforms.

That was about the time when Warren began to be seen at the night spots without Jou-jou and always with the latest of new beauties. But the great world continued to spin down the ringing grooves of change for a long time before Warren fully grasped the truth. And the truth was that, as much as any nun, Jou-jou had renounced the world. It was about that time, too, that Warren's face began to shrivel a little, his brow to contract into wrinkles, and he began to be an old man.

Late one evening, when she was at home and working over reports on her desk, the telephone rang. Warren answered; it was South America asking for his wife:

"Hello! Yes, Professor Royle. . . . oh, yes. . . . oh, yes, indeed. I'll be coming on the soonest plane! Good-bye!"

"What is this?"

"I am going to Brazil; we'll be there for several years," she explained, all breathless and compassionate and firm as rock. "We're following through on a small lead we have—research, you realize, Warren? Cancer! You would not want me to stop *now*—not on a job like *that*. But it would not be fair to you to ask you to wait for me—so good-bye, Warren!"

One day, at a café in Paris, Warren ran into Armand, gray-haired now and deeply tanned. The medical missionary was home on leave from the Cameroons.

"She was my first pupil," Armand smiled. "I was there when she first discovered her mind—it was like witnessing the birth of a star, Monsieur. Every other kind of artist works in material, like marble or canvas, that must some day fall apart—but not the teacher. He works upon the human mind. To help a soul fill its mind with knowledge, and the heart with understanding—that is to share creation with God."

Warren turned and took the teacher's hand.

"Thank you," he said huskily. "It was a great job—you aroused her soul, and I didn't even suspect she had one!"

ONE HEAVEN OF A FELLOW!

CAPE COD, 1947

THE host was an oil magnate. His guest was a clergyman, who, because of heretical views, had just resigned under pressure from a famous pulpit. Over luncheon coffee, the conservative man of business now made a proposition to the radical man of God:

"Dr. Fosdick, will you accept a call to be pastor of Park Avenue Baptist Church?"

The minister shook his fuzzy, brindled hair.

"No, Mr. Rockefeller! Your small church, in the swankiest part of New York, is for the wealthy few. Impossible!"

"Suppose we were to build a much larger church to serve the whole community and invite everybody. . . ."

Dr. Fosdick puckered his lips. He has the perplexed face of a maiden aunt and the eyes of a seer. Then he said:

"The answer must still be no!"

"May I ask why?"

"Because of you, yourself, Mr. Rockefeller—the biggest obstacle of all. I wouldn't care to be known as the pastor of the richest man in the country!"

All blandishments used up, Mr. Rockefeller exclaimed:

"Look here, Dr. Fosdick! Do you think people will criticize *you* on account of my *money* more than they will criticize *me* on account of your *theology*?"

Both men began to laugh—and before long rich man and clergyman were talking of a dream.

Out of the dream there since has risen New York's great gray Riverside Church, to which every week come 10,000 visitors. In these Gothic spaces, denominationalism is ignored. It is a Baptist church, yet only a quarter of its 3500 members call themselves Baptists; the others come from 40 differing religious groups. Now Minister Emeritus, after 20 years of leadership, Harry Emerson Fosdick calls his experiment in Protestant harmony a successful pilot-plant operation; a unified church in miniature.

The venture was led by a zealot, consumed with love for God and man, and galled all his life into passionate insurrection against rule and formula. "I should be ashamed," Fosdick once declared, "to live in this generation and not be a heretic." There have been many liberal theologians in this country but it was Fosdick who dramatized the conflict between old belief and modern intellectual adventure, and made the struggle Page One news. Yet the most famous Protestant in America is known today only by his sermons, books and broadcasts; his full-dress biography is yet to be written.

The mixture of faith and rebellion vibrates in his genes. One ancestral Fosdick was fined two pounds in 1643 for reading the wrong books; another was expelled from a colonial pulpit because he rejected hell. On stormy nights his grandfather feloniously rowed boatloads of fugitive slaves across the Niagara River.

In earliest life Harry also began to rebel; at the age of four he ran away from home and while he forgets why, it was surely an act of protest. At seven, he made up his mind to be a foreign missionary, and asked to be baptized. So small that he had to stand on a box in the pool, he nevertheless got his way.

On a schoolteacher's salary, "Pop" Fosdick and Mother had to count the pennies, but there were always pennies to count. It was a home where mother played the piano, father the flute, and the three children sang; a family that in Victorian days felt no dismay when Mother's parents were divorced on the ground of incompatibility, and that kept unshaken trust in Pop even after he dropped most of their savings in the stock market.

Blue-eyed Harry with the jungle of brown curls seemed a mystifying contradiction—a child so early aware of the wonder of life, yet part of a scrimmaging gang that called him Sticky. He got the nickname because he swiped some candy one day and then had to shake hands with the Methodist minister, who incidentally, was Dorothy Thompson's pa!

Boyhood in the little town of Lancaster near Buffalo gave Harry eight happy years, including *Post Office* and other kissing games.

"It's funny!" he chuckles. "The church people wouldn't let us dance, but they *would* let us kiss!"

But the fun of life was spoiled periodically by hell-preaching evangelists who came into town with long faces and dire warnings of sinners roasting forever. In their eyes, card playing was a sin; theatergoing damnation.

"I hold it everlastingly against them," declares

Fosdick, "that once, as a young boy, because of their idiotic legalism, I refused my own father's invitation to see Edwin Booth in Hamlet!"

In Buffalo high school, while studying Latin and Greek under his father, he first began to look admiringly upon the girls; there remains to this day a fragment of his apostrophe to an early charmer:

"Fairer than a fuchsia—
All that and more is Lucia!"

Soon he had a procession of "best girls," many of whom are still his friends.

"I cannot recall," Fosdick says, "that a loose woman ever attracted me. I should not be ashamed to meet now any girl I ever was friendly with."

He sowed his wild oats in a window box! He was a serious youth; at graduation, he knew he desired a spiritual career and so entered Colgate Theological School. Two years later he won a scholarship for Union Seminary in New York. To help finance himself through Colgate, Harry had entered a contest on vivisection; knowing nothing about the subject, he scribbled a blistering essay and won second prize money. Now to obtain food and lodging in Manhattan he helped to run a mission for bums.

This was the toughest year of his life—he was studying theology at the Seminary and philosophy at Columbia, meanwhile doing two men's work at the Mariner's Temple on the Bowery. But the work had its amusing side; there was the time when "Newspaper Mary," a sidewalk alcoholic, arose after a stirring evangelistic plea, bit a plug of tobacco, spat into a shiny spittoon and nominated the speaker for president on the Democratic ticket.

Another night the sermon was about the prodigal son.

The crowd of beggars sat spellbound, as the orator described the New Testament spendthrift, and his welcome from father—the robe, the ring, the fatted calf. After a moment of awed silence an inebriate on the front bench burped exultingly:

"So he put it over on the old man again, hey?"

On Sundays, Fosdick held as many as nine meetings in Bowery lodging houses, at a time when a 25¢ Sabbath dinner in a hash-house under the Third Avenue El was his best meal of the week. He sold his prize gold medal for $40, bought a ring and hastened to Worcester on the greatest mission of his life—to propose to a girl. Back in Colgate the seminarian had fallen in love at first sight, than which there is no better way. A friendly professor had told him about Florence Whitney, from Worcester, Mass., who was coming for a visit. Would he squire her around? The bespectacled student took one look at dark-eyed Florence, and like the gambler in the song, his heart stood still. Ever since, they had been good friends; now he put the question. Her marriage promise secure, he came back to Morningside Heights and the Bowery slums.

He was ordained on November 18, 1908, and nearly a year later, Harry as parson and Florence as parson's wife began life together in First Baptist Church of Montclair, New Jersey. Fortunate the preacher whose wife knows her job! She needs the wisdom of serpents and the harmlessness of doves to keep peace in a congregation; tact, and charm; energy and patience. And she must be able to criticize her husband's sermons yet never ruffle his dignity. From the first, in this supremely testing role, Florence Fosdick gave a star performance.

Before long, some of the new pastor's outspoken sermons raised the wind in Montclair, and Fosdick knew he was in for a struggle. But long ago, in Colgate sophomore days, he had fought the same struggle with himself. That was when he had begun to feel increasing religious doubts.

"For me," he declares of that time, "truth was becoming an open field to be explored. What one believed had to be discovered! I no longer merely doubted the old stuff I had been taught; I rose in indignant revolt against it." And he wrote home to mother:

"I'll behave as if there were really a God, but mentally I'm going to clear God out of the universe. Start all over to see what I can find!"

The iconoclast was to find among trusted Colgate professors men who held on firmly to Christianity. Most influential was William Newton Clarke, of whom Fosdick says:

"He brought to me the water of life. All the best meanings of religion could be mine again, without the crucifixion of the intellect. He said: 'I am sure the stars are there—even though we have had to change our astronomy!' "

Challenged now in his first official pastorate, Fosdick immediately called in his critics, and rising to his full 5 feet, 8 inches, smilingly promised to quit if they objected to his views. For the remaining 11 years of his stay in Montclair there was never another peep!

"If they had complained of the *quality* of my sermons," Fosdick tells you, "they would have been right!"

It was true that in the pulpit, he was self-conscious and awkward. Now the first pulpit orator of America knows whereof he speaks when he says:

"Demosthenes became a great orator, not *in spite of* his stammering but because of it."

Because of his own awkwardness he set himself relentlessly to self-improvement. Long hours he spent in preparing his sermons, and rehearsing them in his study with only Florence for his audience. Then, one Sunday morning he had a flaming experience in the pulpit; he felt himself filled up suddenly with a strange warmth in body, mind and spirit. "The idea I was dealing with took fire," he told me. Ever since he has been able to hold crowds in thrall. Speakers envy his sermons, especially his stories and illustrations.

"Some people find it hard," he preaches, "to grasp the idea of the Trinity. Yet it is simple. There were also three Beethovens in one. First, the composer—the Creator! Second, the performer, who sat at the piano and played. Third, the personality known to his loved ones, Beethoven the friend. Three Beethovens—yet all one!"

Many of his best stories are humorous; for all his zeal, Fosdick has a theatrical instinct for timing and the emphasis of a professional comedian. A vaudeville actor told me: "There were seven wows in his speech at his testimonial banquet."

For instance:

"The story runs that the chairman of a county council once rose portentously to his feet and said, 'Gentlemen, what this town needs is a supply of fresh, clean milk, and the council must take the bull by the horns and demand it. . . .'"

And in the solemnity of his farewell sermon in Riverside he could still quote:

All our fathers have been churchmen
Nineteen hundred years or so
And to every new suggestion
They have always answered No.

Within a few years after his start at Montclair, the

world outside began to take notice of this boundlessly energetic man; churches and universities invited him. At Princeton he had to blow down a Jericho wall of Sunday comics raised against him by rude students in compulsory chapel; he overwhelmed them with jibes more amusing than anything in *Foxy Grandpa* or the *Katzenjammer Kids;* at the end of his sermon the boys cheered him. In those years, he was writing several books, and lecturing in Union Seminary, while continuing to study at Columbia for a master's degree.

How could one man do so much? Part of the answer he found in solitude; he rented a room in a Montclair office building, where, with a blind door and no telephone, he locked himself away five mornings a week. Alone and uninterrupted, a man can do a lot of work in five mornings.

But after twelve years in one church, Fosdick began to feel restless. He and Florence now had their two girls, Eleanor and Dorothy. A third died at birth; but the still-born child was given a name and is a part of family memory and devotion. The Fosdicks also stayed their first summer on Mouse Island, in Boothbay Harbor, Maine, their patch of heaven on the earth.

Many voices were inviting—a New York church wanted him for pastor, a woman's college considered him for president. But, in 1915, preferring to be free to teach and preach Fosdick became a full professor in Union Seminary. No one suspected, Fosdick least of all, that he was forsaking a cloister for an arena.

Europe having gone to war, Fosdick now began to urge that the United States join the struggle at once.

"What a temptation war is to a preacher," he was later to lament. "If he takes the popular side, which is always for vengeance, how great the thrill he will feel as he moves great crowds! Idealizing war is no business for a Christian pulpit."

He wrote *The Challenge of the Present Crisis,* a sizzling call to violence, which had a great sale, but of the book the author now says:

"I was wrong! The book's main objective I repudiate! War is a great problem to the church; there is no neat solution."

After four months abroad with troops and crews, he came home seething from the abattoir. What many returning chaplains are declaring today, Fosdick was proclaiming in 1918; soldiers were a cross section of the United States and their attitudes a blistering comment on churches.

"The utter irrelevance of our petty, sectarian divisions, must give way," he stormed.

Just when the fiery Baptist professor began to feel the need of a sounding board a group of Presbyterians invited him to be their "Guest Preacher" in New York's Old First Church. Because he accepted, this sedate house of worship on lower Fifth Avenue was soon to wince in the spotlight of national publicity; its pulpit a stage on which Harry Emerson Fosdick was to play the leading role in the religious drama of a century. Whether as hero or villain, depended entirely on your point of view.

Unmolested there for a while Fosdick preached that in an age of scientific discovery one could stay in a Christian church and keep intellectual self-respect. He declared he could never be either a reactionary or a radical:

"The idea that any creed can be final is as incredible to me as that the interpretation of the physical cosmos could stop with Newton or Einstein. . . . But, while ideas of God may change, and ought to, that does not mean that anything has happened to God. . . ."

Here lay his greatest personal danger; he was a rationalist who believed in the supernatural; yet a devout Christian who questioned everything; such a contradiction was found to be suspected on both sides of the fence! And then he preached an incandescent sermon called "Shall the Fundamentalist Win?"

That historic discourse might never have been heard of, had it not been for a man called Ivy Lee. Now Ivy Lee, Georgian son of a minister, was among the earliest and greatest of public relation experts; he told officials of corporations how to win friends and influence opinion. An earnest fellow with modernistic views on religion, Lee applauded Fosdick's sermon as a plea for tolerance; for a church that would open its doors to liberals and fundamentalists alike, without either trying to drive the other out:

"There are many opinions in the field of modern controversy. I am not sure whether they are right or wrong. But there is one thing I am sure of: courtesy and kindness and tolerance and humility and fairness are right. Opinion may be mistaken; love never is."

Filled with admiration for such views Lee published the sermon in a pamphlet and mailed out reprints by thousands.

"The results," sighs Fosdick, "brought the house down."

In explicit terms, the plea for good will simply raised hell. Theology became first page news; the virgin birth, the miracles, the resurrection, the infallibility of the Bible were soon breakfast-table conversation. And while attacks came from conservative pulpits a campaign to prevent such preaching was prepared at a meeting held in the country retreat of John Wanamaker, department store prince.

At the next Annual Assembly of Presbyterians, the issue was angrily debated. On the convention floor the bellicose William Jennings Bryan, most influential Protestant layman, thundered that the issue was the faithful against the infidel. The delegates voted Bryan's way and ordered a full report for next year's session.

What would Harry Emerson Fosdick do? Everyone was asking that question, as the debate waxed hotter all over the country. The Protestant Episcopal Bishop of Massachusetts took Fosdick's side; more than 1200 Presbyterian ministers signed a declaration for him; 8000 others did not. The venerable Henry Van Dyke came from Princeton back to his old New York Church to declare for freedom of belief. President Faunce of Brown praised the rebel for "such power . . . as to win the approval of two continents." The Clergy Club of New York daringly gave Fosdick a luncheon, with 198 pastors sitting at table and applauding. At Cornell University several hundred professors and students testified: "You have deepened our faith!"; so at Columbia, Mount Holyoke, and, mildly amazing, at the Southern Methodist University in Texas. Even the New York Times editorially cheered him on.

But Fosdick was also dodging many a dead cat. The fundamentalists were yowling for him to quit; so were the radicals; he had pleased neither. One called him a "Presbyterian bootlegger, a Baptist outlaw, a theological Jesse James," and he was accused of getting $1000 a month at Old First; this about a man who has seen to it that he has never been paid more than $5000 a year by any church—including Riverside! The radicals said he was a compromiser; he should spurn all formal religion and walk out of the church forever.

From left and right came the question: "How can a man, if he is honest, stay in a church if he no longer believes in its doctrines?"

He did offer to resign but Old First officials preferred to placate the wrath of the Assembly and still have Fosdick go on preaching, if a way could be found. Those harassed Presbyterians pleaded that the offending sermon should be regarded not as an isolated utterance, "but a regrettable incident in the ministry of one whom we have learned to love and honor."

Not so Fosdick himself. He sent his own letter, which was also presented to the Assembly:

"Far from having searching of conscience because I preached that sermon, I should have had desperate and intolerable searching of conscience if I had *not* preached it. . . ."

The final decision was that Dr. Fosdick be invited to become a minister of the Presbyterian Church—else he should not preach in its churches.

Never for a moment did Fosdick seriously consider the proposal; it would trap him under ecclesiastical discipline; sooner or later, he would find himself on trial for heresy. As he decided to resign, William Jennings Bryan cried jubilantly:

"We have won every point!"

Quitting on October 6, 1924, Fosdick told the Old First congregation he would always be against a "denominational closed shop." And it was only a short time later that John D. Rockefeller, Jr., invited him to lunch!

Now you know the extraordinary objections raised to Rockefeller's proposal and you know the millionaire's promises. The amazing sequel was that the Park Avenue congregation backed Mr. Rockefeller's concessions, almost unanimously—one earnest and frightened member did make an opposing speech and then fainted in the pew—and called the rebel to be its leader.

From the fundamentalist forces came the acrimonious comment: "Oil and water mix at last—the water of baptism and the oil of Rockefeller!"

That was twaddle. Leaning over backward not to rule, the millionaire put his contributions into a capital fund, given outright to the church, thus forever stripping himself of any financial influence. Fosdick was his own boss and began to plan the promised church.

Six years later, New York gazed upon the new pearl-gray cathedral on the riverbank. Four hundred feet above the sidewalk rose the great stone tower; archangels at its four corners with gargoyles and grotesques. As, in old European cathedrals, dead saints and living leaders of the time were carved in stone images at the doorways, so the west portal of this twentieth-century church revealed rows of dead and living prophets, including Thomas A. Edison, who was not a Baptist, and Albert Einstein, not even a Christian!

Above toots of ferryboats, and tart horns of autos came an ecstatic clangor from the 72 bells of the Laura Spellman Rockefeller Memorial Carillon. And high above Einstein, the angels and the bells, loomed the solitary figure of Christ, brooding over Manhattan as once, from Mt. Olivet, He had wept over Jerusalem.

In groined arches, colored windows and 50 committee rooms, Fosdick's vast church was designed to speak mystically and practically—an old denomination busy in the latest affairs of man.

"I am a genius as an organizer," Fosdick will tell you. "My genius consists in disliking the details of organization."

So the details were left to three permanent clergymen, a Department of Religious Education and a business manager with a force of 72 full-time and 136 part-time helpers. All these were necessary because of the rapid success of the plan—Riverside Church serves a wide community. Mostly the flock is made up of white-collar employees and owners of small business. They pay the bills; less than 8% of expenses are defrayed by Rockefeller's contributions; the rest comes from 2000 subscribers.

During his years at Riverside Fosdick continued to be a fighting rebel. As late as February, 1939, he preached a pacifist sermon, so fiery that his voice crackled as he demanded:

"Dare we breach the vicious circle of fighting evil with evil?"

Because of these pacifist views a few families walked out of Riverside, but not many. Next he announced a "Protestant version of the Roman Catholic Confessional" and once more the tempest shook its thunders at his fluffy head. But soon he was spending most of his time in his "soul clinic" with those who needed to give conscience a house cleaning. It became almost impossible to see Dr. Fosdick on any ordinary matter of business; your heartache was the key to his office.

The story is told of a Boston clergyman who took the midnight to New York and at nine in the morning called the pastor for an appointment. Fosdick told him he would first have to state his business on the telephone.

"We are going to have a great joint public celebration

and want you to be the orator. And we are willing to pay you $500!"

"I must decline with thanks," Fosdick answered.

"But if I could have five minutes——"

"I just can't spare five minutes!"

Presently the telephone rang again. A Negro clergyman was on the telephone:

"Dr. Fosdick, I think I am at the end of my rope. My troubles are so heavy that I don't want to go on living. Maybe you can show me why I should."

Fosdick canceled all morning appointments and gave this unhappy man two hours. The Negro's wife had cut her throat in the bedroom of their home a few days before. On their knees the two ministers sought peace together.

Later that afternoon the first caller sat in a day coach on his way back to Boston. Beside him—fabulous but actual coincidence—sat a Negro in clerical clothes. The two fell to talking.

"I am very disappointed," said the Bostonian. "I came all the way from Boston to confer with a famous man and he wouldn't even see me. Not even when I offered him a large fee. Terrible how success can swell a man's head."

The Negro parson smiled.

"I came to see a famous man, too! I had to get right with God and go home to my folks, or else jump in the river. Well, here I am heading for home. Thanks to two hours I had on my knees today with my friend. Success ain't swelled *his* head."

No count was ever kept of the many bewildered people Fosdick consoled and guided with techniques of loving kindness. He would agree with his consultants—and then disagree. "Of course I understand perfectly how you feel.

You are right about it, too. But on the other hand, have you ever looked at it this way——"

Today his idea is so widely practiced that seminaries offer courses to prepare students for personal and intimate consultation.

In the later years, many of Fosdick's dreams were coming true, yet when all his battles seemed to have been won, he startled his listeners once more, preaching one of his most effective sermons: "Modernism Is Not Enough!"

Was Fosdick renouncing all that he had fought for? He says, not at all! Still a liberal, he was also still learning; in the sunset of life, the rebel who once had trampled on the incredible now pointed with adoring awe to the incomprehensible. The mystery of the Universe was still a mystery! His enemies had long accused him of sponsoring a purely natural religion, outlawing the supernatural, but——

"I believe in God," he repeated the other day. "Is He not supernatural? I have had experiences myself, and have seen them in others, that materialism cannot possibly explain. Only the basic affirmations of the Christian Gospel can account for them. There lies my central confidence!"

Surely, he thinks, the supernatural help of God is needed now, more than ever.

"In those battles of the past," he says, "the danger was fundamentalism. Today the danger is paganism. Only a united church and the supernatural help of God can overcome the false religions of communism and fascism in the dark years before us! The atomic bomb is here to stay; the one question is whether we human beings are here to stay, too!"

Dr. Fosdick and his work figured largely in another piece by Fulton Oursler. A rather extraordinary case in a mental institution had reached such a withdrawal from the world that the fellow would not speak. Life had piled upon him such tragedy he had locked away his emotions in total apathy. After years, an experimenting doctor set him to stacking books for the planned establishment of a hospital library. While working the patient came across The Power to See It Through *by Harry Emerson Fosdick. He began to read it—his first reading in many years. There followed the immediate return to normalcy—the eventual release from the institution, and re-entry to an active and useful life.*

THE BEST ARGUMENT

NEW YORK, 1952

COMMUNISTS are baffled by Christian charity. Caught within the limitations of their atheism, they can neither understand it, nor foresee the harvest of its consequences. That is why Father Robert Juigner of the Paris Foreign Mission Society was a difficult problem, not many months ago in the Chinese capital of Chungking.

"You are an enemy of the state," the Communist court accused the priest, soon after the Reds took over.

"I am not an enemy, I am a friend," Father Juigner insisted.

His defense was futile. With 80 others, he was herded into a cell designed for only 50. The prisoners slept leaning against each other. Food was almost nonexistent. Armies of devouring vermin swarmed over them.

But the physical hardship was nothing compared to the merciless pressure the Communists applied in a continuous effort to "convert" them to Marxism.

Each day before their miserable ration of breakfast, they were forced to "meditate" on Communism. Then, for four hours, they were subjected to lengthy discourses on Marxist doctrines. In the evening, they spent two hours in an ordeal of forced self-criticism and public confession of faults.

It was in these classes that Father Juigner became the cell's resistance leader. Day after day, he calmly confessed:

"I have been lazy in studying Marxism, I have been inattentive during lectures, I do not believe in Communism."

Infuriated, the Communists bound his hands in heavy irons day and night for sixty days. But every other day he was dragged to a three-hour inquisition before Chungking judges, at which he was accused of the most vicious crimes. His answer was always calm, and always the same:

"I have never done anything against the law of the Government of China."

Upon which a new torture would be applied.

One morning, the huge barred door swung open, and another prisoner was shoved into the crowded cell. For a second he stood motionless. Then, with a despairing moan, he sank to the floor.

A shriek of terror went up from the other prisoners. They trampled each other, fighting desperately to get to the farthest corner of the cell. In the light that fell on the floor, they could see the man's face and hands, a mass of wounds.

Leprosy!

They knew what this meant. If they would accept Communism, the leper would be taken away. How many would hold out now?

Father Juigner acted instinctively. Lifting the leper out of the filth of the vermin-ridden floor, he carried him over to his own blanket. He gave him what little food he had, and that night, actually slept beside him. And every other prisoner took heart from that compassionate and fearless act.

The Communist jailers were confounded. In the face of their cruelest device, not one of the prisoners had wavered. That priest was to blame.

A mock trial was immediately arranged. Father Juigner was quickly convicted of a number of incredible crimes. And his sentence? He was resigned to die. But the Communists had another idea. To put him to death would make of him a martyr and a symbol of resistance. So his sentence was to be banished from China forever. A few days later, on March 16, 1952, the priest crossed the border into the Crown Colony of Hong Kong, a free man.

The philosophy of another prisoner priest whom Fulton Oursler met in Paris held a key-note to the secret of heroism. Father Paul Riquet, when captured by the Nazis, was stripped naked, as a humiliation, and sent thus to a concentration camp in a freight car that held so many prisoners that they had to stand up the whole way. They were 5 days, lightless, in that car and many arrived dead. The second day of the journey was Good Friday and Father Riquet prevented despair in the box car by telling the history of Calvary and the 7 Last Words.

In Dachau Father Riquet's tortures, as so often with the religious, were heightened. He told Fulton Oursler that he doubled his torturers' measures. If they gave but a dram of water he drank ½ of it. If they set him to cleaning latrines, he scrubbed the entire area as well; if kept 3 days and nights without sleep while under continual questioning he stayed awake and worked the 4th night. "Only thus could I keep sane and serene," he explained. "What we are forced to do can break us. What we make ourselves do ennobles us. Self-discipline is glorious mastery. Discipline by others is slavery. This going the second mile and giving thy cloak also tops any enemy. He instinctively knows he is undone and has no power."

(FROM FULTON OURSLER'S NOTEBOOKS ALMOST IN ENTIRETY)

THE LOST 15 MINUTES

NEW YORK, 1949

"Kenneth Long, did you kill your wife?"

The accused man in the witness box turned pale under his freckles; forlorn blue eyes looked at the jury. His reply to the question, thrown at him by his own lawyer, might spell the difference between freedom and the gas chamber.

"Well, did you?"

The answer came in a sad Texas drawl:

"From the looks of things, Mr. Davis—I guess—I *must*——"

One might have heard the fall of a handkerchief in the horrified silence; the prisoner was pronouncing his own death sentence.

Yet his counsel, 41-year-old George T. Davis, turned to the amazed prosecutor with a quizzical smile, as he murmured:

"He's your witness."

From the trial table, Deputy District Attorney Thomas L. McBride rose to cross-examine the defendant in the case of The People of California versus Kenneth

Long. In the hushed Martinez courtroom with its walnut walls, the prisoner was led back over the history of how black-eyed Bobbe Long had been exterminated with a butcher knife.

Married three years before, Air Sergeant Long and the tall, shapely mother of their two children had lived in the factory district of Richmond. Then Kenneth was transferred to an air post in Anchorage, Alaska. The letters of the lonesome husband begged Bobbe to join him in that chilblain region; when the wife finally refused, Kenneth swore that unless she changed her mind within a week, he would come back and kill her.

Because of that written evidence of premeditation, Contra Costa County, for the first time in 30 years, was demanding the death penalty.

On July 26, 1948, one day after the murder ultimatum expired, Kenneth Long purchased an Indian pillow, decorated in purple and yellow. With this garish peace offering in his arms, and return tickets for his entire family in his pocket, he flew to California, determined to know the truth. Like many another inquisitive husband, he was to be staggered by what he found. All smiles, he walked into the Richmond flat.

"How long a leave you got?" were Bobbe's first words.

"Thirty days."

"Then you can't stay here. You might as well know—I'm in love with somebody else."

Kenneth Long literally went on his knees:

"Bobbe! Listen!" he beseeched. "I know it's not our church—but a priest lives around the corner. Let's put it up to him."

Unless you believe *all* of Long's story, it is hard to understand why Bobbe ever agreed, but she did, and when the parish curate urged it, she even promised to go to Alaska. Before a crucifix, husband and wife kissed and made up.

Who can penetrate the mystery of the doomed woman's behavior? Hand in hand she walked home with her husband, talking of the future. Once back in the flat, she locked and bolted herself in the bathroom. She came out, another woman.

"I fooled you," she laughed, and flouncing on the bed, told Kenneth Long that he was not the father of her second child.

In that instant, confusion began to ferment in the man's brain. Afterward, he was to remember how he fell on his knees and prayed aloud; and how he beheld a glittering vision, like the flash of a long sharp blade——

"Knife!" he muttered on the witness stand. "Knife. . . ."

And there his story came to a halt. Beyond it, he could not budge. Blankness, after prayer and glittering blade; a loss of memory covering 15 minutes.

Conscious again, he floundered into a neighbor's flat.

"I think," he gasped, "I killed my wife."

They found Bobbe dead on the rug at the front door, a deep wound in the left side of her chest, and the walls spattered in crimson. On the floor of the bedroom, the butcher knife was sticking upright.

"One more question," said District Attorney McBride, at the end of cross-examination. He didn't believe anyone could lose 15 minutes. But even so—"Why do you say you think you must have killed your wife?"

"Because my wife and I were the only ones there."

"That's all!" boomed the prosecutor.

George T. Davis faced the bench, knowing that the

crisis of the defense had been reached. If the judge ruled against him now, all hope of saving his client might be lost. And the judge was looking at him with a bilious eye.

Only 3 months before, in another case, Davis had accused Judge Donovan of prejudice and bias and got him disqualified from the case. The little jurist with the square jaw and the pointed nose could not have forgotten that. Again, in the selection of the Long jury, defense and bench had wrangled for 8 days until finally, Judge Donovan, pounding the table, quoting from the Latin and mingling erudition with ire, held Davis in contempt of court.

This same Judge Donovan must rule on a proposal of Davis, without parallel in criminal justice.

Unknown to authorities, Davis admitted to his Honor, he had arranged for an experiment in his client's cell. The scientist in charge was Dr. Meyer Zeligs, assistant clinical professor of neurology at the University of California Medical School. As a naval commander in the South Pacific, Dr. Zeligs had worked among sailors and marines with a drug called sodium pentathol, whose potency loosens inhibitions, helping distracted patients to dig up forgotten experiences, buried in the unconscious.

One recent Saturday afternoon the lawyer and the doctor had smuggled into the jail a Pierce wire-recording machine. As Long lay on his bunk, a hypodermic needle was driven into a vein of his right arm; there the needle remained for the whole 50 minutes of interrogation. By dribs and drabs there were fed constantly into the bloodstream, and flowing on to the brain, 13.5 grams of sodium pentathol dissolved in sterilized, distilled water.

Soon Long was breathing heavily; pupils fixed, eyes dilated; constantly teetering on the verge of complete unconsciousness. Davis held a microphone, attached to a 25-

foot cord, against the man's mouth, while Zeligs coaxed forth the story up to the point where Long's memory seemed blocked. But under the drug, that psychic barrier fell away! Though his voice had the thickness of a sleeper, talking through a dream, Long rushed on to uncover that blotted quarter of an hour.

What a Pandora's box the unconscious mind of a man may be, when the stubborn seals are broken! Lawyer and psychiatrist shivered in cold sweat at the unexpected tale the prisoner began to tell.

"I was so astounded," Davis said later, "that I damn near fell out of my shoes."

What the defense wanted from Judge Donovan was permission to play the record of that interview for the jury to hear.

Furiously District Attorney McBride objected. There was no possible proof that sodium pentathol was a truth serum. Moreover, the experiment had been conducted unethically, without notice to the District Attorney. There had been no opportunity to cross-examine the prisoner while he was under the drug. So the whole thing was *ex parte*, one-sided. The scheme enabled the defense to get objectionable things before the jury which the prosecution was helpless to prevent. It was bound to be a highly emotional recital with sobs and tears to sway the emotions of the jury. Anyway, all empiric devices had been ruled out in the courts, even the lie-detector machine. McBride wound up by comparing such sensational notions to "the love philters of Cagliostro. Just claptrap!"

To the amazement of Davis, Judge Donovan disagreed. The record was like an X-ray picture, he decided; it could show on what an expert had based his opinion. Giving orders for no interruptions, and for absolute silence, he nodded to Counsellor Davis to go ahead. On the trial table was placed a box about the size of a portable radio with a long cord attached to a light socket.

"Until this moment," Davis told the judge, "the prisoner Long still does not remember what happened during that 15 minutes. He has no idea what he said under the influence of the drug. Like yourself, and the jury, he will hear his own defense now for the first time."

A lever was turned. Through the amplifier all could hear the unmistakable drawl of Kenneth Long, reciting his story up to the point where Bobbe told him about the child. Then the imperturbable Dr. Zeligs snapped off the machine; first he must make one point clear:

"At this moment, Long begins to recover the memory of what he has forgotten . . . he is about to express his unconscious feelings that were repressed."

The machine was turned on again:

Long: Knife—Bobbe . . . Who is this man? . . . Bobbe. . . .

Doctor: What man? Was there a man in there?

Long: Yes. There was another man there—with a knife.

Doctor: Did you ever see him before?

Long: No.

Doctor: What happened now, Kenneth?

Long: And Bobbe says, "He's going to kill you, Kenneth, so we can have happiness."

(Weirdly now, in the courtroom, there could be heard two sounds of the same voice sobbing—one, the drugged, tormented tone on the record, the other, the weeping of the prisoner as he listened to himself.)

Doctor: What did he look like?

Long: Like me—but shorter. . . . He came out of the bathroom. He had the butcher knife.

Doctor: Did you know he was in there?

Long: No, I didn't know there was anybody in the house besides me and my wife. She had an apartment rented—her and him, as man and wife. . . . She was going to take the kids away where I would never see them no more.

Doctor: What did you do or say?

Long: So I told Bobbe not to let him do it. And this man came into the room with his butcher knife—and he killed my wife.

Doctor: Did you *see* him kill her?

Long: Yes, he stabbed her twice.

Doctor: What did you do?

Long: I couldn't do anything—I couldn't move.

Doctor: *Why* did he stab her, huh?

Long: He seemed to think it was best.

Doctor: Tell me exactly what happened? Hey, hey, Kenneth, are you awake?

(SOUND OF HEAVY BREATHING. SOUND AS OF A HAND SLAPPING A CHEEK)

Doctor: Why did you tell the police that *you* killed her?

Long: He told me to tell them . . . That man told me, "Ken, you call the police, and tell them you did it." . . . And he gave me the knife . . . He went out the back window . . . He was wearing sports clothes . . . blue trousers. . . .

Doctor: What was his name?

Long: His name was Peck.

And now, on the record Dr. Zeligs' voice was pointing out the enormity of this charge. Did Long believe that God was listening to him?

Above the static came the sound of the drugged voice again, at prayer:

"Jesus Christ! You know I am telling the truth, don't you?"

Doctor: Confess the truth to God.

Long: All the killing I ever did was squirrel hunting.

When the gavel sounded again, the judge asked two questions in everyone's mind:

"Is there such a man as Peck? If so, where is he?"

Undoubtedly there was such a man, William Peck, the final romance in Bobbe Long's life, and George Davis demanded a warrant for him, charging murder in the first degree. A prosecution lawyer broke in to announce that police were already searching: "The state wants this man as much as you do."

The very next day, William Peck was marched to the stand. No witness was ever more avidly scanned by judge, jury, counsel and spectators. George Davis whispered to his assistant:

"He *does* look like Long. He *is* shorter. He *is* wearing sports clothes. *And* blue trousers!"

Yet—unless Long's story in trance was the truth—this was the first time the two had ever seen each other.

Peck admitted his relations with Bobbe Long. And, yes, it was true that he went with her to rent another apartment under the name of Mr. and Mrs. Peck.

Where then was he at 5 P.M. on July 26, 1948?

Peck had been sound asleep in his own apartment. The Coxes, friends from across the street, woke him up about 5:45. He went to their flat and had coffee with them;

they confirmed this. There was no evidence whatever to place the man on the scene of the crime, a hundred yards from his bed.

"You can go home now, Mr. Peck," said Judge Donovan.

What would the jury do with all this? Last arguments and instructions resounding in their ears, they retired at 2 P.M. Tuesday afternoon. And Davis began to be afraid. Had he been wrong to rely on his bizarre experiment? Would it have been better to plead justification, extreme provocation, the unwritten law for outraged husbands?

He sat down at the deserted trial table to wait. For him to win, he felt sure there must be a quick verdict; if the jurors took their time, his chances were slight. The half hours lagged and dragged into hours of excruciating suspense.

It was 8 o'clock the next night, that the jury sent word they were in hopeless disagreement. Their first ballot was 9 to 3 and in more than 24 hours it had not changed. Wouldn't the Judge dismiss them?

"I will," sighed Donovan. "Get the District Attorney and defense counsel back in court."

Davis was there but the prosecutor was not. And here, at the end of this fantastic trial, came one last ironic upset. Not until later was George Davis to learn how his client's fate was decided.

Bickering at an end, the relaxed jurors sat waiting in their room; the two women and ten men all felt friendly.

"You know," remarked a lady juror, addressing the leader of the minority, "now that it's all over, I want to tell you I'll never be able to understand you."

"What do you mean by that?"

"A man of your brains! Can't you realize what that

poor devil went through? No wonder his brain went funny."

"Well," mused the other. "Maybe you're right, after all. I could change my vote, even now."

"Why, so could I," said Juror No. 9.

"Me, too," chimed in Juror No. 11.

The final vote was unanimous; by the time McBride got there Kenneth Long was acquitted, only because in returning to court, the District Attorney had lost 15 minutes.

The next day was Thanksgiving.

Of course this strange, dramatic trial raised some unanswered questions in the public mind. *How could Long actually forget those crucial 15 minutes?* Dr. Zeligs testified that Long had genuine shock amnesia, a type of lost memory suffered by thousands of combat soldiers. The news of his wife's love affair, her statement about his child were unendurable shocks to him. Moreover, the reputation and integrity of Dr. Zeligs were unassailable.

But why was there no Grand Jury investigation of Peck? The man's alibi stood uncontradicted. Even fingerprint evidence would have been worthless, for Peck admitted intimacy in the apartment. Oddly enough, the evidence that sufficed to convince the jury of Long's innocence was not strong enough to warrant action against another man.

Some mystery probably will linger forever over this most extraordinary courtroom drama.

THE HARDEST LESSON

CAPE COD, 1951

SOME psychologists believe that character is fixed in childhood and can never be changed. But my friend Dr. Edwin declares that anyone who wants to change himself can do so at any age, if he has the courage.

Dr. Edwin was that rare combination among neurologists, a thorough scientist and a deeply religious man. Friends called him a doctor of heartache. As a prize example of his faith, he liked to tell the case of Frank Dudley.

When the blow fell, in the middle of his life, Dudley did not feel that any part of his character was in need of repair. Born poor, he had put himself and his younger brother through college, and then, on sheer nerve he had formed his own advertising agency in New York and earned a modest fortune.

One autumn afternoon, Dudley checked in at a Boston hotel, never dreaming that three brief telephone calls were about to change his life. First he called his brother's home and when his sister-in-law answered, he said:

"Agnes, how would you and Eddie like to run down here and have dinner with me?"

"No, thanks," Agnes said in the brisk tone which often nettled him. "Eddie has a business appointment tonight and I'm going to be busy, too. When he calls, though, I'll tell him to give you a ring."

Was there in her voice a faintly acrid undertone? Shrugging off suspicion, he called an old college friend, whose answer made Dudley reel:

"We're going to the big party Agnes is giving tonight for your brother Eddie. We'll see you there!"

Bewildered, Dudley replaced the receiver. Something gruesome must be going on. He would soon find out. But the tingle of the telephone bell forestalled him:

"Frank? This is Eddie. How are you, fellow? Sorry I'm tied up for tonight. How about lunch tomorrow?"

Scarcely knowing what he said, the older man mumbled assent. In lonely consternation, he looked down at the street as if the world were rolling another way.

No two men had ever been closer than he and Eddie, especially since high-school days, when in one winter, both parents had died. He had been father and brother both to Eddie and he would have bet his business that nothing could ever sever the ties between them. Naturally they had not been so close since Eddie's marriage. Not by the smallest sign had the older brother betrayed his disappointment in the match. Agnes could never make herself an intellectual companion for Eddie, who was a teacher of history, a scholar; with the right background and influence, he might one day have become president of a college.

Nevertheless, Frank Dudley had treated his sister-in-law with tender gusto, saluting her with a ceremonious kiss when they met, and when they parted. But not once had Agnes kissed him first.

Why had they lied to him? After a sleepless and brooding night and a frazzled breakfast, he could hold back no longer; he drove out to his brother's house.

Agnes opened the door. She was small and dark and quick in her movements. Plainly she was in the midst of setting the room to rights, after a festive evening.

"Eddie's left already," she announced. "He had some class papers——"

"Agnes! Why didn't you and Eddie invite me last night?"

To his chagrin, there was a catch in his voice.

"Frank, I'm really very sorry. It just couldn't be helped. Blame it all on me. Eddie wanted to ask you. But I told him I'd rather not have the party——"

"In God's name, why?"

"You'd have ruined everything, that's all."

"How can you say such a terrible thing?"

"Because it's true, Frank. Why do you suppose we ever came to Boston, except to get away to ourselves? Eddie is a fine and wonderful person—yet you hurt him every time you come around. You just take charge; you're the big successful man who has to impress everybody. You top everything Eddie says, every opinion he expresses, every story he tries to tell—you contradict him and make him look foolish in front of his friends, in front of me, in front of his own child. Well, last night the president of the college was coming to dinner. We hope Eddie's going to be promoted. It means everything to us. Why should you take the spotlight and spoil everything? That's why, for once in my life, I put my foot down."

Her hand was unsteady as she smoothed back a wisp of hair.

"I've always known what you really think of me, Frank. But there's one thing I can tell you—I try to make Eddie happy and that's more than you ever do."

"I'm not like that at all," he cried.

"Aren't you though?" she said miserably. "You ought to get wise to yourself."

Frank Dudley turned away. His sister-in-law looked as if she was going to faint as she shut the door.

Eventually Dudley appeared in the office of his club fellow, Dr. Edwin.

"I'm not sick," he insisted. "But I can't get this thing out of my mind and I can't decide what to do. That woman is my mortal enemy and I won't let her separate Eddie and me. There must be a solution."

Dr. Edwin looked at his friend over the rims of his glasses.

"There is," he declared flatly. "But you won't like it. That sister-in-law gave you the best possible advice when she told you to get wise to yourself. Philosophers have been saying the same thing for thousands of years—'Man, know thyself.' But almost nobody ever has the nerve to do it."

"I think I know myself all right," said Dudley.

"Which self? Like everybody else in the world, you are not one person, but three. You are the man you think you are, the man other people think you are—and the man you really are. And generally that last one is the man nobody knows. If you ever have the nerve to make his acquaintance, you might change your whole life."

A gaunt look had settled on Dudley's troubled face.

"I'll do anything—I'll try anything—to keep things right," he said. "You show me myself, as I really am."

"Not I! Only you can do that. But I can suggest how to start. Why don't you play the game I like to call spiritual solitaire? You become a detective and spy on yourself. Watch yourself! Listen to yourself! Weigh your thoughts and impulses! Don't write or telephone or go to Boston until I say so. When you are ready, come to see me again."

It seemed to Dudley that the old neurologist had failed him. When he went to dinner, he had no intention of playing the game. He sat down at a round table with several other men, most of whom he knew. Presently one of the group began to tell a joke.

As he launched into his yarn, the man's eyes were glowing, all his slight powers were exerted to impersonate the characters. But, as it happened, Dudley had heard the story before, and his eyes wandered away. He was thinking of another yarn, much funnier than this one; he meant to tell it the moment the narrator finished. He could hardly wait for the story to be over. His fingers were beating a fidgeting tattoo on the tablecloth, when with a jolt he remembered his new game. It was almost as if Dr. Edwin had jogged his elbow, while the words of Agnes resounded in his memory:

"*You top everything he says, every opinion he expresses, every story he tries to tell——*"

Dudley was conscious of a chilly feeling down his back as if something weird were happening. He shivered as a shout of laughter followed the finish of the story. All at once, eager to appease himself, Dudley blurted out:

"Gosh, that's a good one! And how magnificently you told it!"

The storyteller turned to him with an utterly grateful glance. The little company lingered at the table, bound spontaneously in that hour of friendliness. Dudley kept leading the applause and thoroughly enjoying it all. As they were breaking up, the first storyteller told him he was one of the most interesting fellows ever—and Dudley had scarcely spoken a word all evening!

This experience was the beginning of a prolonged interior adventure. At lunch the next day with a business associate he learned that a certain man wanted to be elected vice president of a trade association.

"That won't be easy," Dudley objected.

"Why not?"

Fortunately, Dudley hesitated. He must make hesitation a habit, just to keep himself in bounds. What was it he had been about to say? He had intended to reveal how much he knew about the feelings among the associates, how they came to him for advice; he meant to hold forth, to expound——

But again the voice of Agnes ironically echoed in his memory: *"You're the big successful man who has to impress everybody——"*

"That man," he stammered, "is too good for a vice president. He'd make a great president."

"Dudley," cried the other with a whoop of joy, "you talk like a statesman. He's my closest friend, you know—and with your help we can put him over."

But Dudley was inwardly astonished at the meanness he had come so close to committing. If the truth must be faced, he was not much better than a he-gossip, a ponderous tattletale. And why? Simply because he was under a constant temptation to be interesting. He wanted people to listen to him, to think how important he was, how much on the inside of everything.

"From now on, to hell with all that," he said fervently.

But it's one thing to consign vanity to hell and another thing to keep it there. Dudley was tracking down the mental habits of a lifetime and they had a sly way of disguising themselves. He could be—and usually was—analytical and realistic about the failings of others, but he was instinctively romantic about all his own traits. What was stingy in the other fellow was simple thrift in himself.

There were many such discoveries. It startled him to detect the gossip with which he spiced conversation; the little detractions his tongue uttered against men whom he called his friends. More than once he found, to his horror, that he was capable of rejoicing over one man's misfortune and grieving over another man's success. Dudley was shocked, yet enthralled. Even the unpleasant things reported to him from his critics became valuable clues in his quest for truth, often bringing an unexpected bonus of laughter. There were times when Dudley had to roar at his own inconsistencies. And the more he learned about himself, the easier it was to understand others and forgive them.

One day, while packing his bags, he realized that two weeks had gone by and he had not returned to Dr. Edwin. With a package under his arm he called at the neurologist's office, and related his recent adventures in the deep interior of his personality.

"And what about the brother's wife? Are you still angry with her?"

"Doctor, I have taken an inventory of my own damn foolishness, and I am so sore at myself I haven't room to be sore at anybody else."

"Then," sighed Dr. Edwin comfortably, "why don't you go to Boston?"

"The plane leaves in an hour. It happens that this is my young nephew's birthday. His present is in this package. At first I was going to buy him a $200 camera, but I realized that would be more expensive than anything his father could give him. So I got a bigger idea. This is something no other kid in the world could have."

And with the gift under his arm, Dudley hurried away.

His heart was pounding when he came to his brother's door. Agnes looked at him as she invited him in. Presently he sat with Eddie, Jr., on the living-room divan, the gift package opened on his knees. It was a stout black book and the worn cover had no title.

"This scrapbook," began Dudley, "is something I've been keeping for years. It's filled with things about your father, Eddie; clippings from sport pages when he was high school swimming champion; he won over me as well as everybody else. Snapshots. And letters people wrote me when your dad was sent overseas and for a long time was reported missing. Here's a note about that from my second best friend in the world. Look what he said about your Dad. 'You,' he says—meaning me—'you have a brilliant mind, but your brother Eddie has splendor of the heart and that's a lot more important.'"

In the silence, as the child read the letter, finger-tracing every word, Dudley saw Agnes turn her back and go to the window.

"Well, who is your very best friend?" asked Eddie, Jr.

"The lady at the window," said Dudley. "A good friend tells you the truth. Your mother did that for me when I needed it most, and I can never thank her enough for it."

In answer Agnes did something for the first time in his life or hers—she came back to the divan and put her arms around Frank Dudley and gave him a sister's kiss.

On two other occasions this psychological trick of listenning to oneself totally changed a pattern of life that was leading to disaster. One was the tape-recording taken of everything said by a certain famous star while she was on the 4th night of one of her prolonged and habitual drunks. A week after she crept home from the hospital into which she had eventually been poured, the tape was run off. It was late at night and she was alone in her room preparing for bed. She listened to her own mouthings, curses, threats, fears, tears, babblings of times past and stark self-revelation. She never drank again.

An industrialist who had long feared he was slipping heard Fulton Oursler tell of that experiment. He set up a recorder in his office, and one in his home, and gave instructions to have them turned on almost continuously, unknown to him. He recorded himself for a week. Then carefully listened. He heard his own views and inflections on a multitude of subjects, his behavior with dozens of people. He said he broke out in a cold sweat over and over again. He packed up and went to the mountains alone for a week. He came back with fresh attitudes. "But I wouldn't recommend it to anyone else," he said. "It could kill as well as cure."

IN THE MIDST OF DEATH

NEW YORK, 1952

I DO not know what a theologian would say about these facts. But they are facts, beyond suspicion. The information came to Rev. Dr. William Wysham, general secretary of the Foreign Board of the Presbyterian Church from a Korean minister of the Gospel, the Rev. Kyung Chik Han of Seoul and Pusan. He described what is certainly one of the unforgettable episodes of the Korean conflict.

A group of South Korean young men were chosen for a dangerous assignment. They were to cross the enemy lines in disguise, infiltrate among North Korean and Chinese Communist troops, and bring back military information.

Dressed in the uniform of Communist soldiers, obtained from prisoners of war, they crossed the lines in the dark of the moon. But luck was against them. The party, 30 in all, was taken prisoner. But since the men were wearing the wrong uniform, they were not prisoners of war, but spies, and their fate must be death, immediately.

Two companies of soldiers dragged them to the side of a little hill and lined them up for execution. One firing squad was composed of North Korean soldiers, the other of Chinese Communists. The hands of the victims were tied behind them. In another instant, rifles would be raised and they would all be dead.

And then, in the silence just before the command to fire, there came a most unexpected sound of music.

Four boyish voices were raised in song. The melody was "Annie Laurie"; the Korean words were the measures of a Christian hymn called "Bright Heavenly Way." Four young captives were singing that religious ballad from the Korean hymnal, set to an old Scotch air. They were singing it because they were Christian converts and had made a compact among themselves that if they were caught and condemned, they would testify to their faith before they died.

A snarl came from the captain of the Korean squad. Turning to the leader of the Chinese Communists, he said:

"Will you gentlemen please step aside? These wicked and defiant men dare to call themselves Koreans. We North Koreans want the privilege of killing them off."

Glaring at the captives, he ordered them to turn around, their backs to the guns. Two brisk commands—and then a sudden thunder. Thirty captives fell to the ground. It was all over.

But not all over, as had been expected. The 30 spies of the United Nations lying on the ground felt the touch of gentle hands. They heard kind voices telling them to stand up. Were they in heaven? Were these angels? As they staggered to their feet, they beheld the truth.

The entire squad of Chinese Communists lay dead on the ground before them. The North Koreans had executed their Chinese companions and had spared the lives of their prisoners.

"We are all friends," declared the leader of the North Koreans. "We, too, hate Communism. We do not need to kill each other. Let us go over South together."

"And," said the Rev. Kyung Chik Han of Seoul and Pusan, "they came back across the lines, arms in arms—all because of four brave Christian students."

Fulton Oursler felt there should be a collection of stories about the often incredible wonders of mission-and-chaplain work in relation to the Armed Forces. His notebooks show he half-planned such a book under the working title, They Were There Ahead, and an alternate title, God and the Army. In remotest hills and islands natives were found who welcomed and aided the white man, even in uniform. Many already knew the language and knew the ways of sanitation, medicine, rudimentary engineering. Yes, even tin-can shower baths.

WHAT MAKES A JUVENILE DELINQUENT?

CAPE COD, 1950

FOR over a decade I have enjoyed the friendship of Eleanor and Sheldon Glueck, who have devoted the major part of their lives to the study of the criminal personality and the mentally unbalanced. My own steady absorption in the mystery of crime in human nature, sparked in earliest boyhood by Conan Doyle, has been nourished often by long debates and discussions with the Gluecks. Sheldon is Professor of Criminal Law and Criminology at Harvard Law School and his wife, Dr. Eleanor Touroff Glueck, is Research Associate. In 1950 they finished a prolonged scientific study of juvenile delinquency* for the Commonwealth Fund and in November of the same year published their findings, which throw hopeful light on the riddle of hostile character and incorrigible behavior.

If potential lawbreakers could be spotted on their first day in school—before they have ever thrown stones at train

***Unraveling Juvenile Delinquency*, by Sheldon and Eleanor T. Glueck. XV—399 pages. Published, 1950, by Commonwealth Fund. Price $5.00.

windows, set fire to houses, slugged, stolen, raped or murdered—we could save lives, careers, untold heartaches and literally billions of dollars every year. This constant dream of psychologists and churchmen comes much nearer to reality in the Gluecks' survey.

One out of every 100 American boys becomes a police problem; 230,000 boys are brought into court every year. These government figures account only for those who get arrested; at least twice the number are handled unofficially by social and church agencies. How many escape detection altogether is beyond surmise, but juvenile delinquency increases at a frightening rate.

Character prophylaxis—the testing of children early and periodically to detect malformation of personality when the twig can still be bent—is as necessary as are periodic medical examinations.

Searching for factors common to child offenders, the Gluecks began their 11-year survey by carefully selecting 1000 youngsters for what was really an unexampled scrutiny. Five hundred were normal boys doing well in home and school. All the other 500 had been in police trouble; most of them sentenced to reformatories after judges, doctors, social agencies and church workers had tried in vain to help them.

What is the basic difference between good boys and bad, the blessed and the damned? There are dozens of theories, from the baneful effects of slums and bad companions to possession by evil spirits. But no known theory of juvenile delinquency covers all the facts.

In one New York tenement, two brothers were born, a year or so apart. They played in the same alleys, were neglected by the same mother, abused by the same father. One became a gangster and a killer. The other became a detective whose grisly job it was, one day, to bring his own brother to justice.

What made the brothers different? Obviously, environment could be only a part of the answer. The overwhelming majority of boys, born in wrong streets and raised in wrong families, turn out all right. It was the purpose of the new survey to find all the factors.

The investigators decided to match, as nearly as possible, bad boys with good boys of equal age, background, intelligence and disposition. By twos and twos the 1000 lads were laboriously paired to make comparisons acutely significant. So the troublemaker from a family paying $26 a month rent must have his opposite from a similar low-rent family; Greeks to match Greeks, a stepson for a stepson.

Chosen and paired off, the boys were stripped nude, weighed, measured and photographed. A medical examination was followed by tests of intelligence and achievement, a study of constitutional or "somatic" traits, and a psychiatric interview. Family backgrounds and personal histories of the 1000 boys were also explored.

Out of a final maze of decimals and calculations and tables of statistics, there emerges—in the mind of this reader, at least—an astounding creature: a composite juvenile delinquent.

Not in body, mind or spirit is he what you might expect him to be. Even in the cold precision of scientific detail, he appears, with all his dangerous propensities, a lonely and baffled creature, worthy of help. So many of his traits would make for dynamic manhood if drawn into different channels!

To begin with, he has a handsome physique. There is nothing undernourished about him; in height and weight he is superior to most of the good boys. He is more dynamically masculine, a fellow of bone and muscle tightly knit and with very little fat; not round and flabby, nor fragile and skinny, as are many non-delinquents. Neck, shoulders and chest are braced, but he has a tapering torso and narrow hips.

Far from being the underprivileged runt of sentimental legend, the delinquent is likely to have the form of an athlete.

While there is no intention, of course, of suggesting a "criminal type," this portrait of an athletic masculine delinquent does not, in the words of the authors, "in any sense represent merely random variations. It is a meaningful anatomical pattern."

More surprises appear in the health examination. The delinquent is not at all the product of bodily disease or weakness. There is "very little, if any difference in the general health status of the two groups." Except for one thing:

The handgrip of the delinquent is startlingly stronger, reflecting greater vitality.

Thus, another old illusion is dashed. "There is," the report recalls, "a popular notion that juvenile delinquents are on the whole a less healthy group of youngsters. The facts by no means bear out this belief."

A final surprise develops in the health studies:

"There is a statistically significant difference in the proportion of delinquents and non-delinquents evidencing neurological handicaps of one sort or another."

What difference?

More good boys have neurological troubles than do bad boys!

Among the non-delinquents are found more who stutter, who lisp, who have tics, or other defects. Fewer of the bad boys have any psychoneurotic tendencies at all.

How intelligent is this mentally and physically healthy delinquent who, as we know, has repeatedly committed vicious crimes? What is his "aggregate or global capacity to act purposively, to think rationally and to deal effectively with his environment"?

In this survey intelligence or psychological tests were by no means a dominating factor; because ". . . the I.Q. standing alone nowadays is regarded as somewhat naive and not always helpful." Even so, the survey demonstrated that low or moronic mentality is no characteristic of juvenile delinquency.

While in certain tests, the delinquent is a little—but only a little—inferior, he is, in others, somewhat superior. Out of thousands of tests in "hand-mindedness," for example, he emerges to convince investigators that delinquents "evidently have a little more of some sort of creative ability."

It is in temperamental make-up that more positive factors of delinquency appear. Our feelings have more to do with shaping character and behavior than our brains have. These deeper aspects of intelligence are explored by use of the Rorschach test. To the layman the process seems almost mystical, yet psychologists regard the test as a powerful instrument in diagnosis.

With ten ink blots on cards, examiners draw from a child the darkest secrets of his mind. What does the shapeless blotch make him think of? Strangely, the human mind, beholding the crazy designs, tends to find evocative symbols. Telling what thoughts they evoke in him, the boy begins to reveal himself.

The inquirers learn that from earliest childhood, the delinquent has found it hard to "think and act in the ways of the community," which means that he lacks what we call common sense.

He seems constitutionally unable to follow a methodical approach to any problem; his "social assertion" gets in the way. Not self-assertion, which is "the faculty of asserting one's rights, demands, opinions in a direct and open manner, without exaggerated aggressiveness." The delinquent's "social assertion" is his determination to assert his will. He wants what he wants when he wants it, never mind what anybody else says or thinks.

In this dangerous difference lies the boy's defiance of decent and natural restraints; a major symptom. To his nature all submissiveness is odious. As if by instinct, he refuses to respect any rules. Yet, at times, he is of two minds about authority; he may both hate and love his father, fear or envy him. So with others who have power over him; he may live in a mental climate of emotional tension and conflict.

But make no mistake; the boy has little or no feeling of "insecurity." He is not a prey to anxiety, and suffers neither from frustration nor inferiority. He does not worry about losing his job, his home or his liberty. He is loftily sure he is smart enough to take care of himself.

His inner grief and resentments arise because he feels he is a superior being who is not appreciated. With grandiose notions about his destiny, he has no sense of dependency, no normal fear of failure or defeat. Incurable optimist, when the law catches up with him, he is always sure that next time he will "get away with it." He is the most self-reliant of lads; the good boy, whom he scorns, is more often the one who looks to others for help and encouragement. The delinquent does not care what anybody thinks;

he feels no need at all to live up to the expectations of others; basically he does not wish to co-operate.

But, for all his cocksureness, he is forever making blunders. Driven, like everyone else, to get satisfaction for his human needs, he acts on impulse, with little self-control. One can never tell what he will do next. Yet in all his headstrong ways, he shows a certain charming vivacity, a liveliness of manner which makes him outshine many a solid and dependable young citizen.

Psychologists call him an extrovert, because he is apt to get rid of his tensions through emotional tantrums or rugged action. Seldom, if ever, does he allow disturbed feelings to pile up inside his mind; he doesn't brood; he explodes. It is most unlikely that our incorrigible will ever become a mental patient; only 3.2 per cent of the 500 delinquents had marked neuroses.

Perhaps his most significant trait is identified in the psychiatric tests when some of his hopes and dreams began to appear.

Far more than most boys do, the incorrigible lad yearns for adventure. All youngsters have such daydreams, but the delinquent believes in them; with him the need for danger is a compulsion, an unsatisfied thirst.

He and his like are born that way; an uncertain number of boys have always been born that way, and in olden times, it was much easier to do something about it. Then boys could run away to sea; climb the crow's-nest and struggle with man and nature. Or they could join a train of covered wagons and actually stand with their elders and shoot it out with redskins and bandits. Others ran away with the circus or followed the army. Finding excitement, they ultimately matured, if they survived, and finished their lives as more or less exemplary citizens.

Not so today. Ship captains and circus bosses are too afraid of the law and of unions to hire runaway boys. At home, what excitement is to be had? Only in violating the law. To obey his impulses, to find real thrills on the home front, the boy must make himself a criminal.

"This definite preference of the delinquents for adventurous activities," the report declares, "for exciting forms of recreation, is one of the more striking findings of this study."

To satisfy the craving, a boy will spend endless hours in the movies, watching some cheap melodrama over and over again. He steals rides, hops trucks, keeps late hours, roaming the streets long after midnight; he exults in destructive mischief, begins to drink in his early teens, or even before. His haunts are those of his gang—waterfront, railroad yards, poolrooms, cheap dance halls and amusement parks. One half of all the 500 delinquents were active members of gangs, organized for a definite antisocial purpose and having vigorous leadership.

The delinquent was not led into crime by bad companions. The survey shatters that illusion also. From earliest childhood, he shows a preference for other boys as unmanageable as himself. He avoids good boys because he despises them.

"This tendency," the report declares, "is a much more fundamental fact in any analysis of causation than the theory that accidental association of delinquents and non-delinquents is a basic cause of crime."

Although he can never hold on to any possession very long, the delinquent has a broad streak of acquisitiveness; he wants money or whatever may catch his eye, quite above the desire for their immediate use.

Meanwhile, other investigators are studying his home

and family, and there, also, immediate signs and tokens appear.

Most of the good boys live with father and mother; more delinquents come from broken homes, parents separated, divorced, or parted by imprisonment and death. The earnings per person in matching flats are 20 per cent lower in delinquent families. His family is more likely to be dependent on relief agencies and doles.

The delinquent's home is not as clean; is more crowded and has less sanitary facilities. There is crowding in beds and no privacy. "The under-the-roof situation," the report states, "is significantly worse among the delinquents than in the homes of non-delinquents."

So we see that even when matching boys are drawn from the same slums there are differences in family self-respect and integrity which count heavily. When one boy is good and another bad in the same family, however, the differences narrow down to individual temperament, and these symptoms need to be discovered at the earliest moment.

More important, there is a certain cohesion in the better families, a "we" feeling of strong emotional ties. Here we come close to the heart of the whole matter.

The most significant factor in any boy's life is his relationship with his parents and especially with his father. When it is disturbed—as it is so often in sordid surroundings—the child is already in danger. Even if the father is a loafer, a drunkard, the boy may love him if he is kind, but if the father shows hostility or contempt, something is dammed up in the son. He has a deep, passionate need for "emotional identification" with his father; he needs an ideal image, a paternal, older, wiser friend. That deep human hunger for emulation will be turned elsewhere—and perhaps the disappointed boy begins to worship the strongest, boldest, toughest ne'er-do-well in the district. This, complicated with the young panic that overwhelms when the father deserts, or is sent to prison, naturally produces a frightened child looking for a substitute.

The survey shows that the delinquent has long been at odds with his father while most of the good boys on the block remain close to their fathers.

Moreover, the incorrigible has suffered from erratic and conflicting discipline, which has encouraged him to defy all authority. He has taken many beatings for his sins, and learned nothing from them except how to endure pain, which may be of grisly use to him in a criminal career. Physical punishment does not come off very well in this survey.

It is a coincidence that a similar survey has just been completed in England, by Dr. H. Stott, a British psychologist whose work was financed by the Carnegie United Kingdom Trust. Dr. Stott's report, which also covers nearly 500 pages, analyzes only 102 cases of juvenile delinquency, but comes to very much the same conclusions—including a declaration that nursery schools are preferable to the wrong kind of home, or the "minding" of the child by untrained brothers and sisters or hired baby sitters. "The tough nuts," Dr. Stott declares, agreeing with the Gluecks, cannot be induced to take refuge in youth clubs or playgrounds; "the lost sheep" must be sought out in the very early years.

After 11 years of work, the Glueck investigators felt they had found certain characteristics of delinquents. But not all of these traits would appear in the very young child; many develop only with the years. Would enough storm signals show up in a six-year-old to make a forecast possible?

This question was answered by setting up a series of "predictive tables" listing outstanding signs of delinquency which can and do manifest themselves at a very early age.

Was the boy markedly adventurous? Extroverted in action? Stubborn? Emotionally assertive? Did he exhibit "social assertion"—the aggressive infliction of his will on others? Was he defiant? Suspicious? Destructive? Did he display emotional lability—headlong impulsiveness, without thinking things over beforehand? Was he highly suggestible—letting his feelings rule his thoughts, more than most do?

From the factors in the social background, it was also important to know whether the discipline of the father was lax, overstrict or erratic—or firm but kindly. The importance of this type of question becomes evident when the statistics show that of the boys where discipline by the father was lax, 59.8 per cent were in the delinquent group; of those whose fatherly discipline was firm but kindly, only 9.3 per cent were delinquent. Was the mother's supervision suitable or not? Was the father affectionate to his son or hostile? The same question must be asked about the mother. Was the family held together by ties of sympathy and warmth of feeling?

These are major factors from which a character diagnosis can be made. It is a stripping down to practical essentials of thousands of facts, contrasting statistics, and psychiatric observations. From such a streamlined inquiry, simple as it sounds, the danger clues will appear.

But the list of these and other crucial factors, do not, of course, tell the whole story. Something more than statistics must be drawn upon by the good clinician; face to face with a child, he is aware of the uniqueness that belongs to every human personality; he feels *en rapport* and by what some psychologists call "clinical hunches" he perceives signs and symptoms below the surface. The wise operator regards these special insights as "experienced intuitions." It has been said that the "assessment of men . . . is the scientific art of arriving at sufficient conclusions from insufficient data."

Moreover, no child could be expected to show all the symptoms. Any child might have several of them and still not be a potential delinquent. But it is beyond argument a danger signal when most of such factors appear in a six-year-old. The chances are that, if not stopped in time, he will become a criminal. Here, then, was a technique of discovery.

How scientific are such techniques? It is, of course, true that prophetic infallibility is beyond the reach of social scientists. They are working in the realm of probabilities. But there are reliable laws in probabilities and by applying these gauges to young children, it is asserted that from 65 per cent to 70 per cent of the delinquents can be isolated at six years of age, when there is still a chance to help them.

To skeptics the Gluecks point out that Dr. Arnold Gesell, Director of the Clinic of Child Development at Yale University, is able to size up far younger children, rating even infants for adoption as "highly favorable, favorable or unfavorable risks"—and solely by psychological tests.

Assuming that a forecast is correct, what then? Are they sure that a potential delinquent can be guided into integrity and adjust himself to the world? The answer is a resounding "yes"—followed by warnings of difficulties.

"People," Dr. Glueck points out, "realize that in cancer

or poliomyelitis we are dealing with complex diseases and that years of research will be required before cures or preventatives are discovered. But when it comes to the even more complex mystery of human nature, they take it for granted that delinquency is a simple matter—boys just decide to be bad—for which there must be simple cures."

But the problem is not simple and the program for treatment will call for boldness and imagination.

Many techniques are ready and waiting to be used. The notable work done by Professor Ernest Ligon at Union College is a shining example. About 15,000 children have been given new directions in his laboratory, and their basic wrong attitudes transformed. The work of Father Flanagan at Boys' Town, of Floyd Starr in his Commonwealth are two that stand out among others. It is notable that in all of these, one of the greatest techniques is tender and loving care—the quality most often missing in the lives of delinquents. The people working in such projects offer themselves as substitutes for the lost ideal of a boy's love for his father.

Our schools need to be radically changed. Their first task must be the development of integrated personality in children, rather than merely teaching academic tidbits. Unless teachers are thoroughly trained in mental hygiene, many children will continue to knock their heads against a stone wall of adult indifference to their vital problems.

We must recognize the nobler role of teachers as parent substitutes, as "ego-ideals" in the strengthening of character—and teachers must make themselves worthy of that great role.

We must identify and take into account temperamental differences of children—their special abilities and disabilities. Forcing all types into one traditional mold breeds tension and revolt. The answer lies in supplying a rich variety of school regimes to suit various types. For example, city schools might well provide curricula for "hand-minded" boys who like to deal with concrete materials rather than arithmetic symbols and abstractions.

Above all, activities ought to be framed to provide outlets for the excessive energy of those who hunger and thirst for adventure. How can society take a boy away from the waterfront and the railroad yard, and, in a more congenial atmosphere, give him the excitement his nature craves? "Supervised play" will just not do. All the delinquents in the tests had long before been exposed to settlement house and playground—but not one would stay there. All hold such places in bitter dislike and contempt.

But the Junior Police Forces established in some American cities are an example of what can be done. Boys trained to go into danger to help enforce the law are far less inclined to break it. This principle could be extended to junior apprentices for fire department and other careers of danger and daring.

A program of treatment must be set up so that each child may receive individual care and guidance. This would be an expensive process, but worth it. The cost would be petty compared with the treasure now being poured into criminal courts, prisons and parole boards—too late.

Again, we must be bold enough to try to mold the under-the-roof culture of the homes of young children around better goals. Difficult, yes—but by no means impossible. If at six years old a child shows that he is probably going to grow up to be a criminal, and the fault lies partly in his home and his relations with his father, or his family, then society should do something about the home and family—to improve both, or else remove the child into a more healthful place.

More important, looking to the future, we need to work for better homes and wiser families. As a matter of course young persons should be taught in school the fundamentals of happy marital relations and family life long before they ever venture into marriage. Such teaching should not be on a superficial level. It should involve the fundamentals of mental hygiene and ethics as basic tools for coping with the problems of family life in our troubled and exciting age.

We must break the vicious circle of character-damaging influence exerted on children by parents who are themselves distorted personality products of bad homes and families.

For such an ambitious project, men and women need to be trained. It calls for a new type of expert in dynamic psychology, sociology and anthropology—and human sympathy. Few, if any, exist today. Father Flanagan was such a man; Floyd Starr is such a man.

Every finding of this survey shows a crying need for early recognition of the emotional problems of childhood as a part of the normal duty of society. Here, for the first time, is a method, a technique by which the duty can be met. This fact makes the survey of profound importance. But there remains one last, grim hazard. Says Dr. Glueck:

"At the very outset we are confronted by the delinquent culture of our times. We are living in an era of violence. A tremendous network of agencies spreads suggestions and ideas—radio, television, motion pictures, press. We must survive in a highly competitive economic order, where everyone can see corrupt politics making a mockery of moral platitudes. Old fears of breaking the moral laws are gone. As long as our culture is so greatly predatory, as long as prominent large-scale offenders continually escape prosecution and politicians pal with corrupt elements who finance their campaigns, we cannot, without hypocrisy, decry the delinquencies of the young. We fail to present our youth with a consistent, morally wholesome set of values. That is one basic reason why preaching to the young is greeted by them with amused cynicism. They know us for what we are."

Fulton's mail and phone brought many appeals. Like many another who tries to answer constructively he occasionally found his attempts to help were futile, or mistaken, or even boomeranged. The only boy he managed to get into Floyd Starr's Commonwealth for Boys wouldn't stay there. Of three men paroled in his custody, one never reported; one drank, grew hair, and wrote poetry that earned him $500 a year in slim little books; and the third refused steady jobs and fitfully started "businesses" run for the most part out of a suitcase. All three were extraordinarily brilliant, all had a wide streak of sentimentality, even ardent devotions, as long as no prolonged responsibility or endurance was involved. None had any sense of morals or ethics. Oddly enough, they all had humor.

They puzzled him. Crime and criminals always did. Magazines written and printed behind prison walls interested him.

One Saturday afternoon Fulton took his two older children for a special outing "on the town." As they walked home they approached a street-crowd facing the doorway of what really was an unoccupied store. A man high above them was lecturing; a huge health book up-

raised in his hand. And suddenly the 3 Ourslers gulped, for the man was saying—"You take my friend Fulton Oursler! Was he badly off! Underweight. Dragged out, pale—just a walking shadow. He found out from this book what was wrong with him. Constipation! That's what. And today he's vigorous and——"

That was the third parolee! Later, Fulton phoned him: "What's the idea of using my name in your oratory, feller?" And he was answered: "You told *me you'd do anything to help me! Never occurred to me I'd have to* ask *you!"*

Once Fulton received a manuscript about a crime committed by the writer, who was soon to be executed. It was verified by the Sheriff of the county concerned. The writer was a Chinese and wished the price of the story as soon as possible to guarantee the shipment of his remains to his homeland for burial. Payment was forwarded to him with all possible speed. Then, a year later, Oursler was shocked to receive another story from the same Chinese!

"I thought," wrote F. O., "you were decently interred by now in your ancestral plot. How many crimes have you committed, and are they all as fascinating?"

"Did you really fall for that stuff?" the Chinese answered. "The Sheriff and I split the last check. He really rated it for the fine job of faking the papers. We can give you all the crime you can take."

THE NIGHTMARE

NEW YORK, 1951

LAURA, my friend, suspects that I had arranged the whole affair, just for her benefit. Actually it all happened by coincidence—if there is such a thing, which I am often inclined to doubt.

It began when Laura confided in me. She was, she said, in a predicament.

"The simple fact," she told me, "is that I am a coward. Most of my life I have been protected and felt secure. But now, suddenly, my mother and father have been taken from me by death. I am engaged to marry a young man but, although I love him dearly, I am afraid to marry. I feel afraid of life, afraid to face it, afraid of what it will do to me—most of all, I am afraid of death.

"I loved my mother and father and death took them. I love my young man much, much more—but the thought of being his wife and then having death separate us, sooner or later, fills me with terror. I don't believe in God any more —I just want to run away from everything. How can I find help?"

I have never fancied myself as a sage, telling other people what to do. Although I tried to help the girl, the words seemed forced and unreal. But presently an idea occurred to me. That same afternoon I was scheduled to speak on a national broadcast presented by Guideposts, a non-profit religious magazine for people of all faiths, edited by my good friend, Dr. Norman Vincent Peale. I knew that some of the other speakers were men of real inspiration and so I asked my frightened friend to listen in, sure that she would find the answer to her problem.

As the broadcast got under way, the speakers seemed to me to be talking on every other subject in the world except the conquest of fear. I was feeling quite down-hearted, when suddenly a giant of a man was called to the microphone. He was Gene Tunney, undefeated heavy-weight champion of the world. As he began to talk, it was as if he were aiming his words directly at my terrified friend.

"People often ask me if I have ever been afraid. They only make me smile. One Eastern philosopher said that any man who boasts that he has never been afraid has never put out a candle with his fingers. We are all afraid. Intelligent people, those with imagination, are the ones who know the most overpowering fears and there is only one answer to fear—and that is faith. Unless we have something greater than ourselves to believe in, we are lost. We are prey to fears unless we can pray our fears away.

"Talk about dauntless courage makes me smile. I knew what fear was every time I entered the ring. One night I shall never forget. I was sound asleep and I woke up in the dark wondering what was wrong with my bed. It was shaking like a 1910 Ford. Then I suddenly realized that it wasn't the bed shaking at all. It was I who was shaking.

I was trembling all over—with fear. That was the night before my first meeting with Jack Dempsey, and even in my dreams I was thinking of what he was going to do to me the next day. Courage? . . . It is not being fearless, it is finding the strength from God to do what you have to do—whether you are afraid or not."

My friend Laura still believes I put Gene up to it. But what does it matter? He gave her the answer—and the fact that a prize fighter was not afraid to believe in God sent her back to the faith of her childhood. Her married life has been very happy.

SPEAKER OF THE EVENING

NEW YORK, 1945

YOU are standing on the platform or the banquet dais. The audience sits before you. Anything may happen, and now and then it does. For a few moments of panic you are lost. Then you emerge from the difficulty, gracefully or disgracefully, but the lecture goes on.

I am thinking of a Sunday afternoon in Swampscott, Mass. As I walked out on the stage, the genteel club ladies greeted me with a cyclone of laughter. A black cat had marched out from the opposite wing. In such moments of sickening dismay, every public speaker needs a technique, but unhappily there can be no such thing because each new catastrophe is unique and demands its own instantaneous remedy.

At Swampscott I turned my back on the audience, thus joining them in being amused at the trespasser. The maneuver saved me from being a spectacle of embarrassment; also it gave me two precious seconds to think. When I turned, I was ready to announce a fortunate coincidence. I had long loved black cats. And I told those present why!

"Thirty years ago," I began, "I sold my first short story to a magazine published not five miles from this auditorium. Believe it or not, the name of the magazine was The Black Cat."

The ladies gave a well-bred gasp.

"I still remember the letter from the editor," I went on. "There was a picture of a black cat on the envelope. That's the same cat over there; I never forget a face."

By this time the audience was laughing with me, and not at me, and the show could go on. The story happened to be true; otherwise I could probably never have thought up a graceful handling of the incident.

Just before I was to be introduced to the Ad-Sell League, one night in Omaha, a cowboy rode a white horse right into the banquet hall of the Hotel Fontenelle. Without a preliminary word he lassoed a banker's daughter at the head table. Then he invited everyone present to come to a rodeo the following week. On the way out, the horse fell down on the polished floor, but was not hurt; everyone breathed deeper when the cowboy press agent was safely out into the Nebraska night. All that I could manage, when my turn came, was the resurrection of an indefensible pun; I told the audience that the affair left me "horse de come-back." They were kind enough to laugh and the show went on.

Sometimes words won't suffice; you have to act. At the start of one season I was speaking before a woman's club in a small Long Island town. Suddenly we all heard the drone of planes flying over the clubhouse and the moan of an air-raid siren. I interrupted myself to suggest that wardens leave for their posts. Several solemn ladies departed, and I said to the audience:

"None of us knows, of course, whether this is a test

or the real thing. Perhaps some of you would prefer to be home rather than here. Suppose we take a vote. All those in favor of going on with the lecture, please raise hands."

Bless their stout hearts, they all raised their hands, but one poor woman, in spite of her decision, had a nervous reaction; she began to cough uncontrollably. The more I tried to continue my own sound and fury, the louder she coughed, yet she showed no intention of retiring. That was the only time I have ever left a platform in the midst of a speech. Without stopping my discourse, I poured a glass of water and descended to the main floor. As I handed her the glass, I whispered:

"For Heaven's sake leave now, or the lecture will be over."

She drank and went away. But there are times when you don't know what to do, because you don't know what is wrong. There was that blizzard day when I was afternoon orator at a convention of presidents of women's clubs of Massachusetts. Nearly a thousand of them were assembled in Boston's Hotel Statler. Scarcely had I started my talk on crime prevention when a woman in the middle row stood up boldly, put on her fur coat and climbed remorselessly over her neighbors. Once in the aisle, she turned her back on me and marched out of the hall. At once, as if with perfect timing, another delegate in the right aisle rose and followed; then two on the left, more on the right, a regiment from the middle. The whole audience was walking out!

In my ear I heard the bronchitic whisper of Madame Chairman:

"Instead of the steam heat they have turned on the air conditioning by mistake."

"Ladies," I shouted, to as many backs as faces, "please

everybody stand up and put on your coats. The air conditioning has already been turned off; the heat will be on in a few minutes."

After the heat came on the audience reassembled; a patient two-thirds of the original number. Some of the fugitives later booked me, curious, no doubt, to hear what they missed.

Another far worse nightmare does sound incredible, I realize, but it did befall me, and before several hundred witnesses, most of whom are still living—and not one will ever forget. It happened at a meeting of the Square and Slipper Club in Philadelphia. During the dinner before the meeting the chairman confided in me, with what I hoped was unconscious irony:

"Before your speech, we have Doctor Blank, a famous hypnotizer. You know how it is—when the boys come out to a meeting like this, they like to have a good time."

Now, either that hypnotist had mysterious powers, or else he had subsidized several dozen members of the club and rehearsed them as comedians. Having gone through motions of bringing them under his influence, he then induced them to perform various antics. Finally he dismissed all but one man, a prominent and yet somewhat shy member of the club.

"Do you smoke?" demanded the hypnotist. "Would you like to break yourself of the habit? Very well—you will never finish another cigarette in this world. Remember! Awake!"

After the hypnotist took his bow, I was introduced. Having no mesmeric spells of my own, I tried most earnestly to garner the somewhat diffused attention of a crowd still quivering with rowdy hilarity. Presently I became aware that, sitting in the front row, directly in front of me, was the hypnotist's last subject. He did not look very well. He was glassy-eyed and he was swaying; just before the point of one of my best anecdotes, he groaned and collapsed. While I waited, the hypnotist worked over him and presently declared that he was fully awake. When I resumed, I saw that the fellow was sitting where he had sat before, though now he seemed in good health and spirits. Indeed he seemed fascinated with what I was saying; a dubious compliment, I felt. Nevertheless, he kept his eyes fixed on me attentively; he did not look at his hands as he produced a matchbox and lit a cigarette.

Well, the poor man became instantly and quite palpably ill, and there was only one thing left to do, and I did it. I asked the mystic if he would mind putting the fellow to sleep once more, and keeping him in a state of suspended animation until my part of the program was over. The obliging hypnotist complied, and the show staggered on.

But a man does not have to be hypnotized to forget what he is doing. He may be just plain scared. Once at an affair in the New York auditorium of John Wanamaker, an amateur chairman was pinch-hitting and launched into a eulogy of a new novel and its author. Then blankness whitened his face. He could not remember my name or my novel. I had to walk right out and introduce myself to him as well as to the audience.

Of course, most lectures pass off without these haggard contretemps. But again there are times when the unexpected is more disturbing than amusing.

I was lecturing in Boston's Ford Hall. On that series of Sunday night town meetings, the speaker—called in the contracts "the attraction"—talks for one hour and then undergoes another hour of reasonably good-natured heckling. My talk that evening was on subversive activities; originally it had been delivered before a graduating class of the F. B. I. Police Academy. At one point I read to the audience quotations from a magazine article by a radical woman author who had urged young men "to sabotage war and preparations for war." The questions were provocative but in good humor until five minutes before the end. Then arose a distinguished-looking man who said he was a college professor, called me "that man there" and laid me low. He denounced me for attacking a lady who had merely exercised free speech to point out choices open to youth. He was an effective speaker and the audience broke into sustained applause when he sat down. For me this threatened to be a complete defeat, dissipating the effect of a message I felt important to the war effort. There was little time to think, but St. Paul is right; it will be given you what to say and do. I knew the audience had forgotten what I had quoted and all that I did was to read a second time the advice this woman had written: "Sabotage war and preparations for war. Down tools when the order comes to speed up production," etc. Having read slowly, I turned to the professor and said:

"That is not free speech. That is treason."

The audience cheered; the chairman shouted "Adjourned!" and that show was over.

My ultimate agony as a lecturer, however, happened early in my career, in October, 1926, just a week after my daughter April was born. It began when the publicity director of Harper and Brothers called me on the telephone and said:

"A department store in one of the large cities is having a book fair. They say that you can sell many extra hundreds of your novel, *Stepchild of the Moon,* if you will speak at their fair. Will you go?"

I did not like to leave at this time but my wife insisted that I should not disappoint my eager public. So the next morning about eight-thirty found me approaching the entrance to the department store. Half a block away I could see a knot of people waiting to be let in.

"What enthusiasm," I said to myself. "The crowd begins to gather before the store is open."

On nearer view, however, I discovered that the crowd was composed entirely of authors, all there on the same errand as was I. Eventually we were let in and taken to a large auditorium where a crowd of shoppers had gathered. As I looked at them from my chair on the platform I remembered what a famous woman novelist had once told me:

"They don't come there to listen to you but because their feet are tired."

We all made little speeches and then were taken to luncheon, following which we were led to little chairs and tables on a balcony. Each author had his own chair and table, and a stack of his books. He was supposed to autograph these books as they were purchased by eager fans. I did not like this arrangement. It made me feel like a bearded lady selling post cards.

Moreover, and perhaps in self-defense, I have always felt that I was unfortunately placed. To my right sat a dashing, handsome, blond young man, the late Richard Halliburton. To my left sat the gracious and beautiful Martha Ostenso. All the girls went to Halliburton's table and all the men went to Miss Ostenso's table. Almost no one came to my table. As time wore on, the humiliation became excruciating.

The only time I really had a crowd around my table was when two nuns appeared with a deputation of orphan boys, all of whom solemnly shook hands with me, but not one of whom bought a copy of *Stepchild of the Moon.* My despair was almost complete when eventually a little old lady came to my table. She was feeble and there were tears in her eyes as she took my hand between hers and said:

"God bless you. I have read everything you have ever written. I got out of a sick bed to come down to have a look at you. Just think, I am shaking the hand of Bruce Barton."

One would think that this was enough to happen to anyone, even a sinner like myself, in one day, but my sufferings had only begun. When I could go back to the hotel it was only to get into evening clothes in time to attend a dinner of a press club and then, on farther to two other speeches at local gatherings in high schools, with three additional addresses scheduled for the morrow.

I got as far as the press club dinner. There I had to listen to the same authors whom I had heard talk in the morning, repeating the same speeches and once more recommending their own works in unmitigated phrases. They had to listen to me doing the same thing. In the midst of this it suddenly came over me that I did not have to do this, really. I could stop it if I wished to do so.

I stopped it.

I finished my speech prematurely and left the dinner at its close with the determination not to appear at the two remaining functions of the evening. Further, I determined to nourish my spirit by going to a show. The only theater that I could find was a Loew house playing a combination of vaudeville and cinema. The house was sold out but the ticket seller could give me one seat in a box. I remember that as I sat down in the box there was a shooting act being exhibited; a red-faced man was shooting apples off of his wife's head. When this act was over and the house lights came up I was presently aware of confusion in the audience. A good deal of tittering was going on.

As I looked around I discovered to my dismay that the tittering was all directed at me. The audience was pointing at me and laughing. I felt like a man in a nightmare. Why was I the cause of this universal hilarity? A moment later it dawned on me. In all that audience of a thousand or more people I was the only man in a dinner jacket. Therefore, they reasoned, I must be an actor. Undoubtedly I was a stooge for the next vaudeville turn but they had found me out in advance!

When the house lights dimmed again I crept out of the box and down a fire escape into an alley and from there I found my way back to the hotel. I telephoned home and told my wife I was taking the midnight train.

"But what about your speeches?" she said.

"Yes," I echoed bitterly, "what about them?"

Still, some explanation had to be made, so I sat down and wrote a hurried note that at the time did not seem to me too mendacious. I simply wrote to the chairman of the committee on arrangements:

"My dear Mr. Blank. The stork has left a new baby at my house. You can understand, I am sure, that I want to hurry home."

But fate was still barking at my heels. The next morning a fresh contingent of authors arrived for the fair. Among them was my old friend Thyra Samter Winslow. Said the chairman to Mrs. Winslow:

"Did you know that Fulton Oursler's wife had a baby last night?"

"My God," said Thyra, "she had one a week ago. How did she do it?"

I never went to that sort of affair again.

Fulton Oursler loved to speak. He had grown up in the sunset of both oratory and conversation. "Writing is very lonely," he said. "Far more so than reading. But when you speak, or when you hear a voice, and the moods of face and figure affect you, there *is human sharing."*

YOU FIND UNDERSTANDING AT THE TOP

NEW YORK, 1950

ONE Sunday afternoon, many years ago, the city editor of the Baltimore *American* handed me an Associated Press dispatch from Rome.

"The Pope," he told me, "has just made an important statement. See Cardinal Gibbons. Get an interview."

I found James Cardinal Gibbons, Archbishop of Baltimore and one of the most renowned of American Catholic prelates, walking in the cloisters of St. Ann's Church, intent upon his breviary. I was 16 years old, a Baptist, ignorant of ecclesiastical protocol, and a reporter for just three weeks. I waited conspicuously, hoping he would ask me what I wanted. But Gibbons continued to walk and pray.

Finally, in desperation, I barred his way. "Cardinal," I said firmly, "I am a reporter from the Baltimore *American*."

He raised his eyes to the heavens and gasped: "God

bless my soul! I might have lived to be a hundred and never have known that!"

The smile he turned on me was not merely the wise, understanding response of the great soul he was, a spirit like a searchlight; it was also a good old-fashioned American grin. His hand on my elbow, he added with bubbling good nature:

"Son, what on earth do you want?"

He gave me all the information I needed, but after all the intervening years, what I remember is that warm grin, the greeting of a great man, brashly interrupted, yet understanding and helpful. Within a short time I was to learn that truly worth-while men and women are free from smallness and almost clairvoyant in their ready understanding.

I remember President Taft, on the day a monument was unveiled at Annapolis. A few minutes before Mr. Taft was to be introduced, I learned that the reporter of the rival Baltimore *Sun* had a copy of the Presidential remarks. I elbowed my way through the crowd and headed straight for the President. A gentleman in blue and gold grabbed me: he was Major Archibald Butt, military aide to Taft.

"What do you want?" Butt demanded, with a look reserved only for assassins.

I offered him the same awe-inspiring revelation once imparted to the Cardinal.

"I am a reporter from the Baltimore *American*. Have you a copy of the speech for me?"

"No!" boomed the Major.

"But *I* have!"

I heard a volcanic chuckle, looked up and saw President Taft's broad, mustachioed smile. From his pocket he drew a copy of his speech and with a gloating glance at Butt handed it to me.

Even more unexpected was my rescue from a predicament by one of the country's richest men. That takes me back to the year when Andrew Carnegie established a foundation for peace with a gift of ten million dollars. There came a great day when the American Peace Congress met in our town.

My task was to list the names of notables in the boxes. Eventually I came to the Carnegie box; the steel master was even then making a speech from the stage. I took down the names and asked where Mrs. Carnegie was.

Someone said: "Mrs. Carnegie has been taken ill and carried to the ladies' room."

The door of the ladies' room I found to be guarded by a towering colossus who bore a striking resemblance in size and demeanor to John L. Sullivan.

"What do you want?"

I went into my familiar song: "I am a reporter——"

But this time I saw no grin. Instead, the sentinel said distinctly:

"Get out of here."

"I can't. I'm a——"

You may be willing to die for the freedom of the press, but there is no dignity in martyrdom when you are picked up by the collar and the seat of the pants and are about to be thrown out. In that moment of anguish there suddenly appeared a little man with a white beard.

"Put him down!" exclaimed Andrew Carnegie.

"He's a damned reporter," expostulated my captor, but he let me go.

"Young man," said Mr. Carnegie to me, "you just wait here. I will come back and tell you all about my wife's illness."

He did, too.

"Don't make it sensational, but tell what happened, of course," said Carnegie. "And now, young man, shake hands. I wish you success. You know, when I came out here, you were up in the air—but I noticed you were kicking the other fellow. I liked that!"

And I saw it again—the Cardinal's grin, the President's, the millionaire's; the finest expression of an understanding heart.

Not only among the powerful and the greatly placed but among obscure men and women as well I have found the same phenomenon: worth-while people are never snobs, never conceited, never unapproachable. The growth of the human spirit brings it closer to all living.

"At the top and at the bottom—all the best," he said, when he first read this aloud. "All along the line. Neither has the time, or place, or chance for spiritual fat. Each is too worn out for pretenses, each is too busy keeping alive. The busy man can always do one thing more, right now. The very poor and the very rich get the best in aid and attention. The very great man or the most unlettered servant will give the lonely, the needy, the timid, loving concern. I bet if a bleeding runaway kid was trying to hide in this building right now, it would be that famous singer on the 12th floor or the furnace man in the basement who would reach out a hand to him."

As a matter of record, Cardinal Gibbons once helped get Fulton Oursler a raise, when the overbright young reporter wrote as a lead:

" 'Nuns are fools,' said the Cardinal this morning."

A shocked city editor howled in pain, called Oursler and told him he'd sent the story by messenger to the Car-

dinal's residence for his okay. "And if you've misquoted him, you're through right now—not Saturday." Back came the Cardinal's okay and a message: "I note that your young reporter added "fools for God" in the body of the story. He knows his St. Paul. He has done an excellent account." That week there was an extra $2.00 in Fulton Oursler's envelope, bringing his salary up to $10.

THERE IS MAGIC IN A WORD OF PRAISE

NEW YORK, 1952

A POPULAR Broadway comedian once had an excruciating nightmare. He dreamed that he was performing in a crowded theater, telling stories and singing songs, with thousands of faces watching him. But no one would laugh and no one would clap.

"Even at $100,000 a week," he says, "that would be hell on earth."

It is not only the actor who has a deep, primal need for applause. Without praise and encouragement anyone can lose self-confidence. A visitor at the house of a famous cartoonist remarked: "You must be swamped with compliments all the time."

"Not a bit more than I need," was his answer.

We all have a double necessity: to be commended and to know *how* to commend. There is a technique to giving a compliment; a right way to go about it, and especially in exercising care and discrimination in what we decide to say.

The man who glibly tells his hostess that she looks lovely in pink may cause her to wonder if he has seen her in other colors he thought not so becoming. A more discerning guest will tell her: "On you, my dear, pink looks lovely!"

Nor is it a real compliment to praise a man for some obvious attainment. "That was a wonderfully convincing speech you made tonight," a gracious woman once said to a business man. "I could not help thinking what a fine lawyer you would have made." The merchant flushed like a schoolboy at the unexpected tribute. As André Maurois once remarked: "The general did not thank me when I talked to him of his victories but his gratitude was unbounded when a lady mentioned the twinkle in his eye."

No one, great or obscure, is untouched by simple and genuine appreciation. Yale's renowned English professor, the late William Lyon Phelps, once said:

"I never go into a hotel or a barbershop or a store without saying something agreeable to everyone I meet. I try to say something that treats each one as an individual, not merely a cog in the machine. I will ask a barber how he came to take up barbering, how long he has been at it and how many heads of hair he has cut. I frequently shake hands with a redcap who has carried my grip.

"One extremely hot summer day, I went into a railroad dining car to have lunch. The crowded car was almost like a furnace and the service was slow. When the steward finally got around to handing me the menu, I said, 'The boys back there cooking in that hot kitchen certainly must be suffering today!' The steward began to curse. 'Good God Almighty!' he exclaimed. 'People come in here and complain about the food. They kick about the slow service and growl about the heat and the prices. I have listened to their criticisms for nineteen years, and you are the first person that has ever expressed any sympathy for the cooks back there in the broiling kitchen. I wish we had more passengers like you.'

"He was astounded because I had thought of the cooks not merely as cogs in the organization of a great railway. *What people want is a little attention as human beings.*"

And in that attention, in all attempts to make the whole world kin, sincerity is essential. Every self-respecting man despises flattery, "but," said Sir Richard Steele, "there can hardly be imagined a more desirable pleasure than praise unmixed with any possibility of flattery."

Such pure appreciation is still to be found in the world. The man coming home after a hard day's work, who sees the faces of his children pressed against the windowpane, waiting and watching for him, may water his soul with their golden opinion of him.

Sincerity gives potency to a compliment, even if there is some self-interest involved. A New York executive recently entered the offices of a busy firm and asked to see the president. A statuesque and remotely exquisite secretary took it as an affront to her boss that the caller came without appointment. Her frown boded no good, even though she agreed to carry in his name. As she walked toward the exit, an honest question suddenly struck the caller and he said:

"Did you learn your wonderful poise and carriage in some model's training school—or did it all just come naturally?"

Her frown vanished as if by incantation; her face was a sunrise. Without further delay, she led him into the inner sanctum. The indirect compliment was not merely a subtle technique; his question had the irresistible grace of genuine interest.

There was a tense moment one night in Detroit when Father James Keller of the Christophers was speaking on Communism. A heckler stood up and shook his fist as he screamed:

"You can hate Communists but you can't ignore us!"

"I don't hate you! I admire you," returned Keller. "I envy your tireless energy, your devotion, your sacrifices, and your knowledge of your cause. I urge our people to imitate your virtues."

The tense atmosphere broke and disappeared in friendly hand clapping. Yet Father Keller had been speaking only the truth; he had looked and found qualities to admire, even in his foes.

We have to acquire the habit of searching for the good. Edwin L. Kramer, president of the Sterling Manufacturing Company in St. Louis, Mo., is known internationally for encouraging that search.

At family dinner one evening, Mr. Kramer asked his youngsters to report the good deeds they had seen during the day. At first they could think of nothing, but by cross-examination, Kramer taught them what to look for; the grocery man had given some scraps to a poor boy for his cat; a teacher had sewn up a rent in a pupil's sleeve.

"Before you go to bed," said Kramer, "write a post card to the teacher and the grocery man and tell them how your whole family admired their kindness, when you told us about it."

Soon the father decided the idea was worth expanding. In 1948, he designed his Thank-U-Gram, a form resembling a telegraph blank, for carrying compliments. Ever since then, he has been distributing the blanks free to all who ask; more than 10,000 a month are mailed over the world. The only requirement is a promise to send out three a day, praising three persons for worth-while deeds.

"Good is all around us," Kramer insists, "but we have to train ourselves to focus attention on positive values in common experience. Soon the sense of discovery becomes automatic."

The simple principles of the art of praise—to realize the human need for it, to compliment sincerely, and to train ourselves to look for the praiseworthy—help to rub off the sharp edges of mortal contact. And nowhere more than in marriage!

Princess Alexandria Kropotkin tells of a farm woman who one hot day served cattle fodder for dinner—after waiting 20 years for a word of appreciation from her menfolk.

"I've never heard anything to make me think you'd know the difference," she said, when the husband, sons and hired hands declared she must be crazy. The nearest thing to a compliment she had ever received from her lord and master was: "You're a fine one, you are!"

More fortunate was the widow in the Blue Ridge mountains who chiseled with her own hands on a great rock an epitaph for her husband: "He always appreciated."

Women seem to have an instinct for such things; they bloom under compliment and look at life, so to speak, through their hearts. Lyon Mearson, the author, and Rose, his wife, were married on February 23.

"Well," remarked Lyon, "I will never forget our wedding anniversary. It will always be the day after Washington's birthday."

"And I," his bride answered, "will never forget Washington's birthday. It will always be the day before we were married."

The wife or husband who is constantly alert to say the heartening thing at the right moment takes out marriage insurance. One night Sir Max Beerbohm went with his aging wife to a theatrical party in London. As they entered the room he was ambushed by a horde of stage and film beauties, all eager to impress the great critic and caricaturist. Beerbohm turned to the simple and gracious lady on his arm and whispered: "My dear, let's find a quiet corner. You are looking so charming tonight that I simply must talk to you."

Children, too, are hungry for reassurance; when their need is unfilled, the growth of their character is endangered; the want of kindly appreciation in childhood can be a lifetime calamity.

One night a woman came to the home of the Rev. A. W. Beaven, with a heartaching little confession:

"My little daughter often says and does wrong things and I have to rebuke her. But today I noticed that she had not done a single thing to irritate me. When I tucked her in bed and started down the stairs I heard her sobbing, and turning back, I found her head buried in the pillow. When I asked her why she cried, she said between her sobs, 'Haven't I been a pretty good girl today?'

"That question," said the mother, "went through my heart like a knife. I had been quick enough to correct her when she had done wrong, but when all day long she had tried to behave I had put her to bed with her usual kiss—but not one word of appreciation."

Alice Duer Miller believed that praise was one of the basic graces of family life.

"She never failed to notice your first appearance in new clothes," her husband, Henry Wise Miller, declared, "and she took time to admire and discuss them. She would recur to the matter, call another's attention to the new suit. If I had done a chore for her, she would say, 'Harry took so much trouble over this.' Or, after we gave a dinner, 'You were very good with so and so.' 'You were very helpful at dinner.'"

The same principle is potent in all human relations simply because men and women respond naturally and generously to appreciation. In my boyhood in Baltimore, a new drugstore opened up in the neighborhood, and old Pyke Barlow, our long-established pharmacist, was outraged. He had honorably served the district for nearly half a century. Now old Pyke wrathfully accused his rival of selling cheap drugs, and of being inexperienced in compounding prescriptions. Finally, the injured newcomer consulted a lawyer, who was ex-Mayor Thomas G. Hays, teacher of the largest Bible class in town, and a shrewd old owl.

"Don't sue," Hays advised. "Kill him with kindness."

Next day the new druggist, on counsel's advice, began a campaign of his own. When customers reported to him about his rival's attacks, he said there must be a mistake somewhere.

"You see," he explained, "Doctor Pyke Barlow is one of the very finest pharmacists in this town. He'll mix an emergency prescription any hour, day or night. He trusts poor families. His drugs are pure and his care about prescriptions is fantastic. So I'm following old Pyke as my model. This neighborhood has grown, you know; there's plenty of room for both of us—and I am taking the Doc's store as the pattern for mine."

When the older man heard these tales—because praise flies on the winds of gossip quite as fast as scandal—he could not wait to meet the young fellow face to face, hand in hand, and give him some fatherly advice. The feud had been wiped out by a compliment, every word of which was true.

Wherever human beings cluster, praise is needed, and especially in a general conversation. The kind person will help everyone present to feel himself a part of the discussion. A brilliant conversationalist is not one who merely holds a group spellbound; he also draws everyone else in. He will use a remark made by someone else as a springboard: "Mr. Woods said a very wise thing just now about India. I saw how right he was when I was over there, three months ago——"

A friend once said of Arthur Balfour: "He would take the hesitating remark of a shy man and discover in it unexpected possibilities, would probe it and expand it until its author felt he had really made some contribution to human wisdom.

"Guests would leave, walking on air, feeling no special obligation to Arthur Balfour—that was his cunning—but convinced that they were bigger men than they had thought."

Such kindly techniques have power to elevate the spirit and renew our energies. A neurologist tells me that no matter how tired a man may be, a discreet pat on the back can act like a physical and spiritual injection. "The applause of a single human being," said Samuel Johnson, "is of great consequence, especially if it comes at the right time." And, I might add, more especially if it comes from the right person.

"I praise loudly, I blame softly," said the sapient Catherine of Russia. The wise executive cries: "Good for you!" at the top of a hearty voice; he corrects in private.

Expert supervisors know that judicious praise is a

tonic that can spur workers on to surpass themselves. One executive I know writes notes to employees in appreciation of tasks well done; little masterpieces that are preserved as family treasures.

A small word of commendation may be forgotten by the speaker and yet be remembered by the hearer for a lifetime. Margery Wilson, writing in *Your Life,* told of a New England tailor named Silas Conner who made a suit of clothes for a village boy preparing to leave home. The boy was shy about wearing "store clothes," but with earnest conviction the tailor comforted him: "You're a fine figure of a man, sir. You'll bring honor to the town."

Many years later, Colonel A. B. Chandler, noted telegraphy expert, was walking through an old Vermont cemetery. By chance, he noted, fallen in the weeds, a gravestone, on which were carved the words: "Silas Conner, Tailor."

The Colonel restored the tailor's grave; planted grass and flowers and arranged for perpetual care—all because of 14 complimentary words spoken to him half a century before.

Restraint is another part of technique. "Don't lay it on too thick," is an ancient truism. Pope said that praise was like ambergris: "a little whiff of it and by snatches is very agreeable, but when a man holds a whole lump of it to your nose it is a stink and strikes you down." Practice and common sense make perfect, so that eventually the skill to discern what is worth-while, and the best way to mention it, both become like a single instinct; anyone really wanting to be kind will almost infallibly say and do the right things.

Every schoolboy knows the story of flag-waving Barbara Frietchie and General "Stonewall" Jackson, but less celebrated is the history of Robert E. Lee's behavior in another crisis, and within the same 24 hours. On the famous white horse, Traveler, General Lee was riding at the head of his troops as they marched into Hagerstown, Md. Suddenly, a parade of children filed out of a schoolhouse and blocked the road in front of the oncoming Confederate hosts. Their treble voices were raised in singing "The Star-Spangled Banner."

General Lee reined in his horse, and waited until the singing was over. Then he spoke to the schoolteacher:

"Your children sing well today, ma'am. I compliment you."

Lifting his hat he rode on toward Gettysburg's bitter defeat. In the midst of the War between the States, that schoolteacher and her class perhaps hated a little less, understood a little more, because of the gallantry with which Lee met their defiance.

"Give me my roses now," is an old song that will always be true; the compliments of a funeral oration fall on ears that cannot hear.

An old gentleman used to drop in occasionally at an antique shop near Conway, N.H., to sell merchandise. The owners loved to greet him because he was a pleasant and charming man. One day after he left, the antique dealer's wife said she wished they had told the old salesman how much they enjoyed the uplift his visits brought them. The husband replied, "Next time tell him so." Last summer a young woman dropped in and introduced herself as his daughter. Her father had told her so much about the shop before he died that she had come some distance out of her way to meet the proprietors. When the wife related the conversation after her father's last visit, the visitor's eyes filled with tears as she exclaimed: "How much good that would have done my father. He went through life with an inferiority complex." The shopowner says: "Since that day, whenever I think something particularly nice about a person, I tell them. I might never have another chance."

Most of us leave unuttered truths that would make others happy. "A word fitly spoken," says the Bible, "is like apples of gold in pictures of silver."

As the painter, the musician and all other artists find joy themselves in giving beauty to others, so anyone who masters the art of praising will find that it blesses the giver quite as much as the receiver. It brings warmth and pleasure into commonplaces and turns the noisy rattle of the world into music. The more we seek out the good in others, the more friendliness we attract to ourselves. Something good can be said about everyone. We have only to say it.

And of all arts, this one is the easiest to acquire, because the only teacher needed is a kindly disposition.

This is the last of more than seventy-five articles Fulton Oursler wrote for The Reader's Digest.

While writing it he hit a snag in research that threw certain information centers of New York City into a cross-eyed frenzy. He ran up a telephone bill for calls to Boston, to Washington, Quincy and Princeton that would pay for an orphanage dinner. He remembered in a biography of John Quincy Adams that he had written his wife, "A word of praise is as good to me as 6 hours' sleep. I can be on the point of sick exhaustion but a rave of appreciation will set me fit to work with renewed vigor and fire."

No one—but no one—could verify the quote. F. O. was as aggrieved as if someone had deliberately sewn up all his pockets. He bet "a hundred lobsters" he'd find the quote 24 hours after he reached Cape Cod, and his library.

It was a silly bet to take.

He'd have found it.

THE VOICE IN THE CHURCH

NEW YORK, 1952

OUT of a curious question asked during a Kiwanis luncheon, there came something new into the lives of members of a church in the national capital. A man we can call Jim looked across his blue plate special into the eyes of a Rev. Dr. John W. Rustin, pastor of Mount Vernon Place Methodist Church, in Washington, D.C.

"John," he said, "why is it so many churches open their doors only when a service is being held? Why don't they keep the churches open all during the day and evening? People in trouble really need something like that. Have you ever thought what it would mean for a man to come in off the street—into a church—and hear a voice saying 'The Eternal God is thy refuge, and underneath are the everlasting arms'?"

Dr. Rustin nodded thoughtfully. He, too, had considered the idea.

"I would like to go into a church," said the first speaker, "and hear a message. Suppose that a man in trouble could walk into the quiet and solemnity of a church and then hear a voice uttering some of the great promises and reassurances of the Bible. Wouldn't it be wonderful?"

When the luncheon was over, another man who had been sitting at the table spoke to the clergyman:

"You know what was troubling your friend, don't you? He lost his wife only last week."

The clergyman watched the man who had questioned him going out the door. In that glimpse he saw the haggard stare, the drawn face, of a man suffering deeply. They never met again, but the clergyman didn't forget. He knew that man was not alone. There were many others carrying a burden of almost insupportable sorrows.

Nor did the other man forget. Let Dr. Rustin himself tell what happened:

"The next day he sent me a check for $100, saying, as he did so, 'I never make a suggestion, such as I made the other day, without following through with the practical means to develop the idea.'

"So there I was, with an idea and a $100 check, not knowing what to do with either. Six months later, sitting in a restaurant away from home, a young person dropped a nickel in a jukebox, and then, as the first discordant note struck my ears, the idea came to life. Why not build a beautiful little room for worship, accessible to the street, with a mechanical jukebox and instead of inserting a nickel, to press a button and to hear Nelson Eddy singing 'Rock of Ages Cleft for Me,' 'The Twenty-Third Psalm' with an organ background, or with the great prayers of the centuries recorded with a message of hope to those who pass by?

"The dream has become a reality. The worship center has been built—a young man built with his own hands the altar, then when he had finished it, joined the church on profession of faith. There is an atmosphere of quietness and beauty in every detail about this idea. The result has been truly astounding.

"People from other cities, having heard about it, have stopped by to worship. People with acute problems have gone in to find strength and a new direction for living. Just now mahogany pews to match the altar are being built, and fluorescent lights built into the pews will designate the button that can be pushed for the message that will meet the need of the individual who comes to worship.

"Every day during the Lenten season our children's chapel was open, with music appropriate for the season being played at noontime. There was not a day that there were not people in the chapel for prayer and meditation. The churches of America should wake up to this need, and provide places for people to sit themselves down awhile and to feel the presence of the Eternal."

I couldn't agree with anything more. There is some reason to believe that the idea may spread. Surely it is a good thing to seek in peace and silence to rise above ourselves. But even where there is no such place of refuge for the spirit, we can keep in heart and mind the memory of great Bible utterances, the like of which the widower so longed to hear:

> *"The Eternal God is thy refuge, and underneath are the everlasting arms."*

A DEPENDABLE TRAIT OF HUMAN NATURE

NEW YORK, 1942

ONE winter's night, many years ago, when I was no more than 20, I was belaboring a typewriter in the newsroom of the Baltimore *American*. A copy boy summoned me to the office of the managing editor, a bald-headed old walrus with white mustaches like hanging gardens and a perverse sense of humor. Leaning back in his swivel chair, he asked me:

"Do you play the piano?"

"No sir."

"Fiddle?"

"No sir."

"Sing?"

"No sir."

"Then go up to the Lyric and cover the concert. Our music critic just dropped dead. You've got the job for tonight."

An hour later I was listening with uncritical ecstasy to Fritz Kreisler.

This was heaven. The first word I ever spoke was

"music." Mother taught me to say it when I first heard a street organ. Yet there was never any music in my home, not even one of those long-horned gramophones. During most of my childhood the only music I knew was that of a solemn-visaged choir in the Baptist Church. When I was a little older I haunted the parks and listened to brass bands. I read books about Beethoven and Handel and Haydn and Schubert, but I never had heard their chords and melodies.

I did not know the flesh and blood of music and here I was at Kreisler's concert. The possibility of my being appointed a music critic permanently would certainly have seemed fantastic to anyone except to our managing editor, who detested the smug cant of musical criticism—and to myself. Yet I wanted to make good on this whimsical assignment as I had never wanted anything before.

Meanwhile, across the aisle from me loomed the owlish and erudite critic of the famous Baltimore *Sun.* He was competent, but cursed with a showy felicity of patois that glowed with lush words—"nuance," "dynamics," "musicianship." Tomorrow, I could be sure, he would publish a masterpiece. How could I possibly compete with him?

My only hope was to turn in such a charming performance of my own that no one would dream of giving the job to anyone else and I would be music critic forever. During the intermission I went out on a fire escape and thought the problem over alone in the dark. I admit I prayed a little. Perhaps my prayer was answered; perhaps the solution was my own idea. At any rate, when the concert was over I went backstage and knocked on the door of the star's dressing room.

A moist and fatigued Kreisler was receiving a group of Baltimore society women.

"Mr. Kreisler," I said, "I am a reporter and I have to

see you on a matter of great importance." That would sound ominous to any public figure.

Eventually the room cleared, and I was alone with one of the greatest of modern musicians and one of the noblest of men. He listened in amazement as I blurted out my story and finally asked what I expected him to do about it.

"Will you," I pleaded, "help me write my review?"

He looked at me and began to chuckle. Then he did help me. He told me something about the spirit of a new composition he had played, by a young American composer, and dwelt on the exquisite and fragile melodic charm of the "lagoon passage." He spoke of vibrancy in tone, of harmonics, and of playing with muted strings.

I got it all down. At his best, my distinguished rival of the *Sun* could not have matched the assurance, the penetrating understanding, or the joyous enthusiasm for Kreisler's work which the violinist himself helped me to impart to that article.

The job was mine—for good. I studied and worked very hard to make myself useful in it. For five wonderful years I went to concerts and operas in the best seats. I heard Caruso and Tetrazzini and Melba, Nordica, Homer, Garden and Schumann-Heink sing their greatest roles. I heard Elman and Heifetz and Paderewski and Bauer and Carreno play. I saw Nijinsky dance. And when I resigned from that heavenly job it was to go to New York and be, of all things, the editor of a musical trade magazine, with free tickets to all concerts.

From this experience I learned a blessed truth. No matter how embarrassing or desperate the circumstances may be, people are more likely than not to be kind and understanding if you ask them frankly to help you. I have found that to be true not only of great men but of many obscure little people to whom I have appealed.

Frankness and complete trust in the natural kindness of human nature will seldom fail, perhaps because it gives one even greater satisfaction to be helpful than to be helped.

One day while Fulton Oursler was visiting the home of a hard-bitten lawyer friend the two got into an argument over this instinct of kindness in mankind. The host snorted derisively and stressed man's inhumanity to man. As frequently happened between the two, the vehemence became such that one wondered when they would draw knives. Then Fulton dared his pickle-blooded friend to go out in the street just as he was (disreputable in scuffed moccasins, old corduroys and ancient sweater) and tell the first person he saw he was penniless. The lawyer slammed out of his apartment and Fulton watched from the window as the corner cop was approached by a figure that looked twice more disreputable on the street than lounging in his own home. Furthermore he had, as Fulton knew the officer could hardly escape noticing, liquor on his breath.

The lawyer returned chapfallen. With little ado, the officer had fished into his pocket and handed out a nickel (back in the days when five cents counted). "Here," he had grunted, "you can phone someone or take a subway."

Weeks later, the lawyer phoned in great wrath. He had just learned, through his frequent retelling of the episode, a fact he'd never been aware of—and Fulton hadn't known—policemen are required *to give any bereft person fare or phone money.*

WHY THE SUN STOOD STILL

NEW YORK, 1949

ABOUT 25 years ago, a small-town schoolmaster told his boys and girls about Darwin's theory of evolution. For this violation of a Tennessee law, which forbade instruction contrary to the Bible, the teacher was arrested and the world sat back to watch one of history's most extraordinary trials.

Called to the witness box as defender of the faith, was a three-times candidate for the presidency, William Jennings Bryan. The defender of the schoolteacher was Clarence Darrow, eminent agnostic. Furiously, Darrow attacked the wonder tales of the Bible, cross-examining Bryan as a believer in myths and fairy tales.

"Mr. Bryan, do you believe that Joshua made the sun stand still?"

"Mr. Darrow, I do!"

"Wouldn't it have been the earth, itself, that stood still? And if that is what you believe, don't you know that if the earth ever stopped turning, it would be converted into a molten mass of matter?"

The indignant Darrow seemed to be speaking with exact knowledge. But science is never so dogmatic. A quarter of a century after the Scopes trial, a scientist has published a book, declaring that within historical times the earth did pause in daily rotation; and for more than a day, the sun remained visible over Joshua and his troops.

While only incidental to the author's purpose, the book tends to confirm the Bible in other miraculous accounts; familiar tales of wonder emerge, not as myths, but as accurate reporting of actual events.

The savant who raises these possibilities, Dr. Immanuel Velikovsky, calls his book *Worlds in Collision.** As Darwin and Einstein did, he sets up certain original hypotheses, and buttresses them with impressive scholarship. Like a detective among the sciences (archaeology, paleontology, geology, astronomy, psychology, anthropology, and physics), he has put together by deductive reasoning a chain of circumstantial evidence that may deeply affect the world of thinking men.

The links of his reasoning are forged out of the history and literature of ancient and modern tribes and nations from all over the earth; text and footnotes sparkle with confirming data from the Bible and the Talmud, and from other records going back thousands of years—Egyptian papyri, Babylonian astronomical tablets, Mayan and Aztec calendars—and the folklore of Arabia, India, Tibet, China and Peru. The result is an expanse of facts, small clues and great, which hang together in a beguiling and plausible case.

The tale of the sun standing still illustrates one of his principal methods for getting at the facts. Clearly if the sun "hasted not to go down about a whole day" the phenome-

**Worlds in Collision*, copyright, 1950, by Immanuel Velikovsky.

non could not have been merely a local spectacle. The whole area of the earth had to be affected: if the sun hung in the morning sky over Gibeon, then elsewhere in the world there was to be no dawn that day. In other lands there had to be twilight prolonged for the same period.

Apparently, records from all over the earth do agree as to the time and as to the altered portions of daylight and dark in each area. Such concerted testimony repeats itself again and again in other wonder stories. For every such incident which he analyzes, Dr. Velikovsky quotes dozens, scores, even hundreds of confirmations.

For the Bible's most incredible story—the standing still of moon and sun while Captain Joshua routed the foe—there is worldwide evidence. Says Dr. Velikovsky at the start of a long series of citations:

"Allowing for the difference in longitude, it must have been early morning or night in the Western Hemisphere.

"We go to the books with the historical traditions of the aborigines of Central America. In the Mexican *Annals of Cuauhtitlan*—the history of the empire of Culhuacan and Mexico, written in Nahua-Indian (Nahuatl)—it is related that during a cosmic catastrophe that occurred in the remote past, the night did not end for a long time.

"I am dealing with the Western Hemisphere first, because the Biblical stories were not known to its aborigines when it was discovered. . . .

"We could follow a path around the earth and inquire into the various traditions concerning a prolonged night and prolonged day, with the sun and moon absent or tarrying at different points along the zodiac, while the earth underwent a bombardment of stones in a world ablaze."

Which he goes on to do. What happened, then, on that mysterious day? The theory of *Worlds in Collision* rests on catastrophes due to encounters with a comet that befell the earth in two series, one in the fifteenth century B.C. in the time of the Exodus and again 52 years later in the time of Joshua. These astral cataclysms caused strange things to happen on the earth and in the sky.

The explanation of Joshua's miracle is that if a large comet were ever to come near enough to the earth, just such spectacular things would come to pass; the encounter would slow down the earth in its daily turning, and people who think that the sun is going generally around the earth would see, among other mystical sights, the sun and moon as if suddenly halted and held rigid in the heavens. That, he maintains, is exactly what occurred about 1500 B.C., in the time of the Exodus of the Jews from Egypt and recurred in the time of the Conquest of Palestine under Joshua.

The mysterious outlaw in the firmament, the comet which pursued the earth and also brought on the plagues, caused the seas to part, raised a pillar of cloud by day to stalk the wilderness and a pillar of fire by night, was actually a sky-rover born and cast out by spontaneous eruption from the boiling mass of the planet Jupiter. The new comet whizzed around us in space until after centuries it was caught and trapped as a permanent member of our solar system, settling down brightly into a circular orbit, and changing into a showy but contented planet revolving on schedule around our sun—the beautiful star which men call Venus.

The strange birth of that morning star is what Velikovsky's book is really about. All the other parts of his case are dependent on that prolonged and spectacular cataclysm.

In presenting his theory, Dr. Velikovsky begins with humility, confessing the ignorance of science; of "homo ignoramus." What man does not know would fill a bigger book than all the books written. He has yet to learn the simplest and most essential things: what life is, or how it came to be and whether it originated from inorganic matter. Man cannot tell whether life in any form exists anywhere else in the star-hives of the sky, nor what is the mysterious force called gravitation. The birth of the solar system is still beyond the understanding of scientists, on the scene billions of years after the event.

The first step that a scientist should take is to study one planet, the one under our feet; "then, by the deductive method to apply the results to other members of the solar system." This Dr. Velikovsky is trying to do, bringing into his reasoning the new knowledge of electromagnetism and nuclear physics.

He holds that what happens in the heavens is akin to what happens in an atom, where electrons revolve around the nucleus like planets around the sun. They shift their positions, ejecting or absorbing a jet of light. Thus the atom is a microcosm of the solar system and the solar system is a macrocosm of the atom. Someone objects: "We do not read in the morning paper that all of a sudden Saturn and Mars changed their places." True; we do not read it in the newspapers because it is not a daily occurrence, but we do read about it in the ancient records quoted in this new book. The author explains that in an atom, a planet goes around its sun millions of times in a second. Every time it absorbs a jet of light, it changes its orbit. On the grander scale of the solar system, centuries, or even millenniums may pass between a corresponding event there and its recurrence.

The author clearly states his radical new position:

"If these two men of science (Newton with his celestial

mechanics and Darwin with the theory of evolution) are sacrosanct, then this book is a heresy."

Once his idea is understood—that the violent and cataclysmic changes on a miniature scale within the core of the atom have been enacted on a grand but equally sudden scale in the universe of suns, planets and comets—light begins to shine on some old and stubborn mysteries.

Why did the ancient ice fields in India move *from* the equator to the Himalaya Mountains? Why did ice move from what is now tropical Africa toward the south polar region and not in the opposite direction? Velikovsky's cosmological theories account for such unreasonable contradictions; a theory of vast and almost instantaneous change.

Such catastrophes were world-wide, and there were many of them, but Velikovsky, in *Worlds in Collision,* is most concerned with those latest crashes in space—the first series about 1500 B.C. in the time of the Exodus and of the Conquest, and again in the eighth and seventh centuries B.C.

Of course, every astronomer knows that contact with another body of sufficient mass could disrupt the earth's rotation and rhythm. To this day comets by the millions are loose in space, a danger to us, remote but still actual. We know that our earth can and does collide with masses of meteorites; often such sizzling stones fall to earth. Yet even this knowledge is very recent.

As late as the time of our great-grandfathers, no one in the scholarly world believed that a stone, falling from the sky, was at all possible. That skepticism was shared by Copernicus, Galileo, Kepler and Newton, among many others, up to 1803, when a shower of meteorites falling at L'Aigle in France, was investigated by the French Academy of Sciences. Then, for the first time, educated man recognized that some wild thing in the sky could collide with us.

In the Bible accounts, the author finds extraordinary confirmation of the presence of the comet during those bewildering days.

If, for example, the earth found itself enmeshed in the head of a comet, a rain, a very torrent of meteorites, would assuredly fall upon us. Now, in the Book of Joshua, only two verses before the sun is suspended on high, we read how the "Lord cast down great stones from Heaven." Although the man who wrote the Book of Joshua knew nothing of the connection between stones falling from the sky and a stoppage of the earth, he gives a vivid and accurate description.

The first two visits of the comet in the fifteenth century B.C. were separated by a period of 52 years from the time when Pharaoh kept the Jews in bondage in Egypt and Jehovah sent plagues of frogs and locusts, showers of blood and fire, and a darkness that would not lift, to force the old king to change his mind. All these tales Bryan would have believed and Darrow would have scoffed at, but neither could have proved anything, one way or the other. Velikovsky sets out to prove they all happened, just as recorded, the Biblical story of the Israelites closely following the natural astronomical order of events.

For example, during the plagues, the world turned red. Particles of pigment fell, and seemed to turn lakes, rivers and seas into blood; the earth itself looked rusty all over. There are eyewitness accounts of this red saturation, not only in the Bible, but in the *Manuscript Quiche* of the Mayas, and in an Egyptian papyrus by Ipuwer, who, himself, watched the phenomenon. He wrote his lament on papyrus: "The river is blood," and this corresponds with the Book of Exodus: "All the waters that were in the river were turned to blood."

The pollution of fresh waters killed the fish, "and the river stank," says the Book of Exodus. "They could not drink the water of the river." The Egyptian reporter agrees and exclaims: "Men shrink from tasting; human beings thirst after water. What shall we do? All is ruin!"

And not only in the Middle East. The red-stained dust, which irritated the skin of men and animals, and raised boils, causing sickness and death, is reported also in many other lands.

Came next the final Egyptian plagues, a reign of darkness that lasted seven days, climaxed with violent upheavals. The earth was entering ever deeper into the tail of the onrushing comet, approaching its body. This approach, the contemporary reports would indicate, was followed by a stasis of the earth; it shuddered and missed some rotations before righting itself and spinning on.

Nations and tribes in many other places have traditions about a cosmic catastrophe during which the sun did not shine; the long darkness is remembered in Finland, Babylonia, and Peru, all over the world.

According to the Bible account, which Velikovsky does not quote, after those frightening experiences of darkness and earthquake, Pharaoh consented to let Moses' people go. But he soon came to regret his decision, and with his army, rode forth in chariots to force the fugitives back—thus riding posthaste into a miracle about which prophets were to give thanks to God for centuries to come: the crossing of the Red Sea.

Did any such thing happen historically? The logical Velikovsky is sure that it did. The swift shifting of the atmosphere under the impact of the gaseous parts of the comet, the drift of air attracted by the body of the comet, and the rush of the atmosphere resulting from inertia when the earth stopped rotating or shifted its poles, all helped to produce winds of enormous velocity and force, just as described in the Old Testament. The theme of such a cosmic hurricane is reiterated in Mexico, India, Persia and the South Seas. But that was not the full story.

In the midst of such a windstorm, a comet with a head as large as the earth itself, passing sufficiently close, would terrifically affect the ocean tides. The comet raised the waters of the ocean miles high. From Japan to Peru, among the Choctaw Indians and in tribes on the other side of the world, the memory of this rip-roaring time persists, of seas rent asunder, an event so unusual that it became the most impressive recollection in the long history of peoples. For all nations were first blasted by the same plagues and fire, then shaken by the same fury.

And now there also came to pass a pageant in the sky that was profoundly to impress the imaginations of men and their literature. The heavens seemed a battleground, scene of unparalleled terrors and splendor. For, the head of the comet, having previously passed close to the sun, was on fire. Candescent and spectacular, it swung into the earth's own orbit, and the wandering Jews followed a pillar of cloud by day and a pillar of fire by night.

Meanwhile, the head of the coiling comet became entangled in the tail, and that struggle in the midst of the firmament must have looked like a battle between a globe of fire and a dark column of smoke.

No wonder that, as their songs still tell today, and their epics, people in many parts of the earth believed they were beholding a fight between a sky monster in the shape of a serpent and the light god, who won the victory and saved the world. It is difficult to find a people or a tribe on the earth that does not include the same motif in its religious beliefs.

So now came one forever-to-be-remembered phenomenon. A tremendous spark sprang forth at the moment of the nearest approach, when the earth's waters were heaped at their highest, and before they fell down. Which was when, as Exodus reports:

> *And the Angel of God, which went before the camp of Israel, removed and went behind them: and the pillar of the cloud went from before their face and stood behind them . . . and it was a cloud and darkness but it gave light by night. An exceedingly strong wind and lightnings rent the cloud. In the morning, the waters rose as a wall and moved apart . . . And the children of Israel went into the midst of the sea upon the dry ground: and the waters were a wall unto them on their right hand and on their left. And the Egyptians pursued . . . And it came to pass, that in the morning watch the Lord looked down into the host of the Egyptians through the pillar of fire and of the cloud . . . and the waters returned and covered the chariots, and the horsemen, and all the host of Pharaoh that came into the sea after them, there remained not so much as one of them.**

Actually, all the earth was passing through these same events. In China, Yahou's time was the time of Moses in Palestine; in his Chinese chronologies you will find the following reports: The sun did not set for a number of days; the forests were set on fire; a high wave, "reaching the sky,"

*Exodus 14. King James Version.

poured over the face of the land and swept water over the mountain peaks.

In China, as in Palestine and elsewhere, they adopted a new calendar after this catastrophe. And here we are again in the midst of fascinating mysteries.

Our planet now rotates from west to east. Has it always done so? The ancient charts seem to suggest otherwise. Plato knew of these mysteries, for he wrote in *The Statesman* of the "change in the rising and setting of the sun and other heavenly bodies, how in these times they used to set in the quarter where now they rise. . . ." And a little later, he added: "At certain periods, the universe has its present circular motion, and at other periods it revolves in the reverse direction. . . . Of all the changes which take place in the heavens, this reversal is the greatest and most complete."

Velikovsky turns to the natural sciences for an explanation. He points out that this globe of ours is a huge magnet. Now when a thunderbolt strikes a magnet, it reverses the magnetic poles; what before was north is now south, and vice versa. On a grand scale, a short circuit between the earth and another celestial body could result in the north and south magnetic poles of the earth changing places, instantaneously.

Geological records indicate that something of the sort did happen. Velikovsky quotes from McNish, the geologist, as follows:

"Examination of magnetization of some igneous rocks reveals that they are polarized oppositely from the prevailing direction of the local magnetic field and many of the older rocks are less strongly magnetized than more recent ones. . . . This would indicate that the polarity of the earth has been completely reversed within geological times."

Was the cosmic catastrophe that terminated a world age at the time of the passage of the Jews through the Red Sea one of these great occasions when east became west and the side of the earth that had known the morning now knew the evening?

That is too much for Velikovsky to say. But he does assert that the earth then at least changed its orbit, its poles did not stay in their places, and the jolted axis became displaced geographically and astronomically. With these changes came other strange happenings reported in the Bible and elsewhere; Velikovsky devotes pages to the manna dropping from heaven and the falling walls of Jericho as natural consequences of the disturbances.

What had Venus to do with these catastrophes that brought the world to the brink of destruction? "Here," says Dr. Velikovsky, "is a question that will carry us very far, indeed."

As he sees it, there followed seven centuries after Joshua during which people never lost the fear of new disasters, a fear which their best intellects confirmed; more trouble was on the way. Meanwhile these years between saw the labor pains of a new planet when from the fetus of the comet a star was born, and Venus took her low and lovely place in our sky. The dreaded comet became a tame planet, the terrible flying vagabond crouching in peaceful fire close to the edge of the horizon, celebrated ever since as the Morning and the Evening Star.

Is there historical evidence of this? Yes, says the author. By asserting that the planet Venus was born at this time, he has to prove that before the Exodus, only four of the sun's planets were visible, and that in astronomical charts of this period and before, no Venus can be found.

This proof he brings forward; in the Hindoo table of planets of that time, Venus alone among the visible planets is absent although Brahmans of a later period knew of five planets. So it is also in Egyptian astronomy. And there are further references:

From the Chaldeans:	"Venus—bright torch of heaven."
	"Diamond that illuminates like the sun."
	"A stupendous prodigy in the sky."
From the Mexicans:	called comet "A star that smoked."
	"And Venus also a star that smoked."
From the Chinese:	"Venus was visible in full daylight and rivaled the sun in brightness."
Assyrians:	"Venus is clothed with fire and bears aloft a crown of awful splendor."
Egyptians:	"A circling star which scatters its flame in fire . . . a flame of fire in her tempest."

In every country of the ancient world, there are vivid myths of the birth of the planet Venus; never of Jupiter, Mars or Saturn.

Of the second series of catastrophes, the records are much better preserved, for this was the era of the Hebrew prophets. Those inspired ancients were first-rate astronomers as well as poets and seers; they could and did predict, with deadly accuracy, two collisions of their time. Amos warned the people of coming upheaval, and for his gloomy forecasts was put to death. But the catastrophe arrived on time; King Uzziah was at the altar when a great breach was torn in Solomon's Temple by the quaking earth. This first contact was only a prelude. "The day thick with night," foreseen by Isaiah, came upon the land; "the earth," as the Bible reports it, "utterly broken down."

Actually, Velikovsky has said, the prophet Isaiah, as an eyewitness of cosmic upheavals, knew more than modern astronomers about certain phases of astronomy!

And then the long Biblical drama reached its climax in the destruction of Sennacherib, foes of Israel. It is described most laconically in the Book of Kings:

> *"And it came to pass that night, that the Angel of the Lord went out, and smote in the camp of the Assyrians a hundred fourscore and five thousand; and when the people arose early in the morning, behold they were all corpses."*

The identical story is repeated in the Book of Chronicles, the Talmud, and other ancient sources.

Obviously, the simultaneous death of tens of thousands of warriors could not be due to a plague; this spectral massacre happened overnight. The Bible says: "A blast fell from the sky" on the camp of Sennacherib. The death of those enemy hosts of men is explained in the Talmud as caused by gaseous masses, penetrating the atmosphere, which could, in certain areas, asphyxiate all breath.

The fire in the sky, and the gases falling to the earth at that time, all kindred phenomena, are also reported in the

Bamboo Books of China, in Mayan inscriptions, and in records in other parts of the world.

On the evening before the destruction of the army, according to the Bible, the shadow of the sun returned 10 degrees. In China, and elsewhere, the same reports occur and agree that the date was March 23, 687 B.C.

What changes in the motion of earth and moon resulted from these collisions and readjustments, which extended over a period of 800 years, or even longer? The question is far more important than it sounds; it has to do with the puss-in-corner exchange of the North Magnetic Pole and the South. There are charts painted on the ceiling of an Egyptian tomb which show the heavens as they were, over the Middle East before and after these cataclysms—and there is a complete and unmistakable reversal.

The ice ages seem to have ended with catastrophic suddenness; regions of mild climate moved instantly into the polar circle; the polar ice sheet in America and Europe started to melt; gigantic waves traveled across continents, carrying boulders thousands of miles. One does not have to be a scientist to look at a map and see the picture for himself.

A circle, with its center somewhere near the east shore of Greenland, embraces the region of the ice sheet of the last glacial age, or, as Velikovsky prefers to call it, the "Fimbul-winter." Northeastern Siberia is outside the circle. The valley of the Missouri down to 39° north latitude is within the circle.

Darwin was aware of the mystery of northeastern Siberia. In the last century scientists were puzzled by the extermination of the mammoth, an animal far better developed than the elephant which survived. They fancied that perhaps slow changes in the land had forced the great beasts up into bare hills where they gradually died off from starvation. But now we know that the mammoths did *not* die for lack of food. Their bellies were filled, and even their mouths, with undigested grass and leaves, preserved in the bodies of the animals until this day in field ice. That undigested foliage grows today not in the region where the beasts died, but a thousand miles away. Only sudden, natural catastrophes of far-flung violence could explain these and other cosmic conundrums.

The question is inevitable: Was not the North Pole at some time in the past, 20° or more distant from the point it now occupies, and closer to America? So, too, the South Pole would be closer to Australia. The sudden alteration explains why the mammoths were wiped out all at once, as by asphyxiation or electrocution, either of which was possible. They lived in a moderate climate. Came the catastrophe, and the mammoths died. In a few hours, northeastern America changed from the frigid zone of the polar circle into a moderate zone, while northeastern Siberia moved in the opposite direction from the moderate zone to the polar circle. The present cold climate of northern Siberia started when eastern Canada (Labrador) moved out of the polar region.

Archaeological work should be undertaken in the polar circle to establish whether those now uninhabited tundras were not sites of human habitation 2700 years ago. What has already been done seems to justify the suggestion. One writer has called the remains of a city of sophisticated culture found in 1940 at Point Hope, Alaska, on the shore of the Bering Strait inside the polar circle "one of the most startling and important finds of the century," and goes on to narrate:

"Two thousand years is thought a conservative estimate of its age. The excavations have yielded beautiful ivory carvings unlike any known Eskimo or other American Indian culture of the northern regions. Fashioned of logs, the strange tombs gave up skeletons which stared up at the excavators with artificial eyeballs carved of ivory and inlaid with jet . . ."

For those cosmic catastrophes, Velikovsky also finds evidence in the craters and dried lava on the surface of the moon marked in collision with the comet. "The moon," he says, "is a great unmarked cemetery flying around our earth, a reminder of what can happen to a planet."

It is natural that at the close of his book, the author should speculate on what can happen to the world. The solar system is not changeless; if catastrophes have befallen, they may repeat themselves with perhaps a different, even fatal result. In the solar system there exists a possibility that a collision between two planets may some day occur. Trouble might come from the moons of Jupiter which cross their orbits, and from asteroids that cross the orbit of Mars and the Earth, or from the planet Pluto that crosses under an angle the orbit of Neptune.

Moreover, comets—like Venus before it became a star—may again strike the earth; a large comet could run into one of the planets and push it from its orbit; then chaos might start anew. Or some dark star, like Jupiter or Saturn, may be in the path of the sun, and may be attracted to the system and cause havoc in it. So an end to the world, as we know it, is by no means impossible.

This, in substance, very incompletely stated, is Velikovsky's theory. He admits that his case raises more mysteries than he has solved, because his ideas cast a doubt on the long-accepted reality of orthodox theories, and suggest that electromagnetic forces dominate the stars. Here the beautiful dogma of the gravitational principle in our system seems to collapse. Velikovsky accuses modern astronomy of still living in the time when electromagnetic principles had still to be discovered.

Thus, a single scholar has sought a synthesis of knowledge and reason in the fields of science, legend and religion. The result is a theory of our history as a planet fascinating as a tale by Jules Verne, yet documented with a scholarship worthy of Darwin or Jeans.

To science, *Worlds in Collision* opens up a vast new debate; to millions of true believers in the Old Testament, it will come as an unintended and reassuring answer to the rationalist criticism of the last 75 years.

How strange all this would seem to Clarence Darrow, and equally to William Jennings Bryan, if they could know.

Often Fulton Oursler discussed the limitation of man's reason and prejudices in the shadowy chase of logic for the absolutes. If, in the name of religion, *the statement is made that "there is no such thing as matter," a horde of intellectuals raise their eyebrows with horror tinged with mockery. But if* science *says, "there is no such thing as matter; all is atoms, electrons, protons, neutrons, adding up to Energy," intellectuals merely raise their eyebrows with meek acceptance and a nice humility at the meagerness of their own understanding.*

In his first novel, Behold This Dreamer, *published in 1924, Fulton Oursler's idealistic young hero claimed that nothing was so destructive as common sense.*

"What the world needs is imagination," the young hero declared. "Common sense said a man couldn't live under water. Imagination made the submarine. Common

sense said a man couldn't fly. Imagination made the aeroplane. Common sense said a man's voice would carry only so far. Imagination made the telephone, the wireless and the radio. Nothing is as limiting as common sense and reason."

When *Worlds in Collision* by Immanuel Velikovsky was published, its theories and hypotheses absorbed Fulton Oursler as did his talks with Dr. Velikovsky. This survey of the book was published in the March, 1950, issue of The *Reader's Digest*. There arose from press, scientists and churchmen a torrent of indignation. Intellectuals raised an eyebrow this time with injured dignity. Church people accused Dr. Velikovsky of being a rationalist—in explaining miracles as natural phenomena; and scientists accused him of reliance on literary sources, ancient traditions, scriptures, etc. and giving a rational meaning to things they regarded as mythical.

Fulton Oursler smiled and repeated his favorite conviction: "That's nothing to the truths that will one day be discovered—lost manuscripts under rubble—graven stones that will be witnesses—and powers around us and within us which we now barely suspect but which we will recognize and learn to use, even though we only dimly understand them, just as we use electricity and cannot say what it is."

Practical and organized as Fulton Oursler was, the man had in him at the same time a deep respect for intuitive and speculative insights of the mind. Foreseeing the day when science and religion would join hands with mutual respect and understanding, he recognized that this day would not come without the courageous theorizing by which science always advances. It was in this mood that he pursued conclusions such as Dr. Velikovsky's.

More than once Mr. Oursler observed that the artist in his smock and northern exposure, the scientist in his white coat in the laboratory, the priest in his vestments at the altar were all serving and seeking the same Truth.

BETHLEHEM ROAD

NEW YORK, 1950

DURING this holy season of 1950, nearly one hundred top choirs of the country will be singing a new choral composition called "Bethlehem Road." Behind their singing, behind the lyricist's words and the composer's music there lies a story which adds a living parable to my own Christmas this year.

It began last March when an aged mother sent her Hollywood son a birthday present. Her gift was a book of which, I am grateful to report, I was the author.

The son—his name is Robert P. White, and he is the author of a play, two moving pictures and many magazine pieces—for some curious reason forgot to thank his mother for the remembrance. This neglect was exceedingly unlike Mr. White. He is an ex-marine, an ex-newspaperman, and his reputation has been built strictly on the lusty, the profane and the agnostic—so he solemnly assures me. But mother's teaching about politeness had never forsaken him before. "He was angry because I sent him that book," his mother thought. "He'll never, never read it."

Yet strange to tell, Robert P. White read the book three times, and then lent it to a friend from India. She took it to the home of her aunt, the distinguished composer, Alys Greenlund, and presently the musician said:

"I'm nauseated with nightclub and dance hall stuff. I've been doing it for ten years. It's less worth-while than yesterday's newspaper. I want to do a good semiclassical standard piece on some sacred theme for a change. . . ."

Then her niece, the lady from Kwajelein, spoke up and said:

"You can get a theme out of *The Greatest Story Ever Told.* It tells about the trek of Mary and Joseph from Nazareth to Bethlehem under circumstances almost identical with those of today. Wars were raging, taxes mounting, the Jews were being persecuted, and Caesar ordered another census in the hope of finding a few more people to pay taxes . . . and Joseph and Mary and the infant Jesus were displaced persons when they fled to Egypt.

"And furthermore," she added, "the standard prayer is just what it is now: 'Oh Lord, God of Hosts, bring peace to our souls!' "

Mr. White turned to the composer and said, somewhat cynically, I'm afraid, "There you are! The perfect title is '*Bethlehem Road*' and in the lyric give us a prayer for Christmas. The whole world needs a prayer if it never needed it before. . . ."

"Yes, that's fine," she said tartly. "It's a beautiful idea but try and find a lyricist in Hollywood that has the right words for a piece like that."

About two weeks later, Miss Greenlund called Mr.

White to her home and played her new music for him. He listened, enchanted—this was indeed the song of Bethlehem Road.

"Now you must write the words immediately," the composer told him.

Robert White's face looked haunted. He was no Bible student. He did not know one musical note from another. He had never once in his life written poem or lyric. "So," he tells me, "I went down to the desert and in a heat of 105 degrees literally sweated out a miracle."

Another was to follow. As it happened, the manuscript was taken to a talented Negro conductor of a Los Angeles choir, who instantly decided to use the number and then said:

"Give this to the Mills Brothers. I know them. They can use this as a change of pace, I am sure."

But in trying to do that, Mr. White made a mistake. He thought he was air-mailing a manuscript of the piece to a quartet in New York but sent it in error to Mills Music, Inc., one of the foremost music publishers in Manhattan. Five days later, contracts for immediate publication were on his desk. And nearly a hundred choirs will be singing it all over our land this Christmas.

And now the son took a record of the new piece to give as a real surprise to his mother. Before he could put the package in her hands, she looked at him with tears gathering and said:

"You never even thanked me for the book I sent you and I'm quite certain you never read it."

"But mother," he cried, "I did read it and what do you think? I've written a hymn!"

You can imagine that mother's delight and I hope you

can share mine. In a telegram I received ten minutes before I sat down to write out these facts, Robert P. White said:

"Alys Greenlund and I regard this as an undeniable manifestation of an influence above and beyond our own."

So do I.

ENGLAND IN SUN AND SHADOW

LONDON, 1947

I HAVE been talking with a very angry woman, or, rather, she has been screaming at me. One of the best-known writers on both sides of the Atlantic, she must remain nameless:

"I stand in fish queues for two hours. And then in bread queues. And then I have to go home and cook, with no milk, no eggs, no butter—and clean with no soap and no hot water—while you overfed Americans come here and pry. In two years we will all be dead—starved or frozen. Then you can take the country and do with it as you damned please."

It would be easy to be misled by such outbursts, which, I am told, are few. Houses are still charnel cold, rain slops down and polar winds are blowing, now that April's here. Tension aches visibly in pale faces unnerved by one of the harshest winters in English memory.

A clerk in a shop, wrapping a bundle, mutters: "Except for death and scariness, it was better under the blitz. We got more to eat."

Yet I lost count, there were so many window boxes of grime-stained office buildings burgeoning with daffodils and forget-me-nots, all sure that spring will not be far behind. Already, battalions of tulips and iris are shaking their colors. Down the street came a flare of horns and trumpets and drums; a marching regiment with children trooping after.

"The children look well fed and strong," I remarked.

"What good food there is goes to the children," the taxi driver said. "That's so there'll always be an England, as they say!"

And with a rheumy groan, he added:

"That's one reason why liquor is scarce and high, and the beer tastes like it came from discontented hops. But, of course, it's worth it!"

I have been to the theater with a lovely artist and her lawyer husband. You arrive at 7 o'clock; under double daylight saving that means 5 in the afternoon. Audiences don't relish the schedule; one comedian gets a salvo when he says:

"You come here dirty and hungry! You grumble through the first act, rumble through the second and sleep through the third!"

The men sit gloved and muffled in overcoats; the leading man coughs and the star sneezes. Blessedly, between the acts, a pretty maid puts a tray on your lap with cakes and steaming coffee.

At 10 o'clock dinner my hostess said:

"Things do get on our nerves now and then. Sometimes it makes me so restless, I can't sleep. But I don't count sheep any more—I count my friends. By the time I reach 70, I am generally gone. Think of having 70 friends!

I made them all through these tough times; I never had so many friends when things were prospering with us.

"Our recovery may lie in something like that—to grow love as carefully as we grow flowers. I read in the Bible the other day—'Better a dinner of herbs where love is than a stalled ox and hatred therewith.'"

I did not make too good a beginning with Mr. Churchill. On a tour of his home, he led me into a room flooded with northern light—a studio crowded with easels and canvas landscapes. Here Churchill, the statesman, gave way to the maestro among his paintings. My eyes were caught by a fine snow scene.

"This picture," I said, "is the most beautiful of all."

The look my host then bestowed upon me was a triumph of the inscrutable. In orotund voice, full, clear, rounded and resonant, reminding me of the cadence of his great war speeches, he said:

"That one was painted by somebody else. It is a gift from another artist!"

Harrow and alas! Was there a convenient well into which I could hurl myself?

"No," he said kindly. "You were right. My best paintings have been sent away." *

Winston, as every Englishman calls him behind his back, was wearing his familiar shapeless and baggy air-raid suit; on his pink face there was a jocose smile. Flushed from a 3-mile walk, he came into the upstairs drawing-room at Chartwell Manor and dropped affably into a fireside chair. A Siamese cat, climbing on his shoulders, watched

*Weeks later, the author was to read that one of Mr. Churchill's canvases, submitted clandestinely under the name of Mr. Winter, won a top prize in the National Exhibition.

me with eyes of changeful luster. This was the manorial home of many ancestors; here where Henry VIII once slept, Winston Churchill was living as the guest of the government; some day the estate would be a public reliquary of books and mementos of one man's national service, a shrine like the Hyde Park home of Franklin Roosevelt.

His thoughts were on a closer union between the United States and Great Britian.

"The only hope of peace and freedom is in partnership —you the senior, we the older. United, English-speaking peoples can resist any onslaught. Peace through strength! The only thing the enemies of our free institutions respect and fear is raw strength. Let's give it to them."

Such close association was even more desperately needed than when he first proposed it at Fulton, Mo. The fruit of such a union, he felt, would be nothing less than world peace.

"That is how we can show that our way of life will work and prosper and make people happy, and confound the totalitarians who are determined to take away our freedoms of religion and speech and press and assembly and habeas corpus and justice."

There was a glisten in Winston Churchill's eyes as he drew me to the wall of an inner room. His finger pointed to a framed document, showing me a mystery. Surely, I told myself, President Roosevelt had, in 1944, announced at a press conference that the Atlantic Charter never did exist as an actual piece of paper? Some general ideas, he had explained, were scribbled on loose sheets but they had all been left with the captain of the battleship, Prince of Wales, which went down in the China seas.

Yet here, hanging on Winston Churchill's study wall, I beheld the original manuscript of the Atlantic Charter. It was scarred with corrections in two handwritings—and with the promise of the Four Freedoms as boldly intact as they clearly were fixed in Churchill's mind.

In the study next to his bedroom, I counted 12 dispatch boxes gorged with documents for five volumes of war memoirs which he is writing. To Churchill comes a luxury denied any other author; no sooner does he write a chapter of reminiscences than the words are whisked to a printer, set in type and bound into volumes for revision.

More than once I had heard the late President Roosevelt express unbounded admiration for Mr. Churchill. When I mentioned this, he drew me to a suspended frame displaying a card printed with a quotation from Lincoln's Gettysburg speech; below, in F. D. R.'s script, was a message marking an anniversary of their journey to Teheran: "I would travel even farther than that to have the happiness of being with you again."

"Mr. Churchill," I said, "England is sick. Can she ever become strong and well? Some people are saying that there is no way out of the present mess except complete state power."

"People are saying!" he barked. "The British are not a people to collapse when things get hard because of what people say. There is one more exhibit I would like you to see."

That final picture was a set of designs for the floating beach heads, engineering miracles known as "Mulberries," which, taking Nazi strategists by bewildered surprise, made possible the D-Day landings in Normandy.

With the plans was framed an exciting exchange of messages: first, high engineers indignantly informing the Prime Minister that they could not design his floating beach heads; such ideas were impossible. Second, in Churchill's savage handwriting was this command:

"Don't quarrel with me! Quarrel with your difficulties!"

As a result of that dictum, the engineers did solve the problem and Europe was ours. Surely here also was the command for England's new hour of danger!

As I left Chartwell Manor, I had my last glimpse of the stout figure in the air-raid suit standing by the balustrade and waving to me with the deft artist's hand that had guided armies and navies to victory. As I drove back to London in the lavender fall of dusk, there flooded through me the conviction that victory comes only with courage and faith like his.

What stands in the way of British recovery?

I put this question to one of the most interesting and competent men in the Labor government—the socialist Hector McNeill, Minister of State and chief deputy and reliance of Foreign Minister Ernest Bevin.

I reminded Mr. McNeill of some of the criticism to which I had been listening. The quick melting away of the billions in the American loan and the need to ask for more Yankee dollars, was making nonsense of the socialistic program—so the conservatives were telling me. Nationalization, wherever tried, was a flop—in the factories of France and the coal mines of England and Wales, so they were also telling me.

Even one of Labor's own, Mr. S. N. Evans, Member for Wednesbury, reproving a new demand for shorter working hours, in the House of Commons had stated:

"What our comrades are asking for is greater leisure to eat less food, more time to wear fewer clothes, greater leisure in which to see fewer of the more bed-worthy denizens of Hollywood, more time in which to drink less ale, and to smoke fewer cigarettes."

And Robert Boothby, another M. P., wrote: "We are blitzed, run-down, cold, hungry and exhausted. Our people have had to endure hardship, privation, monotony, discomfort and a crushing burden of taxation for seven years. If they are asked to go on doing so indefinitely, they will not rebel; they will simply fold up."

Chess player, reporter and star debater, Hector McNeill heard my questions with good-natured diffidence.

"You have enough coal in the ground to heat all England and run your factories, Mr. McNeill. Why can't you get it out?"

In a Scotch burr of which he is proud, McNeill said:

"Employment in the mines is rising. Men left because working conditions were so poor. With nationalization, they believe the mines will be modernized, so they're coming back. But production is still down, yes. There is some absenteeism."

"What keeps the men away?"

"One reason is lack of incentive. Even if a man earns a few extra dollars, what can he spend them on—except the races, or the 'flicks'! Our shops are empty."

"Could it not be true that the greatest reason is exhaustion?"

"We have had 7 years of bitter effort! And not enough to eat! . . .Yes, but look at what we have had to face this winter—disasters which no government on earth could have prevented. By freeze and flood we lost two million sheep and lambs—food and wool snatched away. Thirty thousand store cattle perished. More than half a million acres washed down by floods. Seventy thousand acres of corn lost, and winter wheat and eighty thousand tons of potatoes!"

All this in an already hungry land! I marveled that there had been no revolt at the polls, and said so. Yet not a single by-election had been lost by the Socialists. Mr. McNeill was certain the people felt the government was not to blame.

"Your enemies are saying that you promised the people paradise and now you are afraid to tell them that you can't deliver it," I said.

"We were elected on a manifesto that you can buy for tuppence and read for yourself. Only one promise did we make. We said we would provide housing. We haven't been able to do it because of all the circumstances. There is a long fight ahead of us; we have got to be frank with the people. If our living standards must go down farther, we can and shall face it. We have the character to do it."

I have just escaped from the Black Museum. That is a moist dungeon under the foundations of New Scotland Yard, and it is filled with souvenirs of chicanery and blood, court exhibits of many dark old deeds—and some younger ones. For example, I handled a pair of binoculars which came through the parcel post one day, addressed to an army officer's wife. Her father opened the bundle and was about to lift the sights to his eyes when some whim made him twiddle the focus wheel. Two murderous steel needles shot forward—they would have pierced his eyes and killed him. Here is an unsolved mystery of New Scotland Yard—but the real mysteries that now worry the police are of another kind.

I asked Commissioner Ronald Howe, debonair chief of the Metropolitan police:

"How many murders are committed in England every year?"

"Between 8 and 12. How many in New York?"

"One every day," I confessed.

There are good reasons for the difference, Howe conceded. England is a tight little island where law enforcement is easier. Even so, crime is increasing—more highjacking, more violence and a moral drop.

But it is being firmly put down. In a solemn courtroom of half-blitzed Old Bailey, I listened to the trial of 5 men who received long terms for highjacking a truck loaded with cigarettes. In Old Street Station, a businessman got three months in prison for buying from a farmer more eggs than the law allows.

"There is no real black market in England," said Commissioner Howe, "compared with France or Italy. The national psychology is all against it. We may have some temporary increase in crime, but this country will stay on the right side."

Later I rode the rainy Thames in a police boat and paused for a cup of tea with Superintendent Tom Fallon at the Wapping waterfront police station. On our way back to Waterloo Bridge, the policeman, pointing to the left bank, showed me the site of the ancient Globe playhouse.

"You know—Shakespeare's theater," added the officer softly. "I wonder how a poet would look at this mess today?"

Today I went to see a poet—the laureate of England, John Masefield. On this blessed afternoon of sunshine, I drove through a land of thatched roofs and chestnut and hawthorn trees, pink and white blossoms falling in the mist, and Scotch broom like a trail of gold leading off into the hills. Here people are legendary garden lovers and surely beauty grows where courage lives.

Down a long lane not far from Oxford, I came upon a good-sized country house and waiting at the door was the poet. The author of more than 75 volumes, which sing of salt fever in men's blood—"I must go down to the seas again"—and of "The tired battalion which fights until it dies"—is now stooped and gray-haired. He led me into a room where his wife was standing by an urn from which came the whiff of fragrant tea. She was a charming and eager lady, wrapped in a coat and wearing a hat. (For all the sunshine out-of-doors today, there is a fireless chill in-doors.) How, I wondered, had they managed the last seven years?

John Masefield had moved to this smiling countryside for peace and seclusion. But with the war came an airfield, used by the American flyers as a base for raids on Germany. Sometimes Nazi planes would pursue them the full distance back and over the poet's room there would be dog fights, flaming planes would tumble from the sky.

The winters had been rigorous; now his stiffened arthritic fingers cannot bend around a pen for long; he must peck out his sonnets on a typewriter. Yet, looking out the window at the cruel havoc of the flooded river spilling over his land, he remarked on the silver glisten over the grasses and the face of the sky, mirrored as in a great green looking glass.

His faith, I thought, was as firm today as when he had written that the spirit of England comes nearer when trouble presses:

No man can praise her, she is full of fault,
No man can blame her, she is full of good,
Kindness, stupidity and hardihood.

Another England lies ahead
With beauty on her bosom as a rose
And sunrise springing at her setting moon.

For all the troubles of today, he said, we should never discount the future of this land and race: "New buds are springing from the ancient wood!"

Today I made my pilgrimage to Canterbury—not the Cathedral, but to the Archbishop. He received me most kindly at his London residence in Lambeth Palace, which is near Westminster Abbey, and has been in ecclesiastical service since 1197.

The Archbishop, Dr. Geoffrey Fisher, has the head of an old Roman senator and wears cloth and gaiters with amiable dignity. I thought he looked like old paintings of William Penn who, when founding Pennsylvania, said, "Those who are not governed by God will be ruled by tyrants."

That might be the summary of Canterbury's hope for England now. Too many people were believing—and being encouraged to believe—that they were only cogs in a state government which nothing could overrule; they were accepting the fallacy that the individual has no importance. The hope of England, the hope of everywhere, was a realization of the uniqueness of human personality, of personal responsibility; of loyalty to old absolutes.

"Perhaps the signal service which Christianity has given to the world was first to create—and then to keep alive—the sense of obligation of man to man. It was created against the forces of indolence, selfishness and lust for power. Today we must strive harder than ever to oppose those forces which would control men for the same evil ends, if given a chance."

Beneath the spires of Oxford, miles away, I talked with another famous Protestant, C. S. Lewis, professor of English at Magdalen College, author of *The Screwtape Letters* and a dozen other penetrating studies of Christian behavior.

Professor Lewis will not thank me for blabbing what, elsewhere, I found out about him. His aged mother is ill and chair-bound, and no servant is to be had. So the Oxford don must stand in the queues; he is a scullery maid with no days off—and he must also teach his classes and read the work his young men have done.

On a bench by the riverside, under ancient trees, Lewis told me how today's young men of Oxford were examining religion. In no sense was there a religious revival. What students were studying was the hope Christianity offered to a chaotic world. With bilious eyes they look at the rationalism which failed to keep two generations—their fathers and grandfathers—out of war. Yet faith was becoming more intellectually respectable and in that there is hope.

And in the Old Palace beyond Christ Church, I found Monsignor Valentine Elwes, in charge of the instruction of Catholic youths, grown from 80 to more than 400.

"Things are tough for everybody," he admitted. "But our young fellows seem to be acting normally. They still talk sex until midnight and religion until three in the morning. But be certain of this—England will come out of this only with God's help."

Today I visited the man who would like to consider himself the most unreligious man in England—George Bernard Shaw.

I had not intended to intrude myself on the old-age

tranquillity of the greatest dramatist of our time but a post card came to the hotel, written in precise and elegant Shavian script:

"As I am 90 years old and completely on the shelf, and this village is very difficult except by car from door to door and the journey costs a whole afternoon, I cannot advise you to waste any of your brief stay on me. But I shall be at home on Saturday next after 3:30."

I waited for the great man in a book-lined room full of incongruities. On the mantel was a golden "Oscar" statuette from Hollywood, awarded for his scenario of *Pygmalion.* Across from his great chair by the barren fireplace was the Holy Bible in 12 annotated volumes, a set of Shakespeare and a fine edition of Chaucer's tales. While I was exploring the shelves, the door opened and Shaw literally bounced in.

Erect in knickerbockers and Norfolk jacket, he had set off his brown tweed with a lavender tie. The hair and beard looked wind-blown, his complexion pink and white, eyes sparkling like a mere youth of 70; the youngest man, he seemed to me, that ever wore gray hairs. He flung himself into the chair with showy vigor, and said: "It's no use trying to get me to write anything; I won't do it. I'm writing all the time as it is."

"What do you think about England now?" I asked.

"Why don't you ask me about America? Your greatest man is that real aristocrat, Henry Wallace. Roosevelt was not an aristocrat, you know; he was only a country squire. But one day Wallace will be President of the United States."

"All your friends in America will hope you live until that happens," I smiled. He threw back his head and chortled. Then I reminded him that 30 years before he had written a play in which he argued that England could govern any place on earth except itself; in the drama, he solved the problem by having a Chinese rule the British Isles.

"Do you think," I asked, "that a Chinese could govern England today?"

"It would take a pretty poor Chinaman not to do a better job than we're getting here now. But that doesn't mean we should go back. It is a question of common sense. The ordinary man must have his chance in two things; education and marriage. The mating part is very important for the future of the race. It is a terrible thing when a young man falls in love with a girl he cannot afford. I, myself, have been in love like that a number of times. It was like an ecstasy, a madness that possessed me. I would look at a girl and suddenly I felt like a man in a beautiful dream. I wanted that girl above everything else in the world. No doubt my reproductive glands were telling me that if this woman and I were married, we would breed fine children—the certain guidance of nature.

"But in every case when that happened to me, I could never have afforded to keep the girl of my dreams for three days, much less a lifetime. We must create conditions so that a man can take his proper mate. There are two brains left in Europe," he added abruptly. "One is Stalin; the other is the Pope."

I told him that only ten days before I had been received in private audience by His Holiness, Pius XII. Shaw was immediately interested; he milked his beard and said: "He is a very great and wise man. You know, I have often wondered—do you suppose that when the Pope was young he was a Shaw fan?"

It was time for me to go. On the way out, I asked him where he did his writing. Against my protests, for I feared to fatigue him, he took me a long way down a garden path to a retired spot at the foot of a slope and there showed me a microscopic one-room house no bigger than a night watchman's shack. It was crammed with books, a desk and a heavy fur covering for his feet.

As we climbed the hill another way, I saw a bronze figure set against a rock, a life-sized Joan of Arc, a very peasant Joan, left hand clenched, right hand against her brow, eyes turned grimly as she listened; her expression seemed to say: "I *do* hear them; I *do* hear the voices."

Shaw walked slowly with me to the car. He talked of a new play that was to be done for a festival this summer and began to demonstrate with a young director's passion how some of the lines would be read. There was then in his unwearied eyes the votive light of the creator, and I was sure that he, the skeptic, could also hear voices!

On the deck of the *Queen Elizabeth,* the brackish smell of ocean is in my nose, and homesickness in my heart —mixed with a sense of guilt. I remember the man in London to whom I gave three suits of woolen underwear and who received them wonderingly as if he held an Arabian shawl, and then began to weep. I thought of shabby coats and frayed old dresses of fathers and mothers who give their coupons to their children; of a sleepless woman counting her friends, and a professor caring for his crippled mother, a policeman wondering what visions the poet might see.

And there came into my head the refrain of an old Northumberland song:

"Fight on, my men," said Sir Andrew Barton,
"I am hurt, but I am not slain.
I'll lay me down and bleed awhile,
And then I'll rise and fight again."

HER BIG CHANCE

NEW YORK, 1951

DAVID Belasco, great stage producer and director, was always a showman, in the theater and out. But once, as he told me himself, when he was giving one of those private performances, he met his comeuppance from a very young and very pretty and very innocent girl.

Any experienced person could have told Elsie, stage-struck country lass, that she ought to forget her ambitions. That's what her mother tried to tell her. Possessed of her dream, Elsie would not listen to mother's argument that the boy next door was her big chance—because he offered her love for a lifetime.

And then, one day, her mother happened to remember something. Many years before, there had been a great snowstorm in which a train was stalled, and the passengers were brought into town. She had taken a man into her house, gave him a hot supper and a room—and he was a man of the theater. His name was Belasco.

"Oh, mother, write a letter for me to take to Belasco. Write it now!"

Reluctantly, her mother agreed. But when the time came to leave for New York, Elsie suddenly became afraid.

"What will I do if he asks me things and I don't know how to answer?"

And the mother, who devoutly believed in her religion, replied staunchly:

"Don't worry. If you must go to New York, hold on to your faith. You're in earnest, you're willing to work hard—God and His angels will tell you what is best for you."

So it happened that Elsie was admitted to the great man's presence. He listened to her pleas for a part, any part, no matter how small, in any play, please, please, please, Mr. Belasco—and he smiled sadly as he replied:

"Impossible, I fear. The only chance is if you happen to have a genius for acting. And that I can find out very quickly—all you have to do is to say two words—but you have to say them right. Just two words—'*Come here*'—and nothing more."

"But how——"

"You are to say them three times, in three dramatic situations. First, imagine that you are a young girl of excitable disposition, very much in love. You have had a quarrel with your young man and you have told him to leave you forever. As he goes out to the door, head bowed, you notice the outline of a revolver in his pocket. You are sure he is going to end his life. Suddenly, everything he means to you, the fact that he is all your future, overwhelms you with remorse and you say to him, '*Come here!*'

"I want to hear you say that!

"Next imagine that you are the mother of a little boy. He is four years old and you have dressed him up in his Sunday suit of white linen and told him to sit on the front step, but he is not to leave it. He disobeys you. He goes out into the street. Suddenly around the corner comes a truck. He is almost killed and is lying in the street, his pretty suit covered with mud. You are shaking with terror. You are also overcome with gratitude to God that he is still alive. And you are angry that he disobeyed you and that his suit is ruined—all this I want to hear from you when you say, '*Come here!*'

"And finally you are the wife of a banker in a small village. The bank has failed. Outside your house is a mob of ruined depositors ready to tear your husband to pieces. But your husband has just put a bullet through his heart and is lying dead on the living-room floor. You open the door, and I want to hear you say to the leader of the mob, '*Come here!*'

"Now, can you say those two words three times for me like that?"

The girl lifted her shining eyes to the master, and something inside her told her just what to answer.

"Not by myself alone, sir," she said. "But, yes—with you to direct me. If you will say the words as I should say them, I am sure I could imitate. Would you say them for me?"

Belasco gasped; she had outwitted him; she got a part.

"And did she become a star?" I asked.

"No," said Belasco. "She did all right in her first show, but she never seemed happy, once she had what she wanted. She always seemed to have a far-off look in her eyes as if looking for something more satisfying. When the show closed, she went home and married the boy next door. I suppose something inside her told her what was best for her to do."

THE MOST UNFORGETTABLE CHARACTER I'VE MET

CAPE COD, 1951

EVERYTHING was ready. The carrots had been chopped into fragments, then smothered in a caul of cottage cheese. On the bare floor of the porch was spread a red Navajo sleeping blanket. Permission had been granted by the golf-club manager for our guest to go barefoot around the course. Hanging in the garage was a sack stuffed with beach sand to be totted over-shoulder on a shore-road hike.

The house was all set for Bernarr Macfadden.

But presently the patriarch of physical culture, apostle of long life through diet and exercise, was calling on the telephone:

"I can't come this week end. Tomorrow's my birthday and I'm going to try a parachute jump from a plane. Maybe I can make it another week end."

"Maybe!" I echoed fearsomely as I hung up. Tomorrow, Macfadden would be 80 years old. What would happen to aging brittle bones when he came plumping down from the sky?

Next day, he sprang through the open door of a plane flying 4000 feet above the earth; he floated across high tension wires, skimmed over trees and rooftops and landed on his feet, upright, unbruised and not even out of breath.

Since the day I first met him, long, long ago, Bernarr Macfadden has never ceased to startle me, his friendship an unfailing adventure in consternation. His character is a complex of paradoxes. No man ever advertised himself more persistently and flamboyantly than Macfadden; his name, his face, his long, bushy hair, his chest, biceps, torso and thighs, all have been exhibited in public, reproduced and magnified in magazines, books, movies, posters, radio and television. Yet in private life he practices effacement, humility and self-distrust. He also distrusts practically everybody else. The most suspicious man I have known, he is also the readiest to test something new. Somebody is always trying to do him in the eye, and, often enough, succeeding. Yet he preserves no grudges.

"Life is too short for hate," he says. "And besides, it's bad for your health."

In a restaurant, a few weeks ago, he spied a man who had done him a costly and bitter injury. Walking over to the table, the physical culture man extended a powerful hand:

"Now that it's all over, I want to congratulate you for your cleverness. No more hard feelings, right?"

Out of story-book poverty on a Missouri farm, Macfadden hacked his way up to the possession of $30,000,000. Yet at the perihelion of his fortune he continued to wear old clothes, old shoes and hats, making them last 15 years or more.

Some years ago, Macfadden, unshaven, barefoot, perspiring and in one of his oldest suits, was taking a long solitary walk on the Atlantic shore and presently found himself in front of an imposing beach-front house. On the lawn was a "For Sale" sign. Macfadden walked around the property admiringly until a woman rushed outdoors, waving the backs of her hands at him.

"Go away, old man," she cried, "or I'll call the police."

"But this place is for sale. I was only looking it over."

"Don't be ridiculous, old man. The place is only for a millionaire."

"Well," said Macfadden, "I'm a millionaire and I'd like to buy the place."

Which he did.

He belongs to no prestige clubs and lives in a monkishly austere flat. Desiring virtually nothing material for himself—he still regards a television set as too much of a luxury—his earnings are emptied into enterprises that propagate his health theories.

Many of these theories were once denounced by orthodox medicine, later to become accepted practice. Today he remains, in medical eyes, a fanatic and a quack, but at 82 he has no doctor—he never has had one—his hair is long and spike-strong, he wears no glasses, has no arthritis, tramps on long hikes in cold storms and blistering heat, jumps over chairbacks, plays tennis, swims, passes a flyer's examination every spring and is planning another parachute jump for his next birthday.

It was because he was suspicious of me that I first met Mr. Macfadden. He had started a new magazine and I, a fledgling writer, had managed to sell to the editor four pieces for the first issue. Four checks were on Macfadden's desk, all payable to me but all still unsigned, when he invited me to call.

"Are you a relative of our editor?" he asked me. "Not even an in-law? Do you mind waiting here while I read your manuscripts?"

Having finished, he gravely signed the four checks and suggested that I join the staff. When I demurred, he tried another proposal.

"Keep your present job. Just come over here an hour every lunchtime. I'll pay you a good salary for an hour a day."

To a struggling young man that looked like easy money. But I soon discovered that the lunch hour was spent entirely in receiving homework; I was up all hours of the night finishing his noontime assignments. Before long I threw in my lot with him, and never once in years of intimate association did we know a harsh word or misunderstanding.

Typical of his tactics was the way he set me to work. He had provided me with offices and a stenographer but gave me no orders. Alone, uninstructed, I fell to writing, while two solitary weeks passed by. But on the third Monday morning I found on my desk a note:

"I am going away for a month and am leaving you in complete editorial charge of our five publications. You know what I want; give the orders and I will back you up. B.M."

For 21 years I remained in the post. During that time he bought and sold, started and stopped, many magazines and newspapers—nursing the successes and strangling the failures. At times our output was more than 16,000,000 magazines a month, and every one of the 16,000,000 teemed with pictures of Macfadden and ads of Macfadden books and correspondence courses on love, courtship, marriage, the natural methods of strengthening eyes, teeth, hair, reducing, increasing, and remedies for all the ills we are heir to.

"He is a charlatan," friends warned me, when I joined his staff. "There is not a sincere bone in his body."

I am glad to report that they misjudged him. What made Macfadden succeed, where imitators failed, was his sincerity, his passionate belief in his doctrine, his conviction that the body, when allowed to do so, can heal itself of any conceivable disease, by its own unaided natural methods; that weakness and ill-health are preventable crimes and that any person's life, with the enjoyment of all its powers, can be prolonged far beyond insurance probabilities. Possessed by an ungovernable urge to spread that gospel, Macfadden shouts at the world, while he builds and buys sanitariums, health restaurants, schools and hotels.

Himself he looks upon as an unanswerable testimonial to the verity of his teachings.

"My mother," he told me, "died of tuberculosis. My father was the town drunk and died of delirium tremens."

When these tragedies made him an orphan Macfadden was a small child. For years of growing up he was shunted from one relative to another, clerking here and farming there. One night he heard an aunt and an uncle talking him over: "You hear the boy's cough? He's got what his mother had; the doctor says he's not many more months for this world."

Ever since that dismal evening, Macfadden has shudderingly distrusted the prognoses of doctors. Through the long, wakeful night, he rehearsed his death sentence, over and again; the memory of his fright returns even now in nightmare. Tossing in the dark, he resolved to fight for life.

But how? Someone told him about a gymnasium in the town, where men could build strong bodies from weak ones, by exercise. But Macfadden could not borrow nor save the $15. Next best, he scrounged dumbbells and exercise booklets from a secondhand shop, accepting every extravagant claim of his "lessons" as scientific fact; the way to strength was through exertion.

Weak as he was, he obeyed the teachings, working harder and longer than he had to in the farm fields. Before long his sustained frenzy of physical effort began to pay off; the desperate boy grew visibly strong, the coughing stopped.

He ran away from the Missouri farm, tramping the roads, riding the rods, stopping for a while with relatives, then wandering off again—taking odd jobs as dentist's apprentice, printer's devil, wrestler, boxer, school coach and salesman of an exerciser. With that grotesque apparatus, Macfadden also sold a pamphlet—and he soon noticed that the people liked the printed matter more than the contraption itself. Out of that discovery he began to print *Physical Culture Magazine* which starting obscurely, caught on quickly and soon achieved a large circulation.

Before long, Macfadden was prosperous, and a sense of power promptly goaded him to action. During long years of poverty, he had observed and reflected on evils of everyday life which, in his view, were ruining the health of millions. Now that he had a magazine, he plunged into a whole series of crusades.

There was first his pet abomination which he called prudery. From work in gymnasiums, Macfadden had come to know the secret prevalence of venereal disease. Boldly he began to print the facts. People were shocked that he dared to discuss such unmentionable subjects. Having published Brieux's *Damaged Goods,* he followed that dramatic tract against syphilis with a serial story on a similar theme and for this sensational yarn he was indicted by a Federal Grand Jury.

His arrest caused a national uproar. President Taft remitted his prison sentence, but a fine of $1000 for "obscenity" had to be paid. Macfadden still wants the money back, with interest, because the time was to come when Washington authorities would plead with him, as with all other publishers, to tell the public the very same truths about venereal disease for which he had been convicted.

He has lived to see many such reversals of attitude. The antivice crusader, Anthony Comstock, once raided his exhibition in Madison Square Garden and arrested the physical culturist for parading a chorus of beauties in bloomers. Macfadden then began his war on what he dubbed "Comstockery," insisting that the human body, if healthy and strong and symmetrical was certainly nothing to be ashamed of. The world has come to agree with him.

Another of his brawls was against patent medicines, linked in early days into a powerful combine. Ridiculing unbridled claims to cure anything from cancer to housemaid's knee, Macfadden reviled the products for being mostly colored water mixed with corn whisky. Others joined in the fight, notably *Collier's Magazine,* and eventually reforms were made. But it was Bernarr Macfadden, not the medical profession, who pioneered in that worthwhile battle.

He fought the distillers, too, and the tobacco manufacturers, and the makers of white flour which—so Macfadden swore—was devitalizing the basic diet of the nation.

But his most exasperated assaults were on the medical profession itself.

Doctors have always scorned him and all his notions as irresponsible and disreputable quackery. Macfadden protests that they should give him a hearing, and examine his methods. Why did they refuse to see that old-fashioned corsets were injurious to women? Why did they ignore his contention that 90 per cent of operations on women were due to venereal infection, innocently acquired? Why would they not test his fruit juice and milk diets in the treatments of various diseases? Why would they not listen to him on weight reducing, sun-bathing, and other natural methods of healing?

When they would not answer, he sent a reporter around to 20 doctors, confiding to each the same set of symptoms. Result: 20 different diagnoses—20 doctors, 20 diseases—ranging from tonsilitis to cancer. One doctor hit it right; the reporter did suffer from all the symptoms he had described, and the cause was constipation.

With many of his theories I could not possibly agree, among them his rejection of vaccination—but that made no difference in our relations. He would remind me that George Bernard Shaw agreed with him on vaccination and let it go at that. Often I found in him admirable enlightenment. For a while he believed—and believes to this day—that alcohol is a deadly poison, and that no one should ever drink whisky, beer, or wine, yet in *Physical Culture Magazine,* in *Liberty* and others of his publications, he fought prohibition heroically and without giving one compromising inch.

"Enforced temperance is worse than drunkenness," he said. "A man must be free to win victory over himself."

S. O. Shapiro, Vice-President of Cowles Publications,

and for years Macfadden's Circulation Manager, proudly tells the story of a hang-over and its cure. Shapiro was conducting a Macfadden sales meeting in Miami. The night before the convention, the chairman admits, he had far too much to drink. Before collapsing in bed at 3 A.M. the last thing he did was to arrange for calling off the morning session. By his own devious ways, the suspicious Mr. Macfadden learned of the situation. At 4 A.M. he came rapping like a raven on the door of Shapiro's room and softly suggested that the circulation manager get into a bathing suit. Together they hiked five miles down the beach, Shapiro undergoing stomach upheavals every few hundred yards, then plunging into the sea. The convention began on time and Shapiro today is a teetotaler and likes it.

Not long after I started with Macfadden, he made an announcement in *Physical Culture Magazine* that he had discovered the secret of sex-predetermination. He told me:

"It is possible for any couple to decide, prior to conception, whether they will have a boy or a girl. I am the father of six daughters and no sons but I stake my reputation on the positive prediction that my next child will be a boy."

In this certainty he was not disappointed; the first son was born, followed by two more. The family called the first little boy Billy. But one day, about a year later, I found Macfadden in his office, pale and grim, writing in great longhand strokes across a yellow sheet of foolscap.

"My little boy died this morning," he told me. "It was my fault for letting him have the wrong kind of diet and I am writing my confession. Please get it in the first possible issue of *Physical Culture Magazine*."

I tried to convince him that the child had died from other, deeper causes, but he refused to be comforted.

"I have often said," he recalled in the editorial, "that whenever I saw a child's coffin go by in a funeral procession, I felt outraged—for it was, almost certainly, an unnecessary funeral. Tomorrow, when the coffin of my only boy is taken to the cemetery, I will have to say the same thing. Billy died because I was false to my own principles. In doting on this lovable little fellow, I relaxed my discipline, I forgot my faith, and as a result my son is dead."

After the funeral, Macfadden disappeared from the office. It was midwinter and for a week he went hiking through mountain snow, while observing a long and rigid fast; making it tougher than ever for himself and so regaining mastery. By this hard road, he believes, in common with mystics and saints, one can find the true path of serenity and achievement, overcoming fear, grief and pain. Once I sat nearby while he telephoned a dentist:

"How much drilling will there be? How long in the chair to finish it all up? Three hours? Well, I can stand that —but I could never stand the thought of shooting any drugs into my body, just to deaden pain. I'll take it straight."

One day, Macfadden was walking down a New Jersey road with a socialist friend. Passing a golf course, near a factory, the leftist quoted an ironic cliché about what fun it was for working children to watch their employers on the greens. The thought was shocking to Macfadden. Later that month he bought the golf course, turning it into a farm school and play place for children.

During two depressions, Macfadden opened "penny restaurants" in New York and Chicago. He believes that foods for strength and health are also the cheapest. Each dish on his menu cost one cent; for ten cents a man was well fed with cracked wheat, cream, honey and other body-building items. A few years later, during an audience in Rome, he told Mussolini that the Italian army's food bills were too high and the nutriment too low. At half the price, Macfadden offered to give Italy stronger soldiers.

Months later, Macfadden received a telephone call from Ellis Island. A consignment of Italian soldiers had just arrived for him; young men to be put on a course of physical culture. Delightedly, Macfadden fell upon those hapless victims of despotism. He barred spaghetti from their meals; he crammed them with cracked wheat and rabbit vegetables, meanwhile putting them through his own system of calisthenics. Finally he sent them back improved, by all standard laboratory tests—and at one third the money spent on them in home barracks. For this demonstration he received an Italian decoration which a few years later he pitched overboard.

In Cape Cod, where he often visited us, the townsfolk tell their own strange stories about him. Natives who do not know the facts are certain we treat our guest unkindly. Some years ago, it happened that Mary Pickford was staying at our house as was Macfadden. There had been some talk of a kidnapping plot against Mary so we asked local gendarmes to guard the house. When these police officers went home, they reported to their wives that while all the rest of us slept in comfortable beds, we made that "poor old gentleman" sleep on the floor, rolled in a blanket. For years, Macfadden has forsworn beds and mattresses, believing that a hard floor is a strengthener of the spine, in his view the center of human vitality.

It was his habit to fly up from New York—often, in his late seventies, piloting solo back and forth—and of course we would meet him at the landing field. But on Monday mornings, when it was time to fly back, Macfadden would refuse to be driven to the airport, preferring to start the day right by walking the seven miles. Any offer to drive over with bags would be refused; he still wanted to make it tough for himself. So tongues wagged again: we made the "poor old gentleman" walk to the airport, carrying his own luggage.

The worst of all the tales grew out of his habit of fasting. One night we were going to wrestling matches at Hyannis and decided to have dinner there. But Macfadden begged off.

"I am near the end of a seven-day fast," he explained. "If I sit at the table with you and smell all that nice food, I'll be tempted. You go in and have dinner—I'll sit out here in the car and think."

You can imagine what they said about that!

When Franklin D. Roosevelt was campaigning for the Presidential nomination in 1932, Macfadden supported him and through *Liberty Magazine* rendered valiant help. Soon after the inauguration, he was invited to the White House, and I heard him say:

"That is very courageous of Mr. Roosevelt. I might easily be an embarrassing guest for him. After all, a lot of respectable people call me a nut, a crackpot, a faker and an old fool. By honoring me, the President might weaken their confidence in him. But he has invited me to be an overnight guest. I would have understood perfectly if he had never invited me."

He hired Mrs. Roosevelt to edit a short-lived magazine called—excruciatingly—*Babies, Just Babies*. Anna Roosevelt worked in the office every day at this time and Macfadden tried to convert her to physical culture ways. One day he confided to me: "There's something contrary in every Roosevelt."

One night we were dining in a suite at the Sherry-Netherland with a Hollywood star who complained of headaches. At the table Macfadden taught her to stand on her head, his way of clearing the brain. In the elevator going down, the fancy seized the actress to try it again and she stood on her head in the little car. At once Macfadden joined her and when the doors opened on the crowded first floor, the two were standing upside down.

In late years, when misfortunes assailed him, I watched him start life anew—stirred by the same principles which had filled him with zeal since childhood when he believed he had only a few months more to live. Meanwhile, he keeps himself busy. He tramps the mountains, he goes hungry deliberately, he jumps and dances and swims. And at night he stands by the piano and sings in a King Lear voice: "I Love Life!"

That is the keynote of Bernarr Macfadden—that he loves life and values it and enjoys it and seeks to prolong it. In strange ways, he keeps himself vigorous, meanwhile scolding and imploring the rest of mankind to take care of themselves, that their days, too, may be long and strong and joyous.

Two men more polarly different than Bernarr Macfadden and Fulton Oursler would be hard to find. Two men who loved and respected each other more, would be even harder. Without a vestige of intimacy (they might not see each other 4 or 5 times a year) there was a fierce devotion between them. From 1925 until he parted from the organization, Fulton Oursler did not work at the pub-

lications, though he retained an office and needed a force of secretaries there and he went to it for a few days every month or two. He carried out all his editorial work from his house on West Seventieth Street, during a year in Hollywood, and 12 full years at his home in Cape Cod.

Often, when asked how many magazines he supervised, he said: "Well, there were eleven when we closed shop last night." But there were always the 7 basic monthlies and after 1931 when he got a telephone call at Sam Harris' apartment while he was reading the first act of a play and was told to take over Liberty, *there was a weekly. (He never finished that play.) In the late '20's he assembled a complete staff for Mr. Macfadden's newspaper, the* Graphic, *but after the first few months he took no active participation in it, concentrating entirely on the magazines "uptown."*

His first experiment at long-distance editing was from Hollywood in 1932 when Mr. Oursler went to do the scenario of his own novel, The Great Jasper, *on a three-month contract but stayed a year. He brought west 2 secretaries, one for Macfadden work and one personal, plus the entire family. The first week he unintentionally made mild history. Going to his first major appointment at the studio (after the usual preliminary greeting-visit had been accomplished) F. O. brought a bulging brief case and a slim secretary. Hollywood Great Ones were famous for keeping people waiting. For over an hour Mr. Oursler dictated calmly in the reception offices, and sent his secretary off with the brief case of Macfadden work handled. When the Studio President finally saw Mr. Oursler he sarcastically remarked that rumor had reached him Mr. Oursler was doing other work on the studio's time.*

"That's right," F. O. agreed. "There was no studio work to do. And nobody *can pay me enough money to waste my time."*

The story flew over Hollywood as only in Hollywood can stories fly. But it was told by the President, who came to love Fulton Oursler like a brother, starting that moment.

After that Hollywood hiatus Mr. Oursler realized distance was small handicap to his work as an editor. Actually it achieved considerable saving of time and energy. He vowed never to live in the city again. He discussed a plan of living year round at Cape Cod with Bernarr Macfadden (who flew cross country to visit several times). Then F. O. arranged long distance to sell his New York house so that he might not be tempted to return and also by long distance ordered an oil furnace and heating system and full insulation installed in his Cape Cod home. Next he set about the happy process of designing himself a library wing to his home for a "workshop."

For 12 years, working by phone, teletype, Western Union and a staff of 4 secretaries who handled the daily mountain of manuscripts, vouchers, art work, duplicate dummies kept in a running state of completion, which arrived at the 11 o'clock West Falmouth Post Office and the similar load that went back on the 4:45 train. A stream of fellow executives, authors, celebrities, who were being ghosted or interviewed, came to the house to discuss plans and their developments. Mostly these were 2–3-day stays spotted throughout the year. Mr. Macfadden came sporadically for a morning's huddle or for several days. Sometimes unannounced he would fly up and circle the chimney until he alerted the Oursters to come to the field to meet him. The night phone talks between them were fabulous. Every 4–6 weeks Mr. Oursler headquartered at the Waldorf, seeing all the Macfadden office staff, agents and others (and catching up with the theaters). Or at Miami Beach, where Mr. Macfadden owned Deauville, and where he had as guests in rotation almost all his workers (down to the switchboard operators before the season was over).

They were 21 tightly packed years, overloaded, overburdened years of radical and historical changes in the world and in individual lives. Mr. Oursler was not a "boss" everyone adored. He neither sought love nor gave it widespread. He was not palsie. He was a mixer only with great effort, and he hated "good times" and "get-togethers."

There were many who did not understand him and felt ill at ease with him: there were some who misunderstood him. But when he rounded out those 21 years with the Macfadden Publications there were those who had held him in highest respect and regard that verged on emotion, chief among them Sam Shapiro, Walter Winchell, Ed Sullivan and Bernarr Macfadden.

HE MADE HIS CHOICE

CAPE COD, 1951

IT was young Terry's first day in a law office. He was a fledgling attorney, fresh out of school and only just admitted to practice at the bar. Through the influence of his older brother, he had been given a small job in a large law firm, and on this first morning, the head of the partnership called him in.

"Now Terry," said the great lawyer benignly, "I want to tell you that you have a great future. It's up to you. Work hard, carry out orders, and in middle life you will be a successful and well-to-do man."

"Thanks," said Terry and meant it.

"Of course, you are starting at the bottom. You are low man on the totem pole, ha, ha! Your first job will be to collect rents from a string of tenement houses and I want to talk to you about that. You are young and you have to learn. Don't listen to the hard-luck stories—and you'll hear plenty, every last one of them phonies. I never knew another such crew of whining, falsifying phonies. Your orders are to bring back the money—and you'll have to bring it!"

"But," Terry ventured, "what do I do if they really don't have the money?"

"Just tell them we'll evict them at once."

"But there's that new clause in the law——"

"I know—and you know—but they don't know. They'll believe you and they'll scrape the money together, one way or another. Good luck, now."

All morning, young Terry climbed odorous stairs of tenement houses, knocked on greasy doors, entered railroad flats and called for cash. And just as predicted, he heard a lot of hard-luck stories. Some of them, even to his unpracticed eyes, were certainly fakes. But were they all pretense? Young Terry doubted it; with every new tenant, his heart grew heavier.

Finally he met Mrs. Flanagan. She was a widow with three small children; she did piecework at home but, having been ill, had earned nothing, so she said, for the last ten days. Terry decided to put her to the test. He telephoned her employers and confirmed that she had not worked. He called on butcher and grocer and iceman and found they had cut off her credit, because she already owed too much. He spent the rest of the afternoon, checking up on Mrs. Flanagan. And the day was almost over when he said to her:

"Mrs. Flanagan, you did not give me the whole story; you're even worse off than you said. And I have found out something else. I find that the landlord has been cheating you by charging you interest. Interest? Usury! On back payments that you owed. I am amazed that a reputable firm of supposedly upright citizens would stoop so low. That's why I just called up the boss and resigned."

"Oh, glory be, you shouldn't have done that, young man. Jobs are hard to get. And you're just starting out . . ."

"I had to do it. Otherwise, I couldn't sue him."

"Sue, you say?"

"For you, Mrs. Flanagan."

"But young man, when you go to law, money is needed and I——"

"Right." And Terry handed her a five-dollar bill, thus emptying his pocket. He had to walk home. And he had to face his brother, who had obtained the job. But his brother, who loved him, folded him to his heart.

Queer thing about young Terry. His first day in court was the suit he brought against his first employer, in behalf of Mrs. Flanagan. And not of her alone, but Mrs. Bernstein and Mrs. Schultz and Mrs. Everybody Else in the tenements known as "Misery Flats." Terry had a score of clients, all of whom had been cheated.

The fact that Terry won his first case was only a beginning. The people of the neighborhood acclaimed him the young friend of the poor. He has been to the legislature, he has a flourishing practice with his own law firm—and he is still an unpurchasable man.

"What I love about it," said his brother, when he told me the story, "was that Terry faced a moral crisis that day —and he made the right choice."

It always takes courage to do the right thing at our own expense. And we are not always rewarded with worldly success when we do. But the dividends of the soul are never lost.

THE UNEXPECTED VOICE

CAPE COD, 1947

ONE of the most stirring stories of faith and courage I know was told to me by my good friend, Dr. Charles H. Heimsath, the former pastor of the First Baptist Church in Evanston, Illinois, and now on the faculty of Trinity University in San Antonio, Texas.

It began on a fine Sunday, many years ago, with Charles Heimsath standing under a brush arbor, facing his first mountaineer congregation.

In 35 years, life in those hills has altered for the better, so I shall not name the place. But on that morning of Charles Heimsath's youth, when he was still a pulpit-scared seminary student, his reading stand was made of unpainted cracker boxes draped with a potato sack. In farm wagons and ox teams, or walking barefoot, log-cabin families—breasting babies to nonagenarians—had come from miles around the county, down to the crossroads service. About 200 sprawled on the grass in clannish groups, old women smoking corncob pipes, the men chewing midnight plug.

Nervousness was already gathering in the young minister's throat as he faced them.

"Silence, please!" he began. "And let us pray."

Heimsath's nervousness deepened when they went right on talking; all through the invocation he could hear election bets being made and mules and hogs bought and sold.

"Maybe they'll settle down soon," he thought hopefully. Raising both hands, and with a smile that was utterly false, Heimsath shouted: "Now folks, let's all join together in our first hymn. Everybody knows the words of 'The Sweet By-and-By.' So come on—everybody sing!"

Through two endless verses and two refrains Charles Heimsath's shaky voice labored on alone, and all the while, in and around the family huddles, small boys played hide-and-seek, with the pulpit as home base.

"I'll try The Lord's Prayer," Heimsath told himself. "They *must* know that."

The prayer, too, was a solo but in the midst of it, suddenly, almost miraculously, the picnic gabble stopped, the running youngsters quit their game, and silence fell like a bomb. As the young minister uttered his amen, his eyes beheld all those mountaineers sitting in rigid attitudes, unmoving as graveyard statues. And every one was watching him as if with but one eye, listening with only one ear—all keeping a secret vigil of their own. And then, as Heimsath, too, heard what they had already detected—a tattoo of racing hoofbeats—there galloped into sight a young man with flying black hair, astride a great brown horse.

With shocking suddenness the rider drew up. Amidst a frightened hush, he looked directly at Heimsath, then scolded his mount forward until he sat towering above the minister and the cracker box; the snorting of his horse riffled the leaves of Heimsath's Bible.

"Never before or since," relates Heimsath, "have I seen such hostility in the eyes of any man."

"You can shut up that book now and go home," he commanded.

Then, wheeling the horse easily and facing the crowd he patted the butts of two black revolvers in a holster belt and cried:

"That goes for all of you. This meeting is adjourned—so go on home. And you all know why!"

As if the words were a signal of release, the crowd broke and ran; nursing mothers scrambling into oxcarts, barefoot families trotting off into the fields. In less than five minutes only the young minister and the horseman were left under the cedar boughs.

"Preacher," the intruder warned, "I told you once—get going!"

Somehow Heimsath found the courage to gasp:

"If I didn't go—do you mean you would really shoot?"

"Would I?" he sneered. "My old man used to tell me that every preacher's head was full of sawdust. I'd just as soon put a hole through your head and find out if pappy was right."

With that, he cantered off, losing himself in the bushes and the poplars and the winding road.

At first all Charles Heimsath wanted was to get down out of the mountains, back into a town again with streetcars and policemen, comfort and safety. His old mare, hired for the summer, was tied to a post near the pulpit, and his belongings, rolled in a bundle, were strapped behind the saddle. There was nothing to detain him. And yet, even as he stowed hymnbook in one rump pocket, Bible in the other, and lifted his foot to the stirrup, he hesitated.

"If you leave the hills now," his conscience seemed to say, "these people will never forget a man who was scared to stand up for what he believed."

"God knows that's right," Heimsath thought. "But what about the fellow with the guns?"

The answer came, of course, from his own heart; he had joined an army that possessed as weapons only prayer and faith and little else. The choice before him was dismayingly clear, and he made it with sheer, downright physical fear as he turned his horse toward the mountain trail.

He did not even know the horseman's name, but a gold-bearded rancher whom he passed on the way gave him directions; when he finally reached the gunman's property, he was in no doubt, for the sign over an opening in the rail fence was like his own bitter voice:

"Keep out! Strangers will be shot at! Signed: Jerry Mason."

Heimsath turned in. He rode up a dirt path and around its second bend he came upon the charred ruins of a cabin, burned to the foundations. Beyond, only a little way, stood a one-room shack with tar-paper roof. Not a tree or bush or flower was there to soften the bleak loneliness of the scene.

"Helloa!" Heimsath called. "Jerry Mason! Where are you?"

Instantly the black-haired youth came to the shack door, rifle in hand. He stared at the minister incredulously.

"Get down!" he ordered.

Heimsath's voice was breathless as he jumped to the ground and gasped:

"Good afternoon, Mr. Mason."

"You got a posse behind you down that road?"

"No—I'm alone!"

"Who put you up to coming here?"

"Nobody!"

"Oh! You just came to dare me—is that it?"

"No—not that at all."

"Well—I wouldn't have believed it—you've got more nerve and less sense than I thought. What do you want?"

"I think," the minister said haplessly, "I would like a drink of water."

Jerry Mason lifted his chin and measured Heimsath with cold calculation.

"Why, of course," he said, with a weird smile. "You can have a drink of water. Why not? Just step right inside!"

In the windowless cabin Heimsath could see a cot, a table and a chair. He noticed, too, that the board floor was swept clean, and that the crockery and pans were stacked in orderly piles on a single wall shelf.

Silent as an executioner, Jerry Mason followed Heimsath, laid aside his rifle, lifted a demijohn and filled a tin cup which he then put down on the table.

"Take it if you want it," he said. "It ain't poison."

Heimsath drank, hopefully studying Mason's face over the rim of the cup. But there was no sign of lessened hostility in the dark eyes.

"Now talk quick," he said. "What are you after on my property?"

Two seconds before, Heimsath could not have told himself what his answer was going to be. He had forgotten that we all have Someone to prompt us when we need it most.

"To apologize," he burst out.

"Are you crazy, preacher—or maybe just stalling?"

And he picked up the rifle.

"No!" The words came rushing from the young minister, trembling, unrehearsed. "I just had to ask your forgiveness for being such a coward. I still am, as you can see for yourself. But this morning, I couldn't even move my tongue. That's why I didn't give you a chance!"

"Give *me* a chance!"

"You didn't get a square deal. The minute you arrived, I knew there must be something awful wrong. Nobody would ever ride into a religious service and break up worship on Sunday morning—not without a good reason! So you had a right to be heard. I should have asked you to get it off your chest. But I couldn't——"

"As if all those yellow-bellies don't know," said Jerry huskily. "They'll never forget—I won't let them!"

"But can't I know what's wrong, Jerry?"

"My mother used to believe all your sort of stuff," he went on coldly. "She was always telling me to be a good Christian. It makes me vomit to remember how I used to sing 'There's a wideness in God's mercy' with her—and halfway believe it, too, until one day Mom took very sick. I fetched the doctor for her—but he ran out like a rat with a knot in its tail when he found out what it was she had."

He grabbed the front of Heimsath's shirt.

"Did you ever watch anybody die of smallpox?"

He shook the minister violently.

"Somebody close?"

He let go and spat on the ground.

"All she ever asked for was a preacher to come and pray with her. I rode down to the settlement. That preacher would only talk to me behind a bolted door—he was too white-livered to come. Nobody else would, either. So I told

Mom I couldn't find anybody at home. I just plain lied to her about the whole thing. I sat there, holding her hand and reading the Bible and saying prayers with her until——"

Walking to the open door, he stood looking out at trees and sky. Heimsath had sense enough then not to say anything. He closed his eyes for a moment or two; when he looked again, Jerry Mason turned, cold and bitter as before, and went on:

"The night she died, there was an accident. The old house we lived in yonder caught fire and the marshal never could figure out how it got started. But when the health department wagon come up here, there wasn't much left but ashes."

The bitterness, softened for a moment, was creeping back into his eyes.

"And now you know! I chase every damned preacher out of these parts."

"Doesn't she still exist—somewhere?"

"I wish I knew! Don't you?"

"If she *can* see what you're doing—do you think she likes it?"

"Why shouldn't I—when they were all so rotten——"

"Not rotten. Just plain scared. You're a strong character, Jerry. But don't you know that most of us are cowards? Like I was this morning. Like the disciples were, when they all ran away leaving Jesus with the sheriff. Your mother wanted you to be a good Christian. Well, that means——"

"I *don't* love my enemies!" he exploded. "I *hate* them!"

What could anyone say now to quiet the sorrow and hatred in those dark eyes? Certainly Charles Heimsath was too young to possess such wisdom. Indeed, it was as if some other voice was speaking when he heard himself ask:

"Was your mother tall—like you?"

"What's that to you?"

"I am just trying to imagine what she was like."

"She was just a little lady."

"Black eyes?"

"No, no—they were blue and looked right through you. She had long white hair and she used to wear it tied in a knot on the back of her head."

For the first time Heimsath walked toward him. He laid his hand on Jerry Mason's shoulder, and said:

"I can almost see her in this room. I can almost hear her voice as she tells you to have mercy on all the frightened people, to make friends. That old hymn you sang with her——"

"Get out of here!" he screamed.

"I'm going. But if you don't believe your mother lives anywhere else, you know she lives in your heart."

"Leave me alone!"

"You're never alone! And you know it!"

Down at the crossroads, Charles Heimsath found ranchers willing, in spite of their consternation, to carry a message for him all through the hills—there was going to be another service under the brush arbor, tonight! Then the minister sat down to wait. Would the people come? And if they did, would there be more trouble?

An hour before sunset, the congregation sat before Heimsath on the grass. Perhaps it was curiosity, but this time he had quiet from the beginning, although many a wary glance was turned toward the upland road. Heimsath announced the opening hymn and his voice rose shakily on the mountain stillness:

"There's a wideness in God's mercy
Like the wideness of the sea.
There's a kindness in His justice——"

And then out of the shadows of the trees Charles Heimsath heard another voice joining in with his; a firm clear tenor of heart-wrenching sweetness, while people all around were chattering:

"Good God! Look! It's Jerry Mason. He's come to meeting!"

And soon the whole excited crowd was singing together as the darkness came down with the stars.

After Dr. Heimsath returned to the seminary to complete his studies, he got a letter from Jerry, asking him to come back and marry him.

"I have done many weddings since," Dr. Heimsath wrote Fulton Oursler. "But none has so deeply moved me. I was not much older than the bride and groom, but I felt they were my children. Jerry is now the Sheriff of the county, the most fearless peace officer in the hills."

WE OUGHT TO MAKE MORE OF IT

NEW YORK, 1952

JOSEPH Auslander, the distinguished American poet, was the witness not so long ago of an object lesson in Americanism.

Mr. Auslander has a friend, and I shall call him Michael Alexander, who was born in the Russia of another day. By great good luck, he escaped from the Communist oppressors of his native land, made his way by slow stages across Europe and finally into the United States. Here he dedicated himself to two projects: one, to establish himself in his profession, and the other, to learn everything he could about the history of his land of refuge.

Mr. Auslander himself is a student of the great adventure that is called America, but he was dumfounded at the knowledge his friend acquired. He knew the life stories of our statesmen and patriots; the influences that worked on the minds of Jefferson and Hamilton, Franklin and Madison, Lincoln and Theodore Roosevelt. He could quote from our documents and from the letters and speeches of our great men, and there was reverence and joy in his eyes and his voice and his gestures when he did.

Of course, he took out his first citizenship papers at the earliest opportunity. And then he took out his second papers. Finally the great day approached for the final test when he must stand before officials of the noble land of his adoption and win for himself what he considered the crown of his life—membership in our free democracy, a citizen with all the rights and privileges and duties of a free man.

Alexander's excitement began to grow. The night before the appointed time found him so nervous and excited that he could not sleep. He lay in bed reciting the Declaration of Independence instead of counting sheep, but the immortal words only stirred him to a deeper ecstasy of expectation.

Mr. Auslander called for Alexander early in the morning and the two of them went to the naturalization office. When they arrived at the office, Alexander blinked at the scene. There was a man behind a counter and a long line of people waiting. The official had papers and stamps, and as each candidate appeared before him he mumbled questions, listened to mumbled answers, signed papers and motioned to the next in line to move up. Alexander shuffled his way in the procession and finally stood before the official. Without looking up the clerk said:

"Name?"

"Michael Alexander." The words, followed by his final name of many syllables, boomed and roared throughout the room like thunder. There were other routine questions and then the clerk said, "That's all."

"No!" thundered Michael Alexander. "That is not all. I will not move on. This is the most important moment of my life. I am becoming an American and you wave your hand and say 'next.' No. This moment is sacred. It is not a little moment. It is the biggest moment of all—'Fourscore and seven years ago our fathers brought forth on this continent a new nation, conceived in Liberty and dedicated to the proposition that all men are created equal. Now we are engaged in a great civil war, testing whether that nation or any nation so conceived and so dedicated, can long endure'. . . ."

The crowded room was hushed as that resonant baritone voice roared on, simply and devotedly repeating immortal phrases. There had been no greater hush at Gettysburg. As he finished with the line ". . . and that government of the people, by the people, for the people, shall not perish from the earth," the silence seemed to deepen and no one moved until the clerk shoved back his chair. He stood up and extended his hand to Michael Alexander.

"I guess you're right," he said. "It is a great thing, just as you say. We ought to make more of it."

And Michael Alexander, chin up, that shining light still in his eyes, stalked out of the room and joined his friend the poet for breakfast.

Fulton Oursler and Joseph Auslander had a common bond in the love of the poem The Hound of Heaven *and interest in the life of Francis Thompson. Joe and his wife Audrey (the great-granddaughter of Shelley) often shared Sunday afternoons of enthusiasms for things poetic, religious, philosophical and especially Irish, for Joe had lived in Ireland long years with the poet* A.E.,

Yeats, and their coterie, and he and Fulton Oursler both loved the land.

Often, with overdramatic earnestness, F. O. would insist he was eligible for the Friendly Sons of St. Patrick. "I belong," he would argue gravely, "to St. Patrick's Parish in New York and to St. Patrick's Parish in Falmouth, Cape Cod, and what's more, you must understand that my name really is O'Ursula."

If he had lived one more day, Fulton Oursler would have been able to keep an appointment to meet Louis Auslander, the first child born to Audrey and Joe after 19 years of marriage.

THE SHADOW OF A DOUBT

NEW YORK, 1951

SOME forty years ago an Omaha gambler was put on trial, accused of trying to blow his worst enemy to smithereens. The result was an astonishing courtroom upset; the case of the picture, the steeple and the two girls in white remains today a classic of criminal defense and of legal resourcefulness when everything seemed lost.

The imagination to find a desperate chance and the daring to take it, belonged to the defense attorney, John O. Yeiser. People said that Yeiser, with his rubicund face, mane of brindled hair and rugged voice turning soft as a woman's when pleading to a jury, was an eccentric, a queer geezer, a rum customer.

For one thing, he had written a book to prove the immortality of the human ego not by Bible quotations, but from scientific evidence implicit in the mysteries of time and space and the dialing of sun and moon and stars. Stranger still, he had often been known to brush aside a princely fee, refusing a client simply because he did not believe the story. But give Yeiser faith in an accused man and there was nothing he would stop at to acquit him. Like the Erdman case, with its belfry and belles and its blacklegs.

On Monday, May 23, 1910, Yeiser read great headlines in his morning paper, proclaiming an attempt on the life of the town's most powerful politician. Let us call him Jack Plenister. He who once had run faro rooms and roulette wheels in frontier towns now was master of a political ring and gossip was that he collected a percentage from every game of chance within 500 miles of Omaha.

On the bright afternoon of the day before—indisputably established at the trial as precisely at 2:50 P.M.—Jack Plenister, coming back from a walk, noticed a suitcase on the front porch of his house. About to pick up the bag, he spied a thin white thread running from the keyhole of the luggage piece, across the veranda to the porch railing. So Plenister telephoned for police.

On the banks of the Mississippi, detectives cut away a part of the lid and thus opened to view the bowels of a mechanical ambush. A revolver was lying inside the infernal machine, the string tied to its trigger, and the weapon nesting in a stack of dynamite sticks, enough to depopulate a city block.

Reading the news reports, John Yeiser looked dubious. Why such a transparent rig as a self-advertising white string stretched halfway across the porch? Not that he suspected Jack Plenister; the machine politician was a fundamentally decent man, but many of his supporters were ruthless. The lawyer's doubts deepened as afternoon front pages blazoned the news that the case was solved; the guilty man already behind the bars.

Who was the dynamite plotter and what was his motive? The prisoner was Frank Erdman, a hanger-on in the gambling crowd; a small-time back-street picaroon. Recently he had quarreled with Plenister and the gang had kicked him out. For weeks, so rumor went, Erdman had been in hiding, fearing a beating from his former friends; "a disgruntled henchman, out for revenge" was the station-house theory of the crime.

With jaunty air, all bland and smiling, John Yeiser appeared that same night at the county jail and offered his services to Erdman free of charge. But Erdman shook his head morosely.

"It's no use. Everything is against me. Sure, I hate Jack Plenister. What's more, I've got no alibi; I stayed in my furnished room until late yesterday afternoon—but nobody else saw me there. I've got no friends, no witnesses, no bail. This thing is a frame-up to put me away for the rest of my life and they're going through with it. Better not waste any valuable time on me; nobody in this town is powerful enough to beat the combination."

Nevertheless, John Yeiser became Erdman's counsel, and as the case came to trial he told his client he felt sure he could deadlock the jury, if nothing more. "They haven't enough evidence to prove you guilty beyond the shadow of a doubt," he declared.

Equally confident he remained, even when seven witnesses, one after another, swore they had seen Erdman near to Plenister's front porch just before the suitcase was found. Unshakably affable in his cross-examination, Yeiser forced each of the seven witnesses to admit that he was connected, one way or another, with the gambling syndicate, and so had an interest in the case.

But then the prosecutor called his star witnesses—the two sisters in white.

Everybody in the courtroom had been wondering

about those two young girls, because all seven witnesses had mentioned them. Each had sworn that he had noticed two girls in pretty white dresses walking past the Plenister cottage. Now, first the younger, then the older of the sisters took the stand. They told a simple, direct, and utterly damning story.

May 22 had been their Confirmation Sunday. After services in church, they had strolled home, going by the Plenister front porch at 2:15 P. M. They were precise about the time and emphatic in their declarations; they had seen Erdman entering an alley behind the house, they remembered his limp, his cap, his checked suit.

Across the courtroom sat the prisoner, wearing a checked suit. When asked to rise and come nearer to the bench, he walked with a visible limp. When they clamped a checked cap on his head, he admitted it to be his own.

With heavy heart, Yeiser faced the older girl. The most any counsel for the defense could do with such an obviously truthful witness was to grope and probe for contradictions, hoping to shake the jury's confidence in her accuracy. He began to lead her back through a chronology of the walk home:

"What did you do when you came out of church?"

"We had our pictures taken."

"And where did you go for that?"

"We did not go anywhere. A boy from our class took it; we all just stood on the church steps."

"Do you have a copy of the picture?"

"Yes, Mr. Yeiser. Right in my purse."

At this point, the judge declared a two-hour recess. Carrying the snapshot in his pocket, John Yeiser walked helplessly into a cafeteria. At a solitary table he sat brooding over his New England boiled dinner. He still felt convinced that Erdman was the victim of a malevolent and outrageous frame-up. But how prove it now? The testimony of these two girls in white had made the state's case invulnerable. There was the photograph, showing church steps, three boys and, all in Confirmation finery with nosegays pinned on long white dresses, six girls, the two sister witnesses among them. Nothing there to give any hope.

And yet, even then, some undefinable hope was stirring deeply in John Yeiser's subconscious mind; a mysterious hunch, intangible and impalpable, beginning to take hold. What was it that seemed to be joggling his mind; some unnoticed clue, or baroque detail that his conscious mind had so far overlooked? Could it be the shadow?

There *was* a shadow on the snapshot. It covered a large area on the right side; an irregularly and fantastically shaped blotch of darkness. Exasperating to have something poppling up and down on the surface of his mind, but still eluding him! Yeiser sat back and tried to make his mind a blank, but memories of his book on immortality came rolling in like an invasion; thoughts of stars and celestial systems and the dialing of time——

Suddenly an idea fairly billowed through his brain. He sat unmoving for a while, in a catalepsy of self-control lest he leap to his feet and emit a war whoop. With the most casual air, he left his unfinished lunch and was presently standing on the church steps. Above him loomed the spire of the belfry; a tower in which a hanging bell now struck one brazen note. The clangor was still reverberating in his brain as he hopped back into the taxi and gave the driver a new direction. Fifteen minutes more and he rode through the entrance of Creighton University and got out in front of a squat, brick building with a Norman round tower topped by a revolving dome. Knocking on the door, he told an attendant:

"I would like to see the astronomer."

Next morning the courtroom was jammed. Word had flown about town that John Yeiser was going to spring a surprise; he had obtained an adjournment the previous afternoon on the ground that he had unearthed new evidence.

The first witness called for the defense was a tiny man in the garb of a Jesuit priest, the Rev. William Riggs, who sat on the stand with his square, ecclesiastical hat in his lap.

"You are the professor of astronomy at Creighton?"

"I am."

"I show you a snapshot. Is it possible, Father Riggs, by looking at this photograph for you to tell at what time the picture was taken?"

"Yes," answered the priest. "I can tell you the time within one minute."

"And how can you be sure of such a thing?"

"By the angle cast by the shadow of the steeple on the picture."

"And what time was the picture taken, then?"

"At 3:20/100 o'clock in the afternoon of May 22, 1910."

Here was expert evidence that turned to no account whatever the tales of seven witnesses and the mistaken memories of two girls in white. Honest mistakes they were, no doubt about it—but in their timing those two girls were mistaken by more than an hour, beyond the shadow of a doubt. If they had really seen Erdman, it must have been nearly an hour after the suitcase was found.

The importance, the significance of the chronological error, astounded the judge and dumfounded the district attorney. The courtroom was silent for what seemed an incalculable period of time. Suddenly there was such babble and chatter that the jurist rapped loudly for order, while John Yeiser, eyes aglow with jubilant brilliance, turned to smile at his flabbergasted client.

That minute, the case against Frank Erdman crumbled. No cross-examination could shake the calculations of the astronomer. All night he had toiled over his figures, spurred on by the possibility of saving an innocent man from life imprisonment.

To be sure, even though the jury brought in a prompt acquittal, there were doubters. No one, skeptics declared, could fix time just by a shadow on a snapshot. But one year later, to the very day and hour, John Yeiser and the district attorney, the judge and the jury held a reunion on the church steps and had their picture taken there. And when the print was made, the shadow of the steeple fell across them at exactly the same angle as in the snapshot of a year before.

Here is one of the author's favorite cases. He had a "facts file" on several thousand crimes, which he donated a year or so before his death to Fordham University Library along with all his crime books. He rather hoped it might be built into a major crime research center, appropriately enough, in New York.

TWICE TOO OFTEN

NEW YORK, 1952

THE radio advertising man picked up the telephone; his wife, so his secretary signaled, wanted to talk with him.

"Art dear, look, I'm awfully sorry, but—could you get home early this evening? There's a committee meeting at the church and the sitter can't come——"

"It would take a lot of rearranging. I'm supposed to be at a broadcast—we work over those commercials up to the last minute——"

"But I've promised to be there. I've got to . . ."

"Oh, if you've got to," Art broke in abruptly, "I suppose I've got to, too. What time, 7:15? O.K. I'll be there."

As he hung up, Art regretted his tone. He had made his attitude toward religion clear to Betty from the start. His feelings had been permanently poisoned by a violent, hell-invoking father. But he was very much in love with his churchgoing wife, and he was perfectly willing to see her take an ardent interest in parish life. Except when it inconvenienced him—like tonight!

For that night, February 17, 1950, Art did manage to find a replacement without too much trouble. He caught the 6:18 home.

And, as it happened, on that night, the Long Island Railroad's 10:03, the after-broadcast train Art would otherwise have taken, ploughed head-on into a New York bound train just outside of Rockville Centre. More than 30 persons were killed; scores of others injured. And the lead car, the smoker in which Art Corbett habitually rode, was the one in which most of the deaths occurred.

Next morning, with the reports of the tragedy before them in the paper, Betty Corbett said to her husband:

"Thank God, Art! That's all I can say."

"What's God got to do with it?" Art demanded. "There's the trouble with you religious people. Every time some coincidence happens, it's God. I'm going to tell you something about the mathematical laws of chance."

And Art Corbett proceeded to lead his wife through a maze of figures which proved to his satisfaction, anyway, that his fantastic escape had nothing whatsoever to do with God.

A few weeks later, there were some promotions handed out in the agency, and Art was among two or three younger men who took a step upward. The new job changed his schedule considerably. He began commuting at more normal hours. The 6:12 out of Long Island Station became his usual train.

The summer passed pleasantly and uneventfully, and it was not until November 22, 1950, the day before Thanksgiving, that Art received another memorable phone call from Betty. This time she asked him if he could come home an hour earlier than usual.

"Church again?" he snapped.

"Yes, it's an early committee meeting, because there's a rehearsal for the minstrel show afterward, Art, and I want to get supper over. . . ."

"It's O.K., Betty," he laughed. "No problem any more, now that I'm practically a V.I.P around here."

He took a 5:15 train home, and felt rather pleased with himself for having kept his temper.

That night, at 125th Street, between Lefferts Boulevard and Hillside Avenue, the 6:12, in one of the most terrible tragedies in the history of American railroads, roared through a caution signal and smashed into the last car of the 6:09, where, for some unknown reason, it had halted outside the station. Seventy-seven persons were killed, and at least a hundred injured.

Once more, the lead car in which Art Corbett would have been seated, was demolished.

The next morning, Betty Corbett said nothing. She just waited. Art looked up from the black clouds of headlines and said:

"Betty, I have only one thing to say: 'Thank God!'"

Since then he has discovered that going to church every Sunday is an invariably uplifting experience which he recommends to all his friends. He calls these recommendations his "personal commercials."

A FORMULA FOR PRESENCE OF MIND

NEW YORK, 1948

YOU have been asleep for hours. You open your eyes. The room is dark and dawn is still far away. You listen. You hear a footfall on the staircase.

What should you do? Lie quiet and pretend to be asleep? Scream? Shake your spouse awake? Grab the telephone? Turn on the lights?

Or perhaps you are walking home from the theater with your wife. In the middle of a deserted block, a man steps from an alley and points a gun at your chest.

Should you grapple for the gun? Unnerve him by shouting for help? Bluff him by refusing to obey his demands?

In such crises, according to my late friend, Deputy Commissioner George S. Dougherty, even the most timid persons often show admirable self-control. From half a century in police and private detective work, Dougherty reached the conclusion that a frantic desire to save his own hide is likely to put any man in a panic, but concern for others often summons up mysterious energies of courage and resourcefulness.

"One touch of nature is a powerful aid in such emergencies," Dougherty told me. "Criminals are only human beings after all, and the man or woman who can start a conversation with them has practically a certainty of escaping without injury. I do not care how low or vicious a man may be, there is always in him a part of our common humanity. All people are reachable somewhere and if you can learn to subdue your own panic something in the very danger itself will inspire you how to act."

And then the man hunter told of a lawyer and his wife, who, one winter night, decided to walk home from the theater. As they reached the middle of a deserted block, a masked man halted them with a revolver. As he lifted his hands the lawyer said to his wife:

"Don't be frightened, Agnes. He won't hurt us," and, to the bandit:

"You can take everything, but I must speak with you privately." At the curb he explained: "My wife is soon to become a mother. Please don't do anything to frighten her."

The bandit took the lawyer's almost empty pocketbook and fled, leaving untouched the wife who was wearing jewels worth more than $50,000.

We all would like to believe we could think up such a ruse upon the instant, but how many of us would be unshaken enough to do so? Does self-possession, coolness amid surprise and imminent disaster, belong only to a superior few? Or, more often, is it a trait of the stolid and the unimaginative?

There are no glib answers to these questions and virtually no literature on the subject of presence of mind. Army tests and those made in psychological laboratories can assay a man's natural readiness or lack of it, but to find the reasons for having or not having it is a difficult matter. Psychiatrists say that over-zeal and under-zeal are equally destructive of poise, self-possession, quick determination, immediate action. Still, the mystery remains. Two men are crossing a street when suddenly a truck swings around the corner at 50 miles an hour. One pedestrian is so frightened that he stands paralyzed, and is run down. The other is so scared that with incomprehensible power he jumps twice as far as he ordinarily could jump and saves his life. What is the difference between the two men?

Avoiding the involved psychiatric theories of the will to live and the will to die, a famous neuropsychologist who is also a man of deep faith, agreeing with Detective Dougherty, believes that the riddle's answer lies in the nature of the soul. The more spiritual the man, the more completely is he ruler of the self and its ignoble emotions, such as fear; his concern being for the larger good, he does not go to pieces when he is in danger. Such was the experience of one of my favorite friends, Blackstone, the illusionist. Several seasons ago, the prestidigitator was performing before a packed audience in a midwestern theater. Suddenly, in the midst of the magic rose-tree trick, he called out to the stage manager: "Ring down the curtain!" Then seizing a coil of rope, he walked down to the footlights:

"Friends," he cried in flamboyant haste, "you have all heard of the Hindu rope trick. A rope is thrown into the air. It stands erect. A boy climbs the rope and disappears. I intend to do that trick for you right now. But if I perform it on the stage you will all suspect mirrors, wires, or lights. No! I shall exhibit it in the middle of the open street. Will you all pass right out through the front door, beginning with those in the last row? Thanks."

In two minutes the whole crowd was outside. As Blackstone and his troupe marched up the emptying aisle to the lobby, flames were already crackling around the edges of the curtain.

While he did not perform the rope trick (no human being ever has done that), Blackstone, by brilliant presence of mind, averted a panic and saved uncounted lives. In doing so he surpassed himself for he has a psychic fear of fire that is almost pathological. Concern for the lives of others was perhaps the source of his inspiration. Dwell on your own peril and you may be reduced to gibbering, ignoble panic. Think of others and you may well find yourself doing the precisely correct thing.

I remember a grisly story out of my youth, when the Woolworth Building, a pioneer among the great New York skyscrapers, was being erected. In those days safety precautions were primitive. Naked girders pierced and crossed the heavens while workmen pattered back and forth on narrow steel, leaning against the wind to avoid being blown off, and with nothing between them and the street, 50 stories below. One spring noon, three riveters squatted on a beam, their feet dangling in dizzy space. The air was warm, the sun was high and they were weary. When lunch was finished, they sat, peacefully enjoying the rest, until the man on the right noticed a dreadful circumstance.

The man in the middle had fallen fast asleep.

Obviously, if the dreamer awoke with a start he might plunge below. Moreover, in his befuddlement he might clutch at anything and so drag one or both of his companions down to destruction with him. If those men had been cowards, they would have departed, then and there, leaving the dreamer to his fate.

Instead, very quietly, the man on the right explained matters to the man on the left. In low tones they considered ways and means; they knew they had to wake up the sleeping man gradually. So they began discussing, in tranquil tones, his favorite recreation, fishing, until the man in the middle opened one eye, slowly caught the drift of the conversation and unstartled and safe slipped back into full consciousness.

It is a fact, however, that all three of them took the elevator down to the street immediately afterward and they worked no more that day.

The magician was thinking of a thousand spectators, the riveters of their dozing companion; it is a challenge to the crass materialism of this day to realize that unselfish concern for others often brings more nerve and illumination than the instinct for self-preservation.

Sometimes salvation depends on the supreme wisdom and courage to do nothing. One day a family of three were driving down the Tamiami Trail between Miami and Tampa, a narrow highroad raised out of swamps, and with deep ditches on either side. Suddenly the brand new four-door sedan skidded, swerved, and plunged over the side and settled down on four wheels completely submerged in 12 feet of water.

"Shut the windows," cried the father. Once that was done, the well-made car was watertight. "Now," he added, "don't move. Take little breaths. Make the oxygen last. Lots of people saw what happened. We're going to be rescued. Meanwhile—let's say, 'Our Father——' "

The waiting seemed endless, but the reasoning was correct. Several witnesses speeded on to telephone the police. With the emergency squad came a diver. When he lowered himself to the bottom, and turned a flashlight into the car, he saw all three passengers sitting quietly with closed eyes and folded hands. They had remained so for 30 minutes, until rescue arrived.

Not all such occasions are so desperate, although they may seem tragic at the time. There is a backstage story actors love to tell of a star who just before the final curtain, was supposed to put a pistol to his head and end it all. But when he pulled the trigger there was no blank-cartridge explosion; only a mocking click. Three times he pulled, three clicks his only reward. Upon which, the revolver dropped from his hand as he clutched the left part of his shirt and shouted:

"Ah-h! The old family heart trouble!" . . . and fell, apparently lifeless, to salvos of applause.

There is an old debate as to whether men or women excel in presence of mind, but newspaper reporters and detectives of my acquaintance are inclined to give the honors to the ladies. While they may squeal in mortal fright before mouse or spider they can, in defense of loved ones, often humiliate a wildcat. Insurance men, too, have testified that women are the greatest firemen in the world. Underwriters say that a glass of water will put out a fire in the first minute, a pail of water the second, but after the third minute you need the fire department. The housewife is usually there with the glass.

There is a tale that for years has been repeated in fiction and as fact that illuminates the question. It happened at a dinner party in India. Around the candle-lit table sat army officers and civil servants of high degree and their wives. The talk had turned to poise and self-control, and the old dispute: which was more reliable in a crisis, man or woman? The males all expressed their opinions with deep conviction. Women, they said, were the masterpieces of creation: they had tenderness, sacrifice, understanding. Their one defect was that they went into hysterics in a crisis. That was when you needed men. All the ladies placidly agreed, except the hostess. At the height of the discussion, she called a native boy: "Ali! Kindly fetch a bowl of milk at once and put it on the floor."

With a terrified roll of his eyes the boy ran to obey, placing a jade bowl on a flagstone, close to the mistress of the house. Then he stood back, holding a looped whip in his hand, as, from under the deep white napery of the table there slithered out a long bloated thing, yellowish brown with white and black marks and a head with a swollen hood. The cobra buried its head in the milk and the native boy fell on it and killed it.

"Well," puffed a red-faced colonel, "how on earth did you know that snake was under the table?"

"It was coiled," replied the hostess, "around my ankle."

Who is it that is blessed with presence of mind? Most likely, he—or she—who has conquered self; who knows that all fears are puerile in face of a common end, and that the trick of life is to live it nobly.

This article grew from a stimulating discussion of the subject at one of The Reader's Digest *editorial luncheons. The mysteries of personality were often debated. As the piece states, there is "virtually no literature on the subject of presence of mind." Fulton Oursler planned to track down the similar bafflement of why certain men and women have ambition and others have none. What kind of people are they? The desire to get ahead does not seem confined to poverty or hardship, to race, or to climate. What is the goad? Who pulls up and on and ahead? What have they in common?*

Mr. Oursler felt all mankind had recognized but latent powers; more imagination, logic and reasoning than he used. Other half-accepted gifts were too precious to be entrusted to us. He called them God's secrets. Intuition. Premonition. Hunches. Telepathy. Prophecy. The wells of forgetfulness. Some day—to the worthy—God would endow us with control of these treasures. Some people had special access to one or two already.

But what makes a boy or girl ambitious?

These questions and suggested answers are in his notebooks, which is where and how article- and story-ideas were seeded and developed.

SWINGTIME AND CHERRY BLOSSOMS

CAPE COD, 1937

WE had not known that we were homesick until we came to Takaradzuka. That nostalgia was a paradox more complicated than we suspected, a mystery not to be fully appreciated until years afterward. Our visit to the Kansai district was due solely to curiosity.

The wife of a Peiping doctor had told us about the Japanese girls' school for American dancing. One day at the Shanghai track she said:

"It simply goes to show how the Japanese mind works. In the Takaradzuka school there are six hundred beautiful and talented girls, specially selected to take five-year courses in American jazz in a Government-subsidized seminary. The purpose is to make sure the Japanese theater shall have a supply of native performers, and that the people shall believe that syncopation is a Japanese instinct. And perhaps it is."

Naturally when we landed in Kobe we made inquiries about Takaradzuka. Soon we were in a car and on our way, with a tiny guide called Mr. Higuchi. Three thousand feet above the harbor we followed what they call the skyline driveway, along the crest of the Rokko mountain range, and then began to skid gently downward until we reached level land and Takaradzuka.

Observed from its outskirts the town, forty minutes from the two large cities, Osaka and Kobe, was an incoherent scramble of buildings in modern architecture; parks and pond water and thin little lanes full of late cherry blossoms and early wisteria and frantic cyclists ringing their bells.

Higuchi wanted to show us everything. He pointed vaguely toward nondescript structures and foliage where wonders were to be seen—little lakes with boats for hire, a tropical zoo with seal ponds, elephant sheds, wild animal cages, a monkey island, billiard rooms, dance halls and a studio where we could have our pictures taken. He extolled the classic decorum observed in the tearoom, succulent cooking of Chinese, Japanese and foreign restaurants, and the perfumed conveniences of public bath rubs for men and women.

We asked to be led at once to the great sight of Takaradzuka, the Recreation and Opera House which encloses not only the School for Girls, but three full-sized theaters, one of them among the largest in the world.

Even when we had reached the entrance, paid our yen, and passed through the turnstile into an open space surrounded by the theaters and an amusement park, Mr. Higuchi hung back. Would we not fancy a turn in the children's recreation ground; later I learned that Mr. Higuchi, aged fifty-seven, had a happy passion for midget auto racing cars, one ride, ten sen.

As we labored with his disappointment—he was blue

as the mountain ranges framing the whole scene—three laughing girls hurried by. They were wearing sedate green aprons, like uniforms, over flowered kimonos. Their pretty faces were young but held the settled and honest look that comes from a difficult discipline. One almost always sees that expression on the faces of young musical and dancing students. These were some of the six hundred Nogi girls probably passing from one studio classroom to another; girls signed up for five years in this place to learn tap dancing, singing, and all the arts of Broadway.

How had such a school come to be? Later I was to learn that since 1913 such a school had been here; in 1918 it was formally recognized by the Japanese Department of Education. For two years students are taught the fundamentals of Japanese training, in which the sterner womanly virtues are emphasized. The next three years are devoted entirely to nip-ups, back-flops, cartwheels and double somersaults. These girls live nunlike lives, they work hard and they are sustained through the training period by the feeling that a bright future is in store for them. The performers of the opera company—in a single production there may be twenty principals and anywhere from thirty to two hundred chorus girls in line—are drawn entirely from the graduates and undergraduates of the school. In addition to their five-year course of study they must also sign a contract for five years in Japanese playhouses—and for salaries that would not be beauty parlor money for American girls.

Higuchi marched us by a parking space filled with undersized bicycles and thence into the lobby of the Grand Theatre. A spacious hall with a grilled roof, it had comfortable seats for those who must wait, charcoal burning in great urns for smokers, booths at which baubles and kickshaws were sold, a check room for the Japanese stilted sandals called getas. Crowds of men and women moved quietly about. Some were in Japanese costume with babies asleep in pouches on their backs. An enchanting sight, those Japanese women in their lovely kimonos, obis, getas and tabis. We mingled with them for a little while, then passed on into the main auditorium.

The Grand Theatre as it is called, where the "star troupe" was performing, was one of the largest theaters we had ever seen. Although it is in the country, yet on this rainy Monday afternoon nearly every one of four thousand seats was taken. We had to buy tickets for what down in Baltimore we used to call "African Paradise," far up near the roof. From this lofty perch we looked down like foreign birds upon a strange scene. The vast interior with its two balconies was done in modern German style, with shrewd and restful house lighting. A large orchestra was playing and just as we were seated the curtain fell on a preliminary act of traditional Japanese entertainment.

The audience sighed and broke into talk with a kind of light, high-pitched and gentle expectancy. Soon the principal attraction was to begin, a piece called—in translation—"The Manhattan Rhythm," a musical play alleged to have been written and directed by Utso Hideo, with music by Sakai Kyo and Tsukui Yuuki, all strangers to us. Then the orchestra blared and whined, the curtain soared and there on the vast, brilliant stage was a long chorus of beautiful Japanese girls dancing and singing in smart top hats, white ties, tails and ebony sticks—a full threescore of yellow, slant-eyed phantoms of Fred Astaire and Ginger Rogers moving with Alabama abandon in a swingtime parade. With knowingness and skill some Nipponese George White had scolded and coaxed these girls into line. They had a Broadway precision of attack in every tap of toe and heel, and in everything an innocent joy of ragtime—a pleasure with no evil in it, childlike and innocent—that feeling was in the high head tones of their singing, the merry flip of hip and shoulder—*boom-a-laddie, boom-a-laddie, boom-a-laddie, boom!* It was as if all Japanese youth had watched a Broadway show and said: "You mean—do it like this," and did it a little nicer than that.

The song they were singing was a New York ditty with a squalid little tune from the slums of melody; I had heard it in New York before we sailed to the Orient. As the chorines of Takaradzuka sang its wilted measures in their native tongue, I remembered that program and looked again. Yet—it said, in so many words, that the music had been composed by Sakai Kyo and Tsukui Yuuki. But then, I reflected, even on Broadway, songs have been attributed to others than their composers. When the Japanese set out to copy, they copy not alone a feature, but a system.

The only trouble I had was in trying to understand the plot of the play, but then I had often had that trouble in New York, too, and here the Japanese had actually improved on Broadway. In the program I found a synopsis of what was going on—a device which I recommend to friends in Longacre Square.

I quote the synopsis:

"In order to raise funds for her daughter, Juliana, to go to Broadway, the mother and Louise sell flowers. But no matter how much they earn, all their money are taken by their debtor, Angels. Louise gets acquainted with Goldman, a wealthy man who offers to lend them enough money for Juliana to make a start in Chicago.

"Angels captures Juliana on her way to Chicago and forces her to work in his bar as a cheap singer. There he takes Goldman and shows him the girl whom he thought had left for Chicago. Goldman is outraged at the insult done to so fine a girl as Juliana but is helpless to save her as Angels' men had surrounded him. His friend, Eddie comes to his rescue and Angels puts the room into darkness. In the uproar Juliana finds Goldman and with tears of joy thanks him. Angels shoots, aiming at Goldman, but Juliana is shot instead. The curtain descends on the dying Juliana in the arms of Goldman.

"And this is the end of the revue called *Manhattan Rhythm.*"

All the parts were taken by girls and some of them imitated men much more convincingly than some of the Rosalinds and Portias and Violas I have seen in the American theater.

A climax was reached when suddenly across the whole stage was flashed an American flag symbolic of a great moment in the plot. The audience sat in perfect silence while the flag was displayed. I occupied myself by counting the stars in the blue field. There were only thirty-six, which, as I whispered to my wife, showed clearly that the Japanese underestimated our resources.

When the show was over we came downstairs and in the lobby purchased a souvenir phonograph record of the troupe singing that familiar ballad. Even on the phonograph label the authorship was attributed to the Hon. Mr. Kyo and the Hon. Mr. Yuuki.

As we walked through a tunnel of cherry blossoms onto a little crooked bridge over a little lake, we suddenly felt saddened. The memory of those piping, adolescent voices, singing a cheap little ditty filched from home, had filled us with a sudden yearning for our own place in the world. That we thought was strange—but stranger still it was when we came home.

For whenever we played the Japanese records a little mist came, and we were homesick for the dancing girls of Takaradzuka.

Three weeks after the author's return home from a vacation trip to Japan and China, Shanghai was bombed. He had sailed the morning after the lesser fireworks of Windsor's Coronation celebration. Behind were left friends that had become peculiarly dear to him in a short but somehow special knowing. What Fulton Oursler saw and learned of Asia seemed an oddly personal experience, a part of him. "I could believe I was an Oriental in a former life; all of this is in my sweat!" he grinned.

The morning he saw the newspapers' photos of the bombing, he could not work. He sat, rocking, at the picture window overlooking Buzzards Bay; rocking and smoking. He put on one of the phonograph records he writes about. When it was finished, he lit another cigarette. "In a few minutes," he said, "I'll get on the phone. Right now I don't believe any of it. Right now I feel the headlines and pictures that are ahead of us in the coming years will be unbearable. It's all cracking open. Right now I long to cry and cry. . . ."

SOMEBODY IN THE CORNER

NEW YORK, 1947

EVERY Christmas Eve, the women of Renshaw, in Nova Scotia, gather at nightfall on the railroad platform. Their children in bed, they come to wait for fathers and husbands, who, having shopped all afternoon in the county seat, are bringing home the Christmas playthings.

When Dr. John Sutherland Bonnell, Pastor of Fifth Avenue Presbyterian Church in New York City, was a very young man, he knew a woman named Emily Sanders who, year after year, waited there on Christmas Eve in the frosty starlight, all in vain. This is the story of the man she was waiting for. And while I have changed names and altered facts, here a little and there a little, this is a substantially true account of what Dr. Bonnell told me befell him there, long ago.

It began on a June day, when Bonnell was a divinity student filling a summer "practice pulpit" in that orchard land of Evangeline. Bumping along a back-hill road on his secondhand bicycle, he was caught in a sudden and furious thunderstorm. Ahead of him, through the downpour, he could see a barefoot little girl sloshing across a rickety wooden bridge.

"Stop crying!" young Bonnell called to the red-haired moppet; "the bridge is wet enough already."

From behind the seat, he unlashed a collapsible umbrella, and then, with the child straddling in front, and the umbrella held shakily over them, he tried to guide the bike with one hand, on down the hill.

"Where do you live?" he shouted into her ear.

"Second house just at the bottom."

"What's your name?"

"Mary. My father is Frank Sanders. Does that mean I have to get off?"

There was no time to pursue the strangeness of her question; they had arrived. Standing in the doorway was a tall, gaunt woman and the only well-kept part of her was the sleek hair wound up in tight golden braids. Already the bloomy flush of life was gone from this woman and yet there was in her eyes a look that was for old happy, far-off things.

"How was it you happened to have an umbrella when all day it's been sunny?" she asked the student pastor suspiciously. She pulled Mary inside, with her three other children.

"I'm the summer preacher at the crossways Church," Bonnell explained, smiling. "At prayer meeting the other night we asked God for rain. So I thought I had better pack an umbrella."

Her gaze was pitying. Motioning him inside, she fastened the door and began peeling off Mary's soaked clothing. On the wall, Bonnell was noticing three faded photographs of the same man, a boxer in trunks, balled fists lifted in a John L. Sullivan guard.

"Who's the fighter?" he asked.

From all four children came a shrill chorus: "That's Pop!"

"He used to be light heavyweight champ!" screamed the older boy.

"He still packs a terrific right!" yelled the other.

"Pop's strong!" said Mary softly.

As the mother hushed her gossipy brood, Bonnell changed the subject:

"I hope you and your husband will bring the children to church."

"You might as well understand," the mother announced stiffly, "that your congregation don't want us. And we sure don't want them. No, there's no mistake. They all think my husband is no good. As long as I stick to Frank, they won't help us. So——"

There was a sudden violent blast of wind as the door was flung open and a man stamped in; a dripping wreck but still recognizable as the boxer on the walls.

"You that summer Reverend?" he demanded.

"Yes—I'm John Bonnell——"

The light heavyweight pointed with backward thumb toward the stormy outdoors; the student pastor had to wave good-bye to the silent wife and children, and ride off.

It was, therefore, a prodigious shock to Bonnell at the Sunday service to behold Frank Sanders, scrubbed and shaved sitting all by himself in the back pew. Why had the dilapidated slugger come to church?

Since Sanders had turned Bonnell out of his house, the young minister had been making inquiries. Sanders' wife, Emily, earned the family money as laundress and spare helper, while he hunted rabbits and wild geese, and fished in the ponds. A lot of his time was spent with his lone friend, whom everybody called Doctor Tom. This broken-down antisocial hermit of a professor kept Frank in whisky, and sent him on errands, fetching newspapers and mail to a reeking bachelor cabin on the other side of town. Bonnell had good reason to wonder about the business of the atheist's apprentice in his congregation.

After the service, Frank remained stolidly in his pew until all the respectable parishioners were waiting outside by the graveyard gate; they thought the student pastor was facing a fight.

"Mr. Sanders," Bonnell told him, "you're welcome here."

"Don't get any ideas, Reverend," Frank retorted, rising with a wink. "I don't believe in pious balderdash."

"Is that boxing lingo?" Bonnell asked. "Sounds more like your friend, Doctor Tom. Frank, why did you come?"

"Reverend, you want to attract crowds to your meetings, don't you? Well, you're going to get 'em. Because I'm going to be here every time you have a service. That's bound to set people talking. They'll come in droves, hoping for the knockout—want to see me plead to be saved from my sins. Hah! You realize I'm never going to do any such thing!"

"Then why," Bonnell demanded, quite bewildered, "do you want me to have crowds?"

"For the nice help you gave our Mary in the rain, Reverend. When I ordered you out of my house I didn't realize—so I've got to square myself."

Chin up and whistling, he walked off, his face toward the hills, and his friend, Doctor Tom. . . .

Never before had the little gray church with the red steeple held such crowds; the splintery pine benches could not seat them all. And Frank, keeping his promise, was invariably there, in the last row, and at first, alone. Later he brought in the whole family, starched, and well-behaved. And later still, Bonnell learned that he had taken a job in the planing mill; for more than a month he kept sober.

But one morning the student pastor was stopped in front of the general store by a puffy, red-whiskered man who barred his path and held up a bottle.

"Look, Rev!" he panted. "If I fill this with water, can you change it into good hard liquor?"

Getting no answer from Bonnell, he turned to Frank Sanders, just coming out of the store.

"I suppose," he shouted, "he's got you to believe in the miracle of changing water into wine!"

"Doctor Tom, I can tell you a bigger miracle than that," Frank grinned. "He's turned rum into food and clothing right in my now happy home."

"Balderdash!" tittered Doctor Tom amiably, holding on to Bonnell's lapel. "Listen, Rev! Suppose you think you're converting Frank. Well, let me prophesy what's going to happen, immediately after you go back where you came from. Good old Frank will quit his job. Immediately! He'll junk his family, immediately! And he'll come back to me! Immediately!"

"And you consider that a good thing?"

"At least he can have a little fun for himself out of this so-called life. You won't get him. I'll get him. You'll see."

Off he waddled, toward the hill road, but over his shoulder, he called back:

"Ask Frank what he'll be doing next Christmas Eve."

There was deep worry in Frank's eyes.

"Whether I can stick it out after you've gone back to school, Reverend, I just ain't sure. This is a lot tougher fight for me than you might realize. What keeps me going, is listening to you—you're like my trainer in the corner, my second; you keep up my nerve. Everybody needs somebody in his corner."

"Everybody has Somebody," Bonnell told him. "You can count on Him, too."

Frank Sanders flashed the young minister a blank look of doubt.

"You can't see Him though," he muttered. "He ain't got skin on. I won't be able to see Him next Christmas Eve."

That was the crux of his fear. For the last five years Frank had gone into Earlton with money for Christmas toys and then drunk himself into a stupor.

"That's what Doctor Tom is counting on now," he finished miserably.

"Frank," Bonnell said impulsively, "if you can keep going steady right up to the morning of December 24, I'll come back up here to see you through Christmas Eve."

"Reverend," Frank cried joyfully, "that's a deal!"

After the first week in September, when the student pastor went back to Halifax, the church at Renshaw was shut up until spring. A letter from Emily Sanders told Bonnell how Frank was sticking to his job and even talking about building some fine new pews for the church. But the hardwood he wanted was scarce, except for a big stock in Doctor Tom's back yard, and the professor refused to sell unless Frank Sanders would take a drink with him.

"So far," wrote Emily, "Frank hasn't taken it, but he will do almost anything for the church now."

It may seem strange, that by the time the holidays came around, John Bonnell had forgotten his Christmas Eve appointment. But he had been completely absorbed in school work all that autumn, and now his folks were planning a jolly time over the holiday fortnight; they had invited as their house guest a young woman in whom he had become deeply interested. He was even considering a Christmas morning proposal beside the yule tree.

What reminded him, just in time, was a run-through of his diary. He was making notes for Christmas greetings and suddenly came upon the name of Frank Sanders.

By telephone calls, he made his excuses, and grabbed the first train for the Grand Pré country. At noon he was once more at the Sanders house in Renshaw, but he was too late.

"Frank's gone to the county seat with all the other men," Emily told him. "He took the money for the toys. But when you didn't arrive on the morning train, the heart seemed to go right out of him."

"I'll go right after him," Bonnell exclaimed. "I'll hire an automobile."

But in those innocent days, Renshaw had no cars for hire. The young minister was marooned in town.

That night, when the return train from town was due, John Bonnell stood with Emily on the platform. What would they see when the train arrived; Frank Sanders drunk or sober? They were afraid to look at each other; afraid of the answers already in their eyes. Presently, in fur cap and smoking a cigar, Doctor Tom accosted them.

"Well!" he exclaimed, with a snort that would have done credit to a bull moose. Raising his voice so that everyone could hear, he added: "What are you keeping this poor woman waiting here for? Emily Sanders knows as well as I do what's coming home to her on that train. Immediately!"

"Pray, Reverend," murmured Emily. "That train ride home is the worst part. Everybody has a bottle to pass around. Pray hard!"

"Pray, hah!" sneered Doctor Tom. "That *shows* you're not sure. Well, I'm sure! Enough to bet good hard cash! Who'll take me up? Who has five bucks that says Frankie Sanders gets off that train sober—who? What! Nobody? Three dollars? Two, then. Surely for two measly bucks somebody in this crowd will bet on good old Frank. Think, neighbors—you're betting on a human soul. So the parson says! How about you, Rev? Will you bet a buck?"

"I don't believe in gambling," Bonnell told him.

"You mean you don't believe in Frank Sanders—not even a buck's worth!"

To this day, John Bonnell does not know whether it was righteous wrath or just plain temper. Then as now, he detested gambling. Yet he said:

"I'll take your bet. If Frank Sanders comes home a sober man, you will give the hardwood stored in your back shed to be made into new pews for the church. Otherwise, I pay you the price of the wood."

"It's a bet?"

"It is," Bonnell concurred shakily, "a bet!"

No one would ever have expected Doctor Tom and John Bonnell to shake hands. Yet they did, and none too soon, for already on the snowy night they heard the far-off whistle of the train. Shamelessly holding the hand of another man's wife, John Bonnell prayed to Almighty God that he would win this, his first and last wager. He can still remember the confusion of his feelings; the torment of soul; in the woofed phantasies of those last waiting minutes it seemed to him that here at this provincial crossroads was all the trouble of the world, the struggle of good and evil making the wind-swept platform an everywhere—and the result very much a doubt.

Now they could hear the bell, loud and strong, and all

stood in the yellow flame of the headlight, gleaming on walls of snow, as the engine, hauling two dim-lit coaches, came snuffling to a stop.

Farmers and breeders and orchard men streamed off the train but there was no sign of Frank. Doctor Tom looked around him with a toothy smile, as Bonnell climbed aboard and marched through the cars, peering under seats and in the washrooms, like a woodsman looking for a wounded animal. As he came out on the back steps, Bonnell shouted:

"Hasn't anybody seen Frank Sanders?"

The engineer, bending far out the window of the cab, called hoarsely:

"Sure I seen him. About two hours before train time. He was going into the Blue Nose Tavern."

That was all they needed to know. There was an audible sigh from the crowd as they turned and surged on toward the bridge over the tracks. As Bonnell took Emily by the arm and they started off together, he came as near to weeping as is good for a senior divinity student. How he hated himself for not anticipating. Why hadn't he brought toys himself, to make sure?

Beyond the bridge loomed a wagon, drawn by two white horses. The driver stood up and waved his hat:

"Merry Christmas, everybody!"

And then suddenly Bonnell saw—and all the others saw with him—a familiar figure clambering from behind the load of barrels and casks. It was Frank Sanders jumping to the snow-packed highway, and the driver was handing down to him a doll and a drum, a ship and a toy cradle, a whole Santa Claus cargo of Christmas toys.

"Hey, Emily!" Frank was yelling. "Don't get scared.

Ain't had a drop! Thought it was safer not to come home on the train. Too much temptation, with bottles being passed and all. So I hopped a ride home on the Blue Tavern's truck."

Emily ran toward him and then for the first time Frank Sanders saw Bonnell.

"Rev!" he yelled. "You *did* come! Well, thanks. But you were right. There was Somebody in my corner all the time —even among the beer kegs! Knowing that fixes everything. Come on home and help trim the tree."

"First," John Bonnell told him, "I've got to see Doctor Tom—and make sure the church collects my winnings. Immediately!"

Dr. Bonnell himself wrote a moving postscript to this story:

"When I returned to Renshaw the following June, I hurried to the little gray church. For a long time I stood there, looking at the new oaken pews gleaming with fresh varnish, recalling with a grateful heart a memorable Christmas Eve."

This story, still unpublished, was bought by The Reader's Digest. *Use of it was very kindly given to* Guideposts, *a small nonprofit publication for all faiths, Protestant, Catholic and Jewish. It was started, 1945, by Dr. Norman Vincent Peale and Raymond Thornburg. It has, in nine years, grown to 650,000 circulation by subscription only. After a year and a half of existence, the offices of* Guideposts *were burned to the ground. At that time DeWitt Wallace took an interest and also brought the crisis of this little publication to Fulton Oursler's at-*

tention. Both men gave inestimable encouragement, advice and practical help to the publication, because of their own belief in the aims and purposes of the magazine—understanding and amity between religions.

ONE TOUCH OF FIRE

NEW YORK, 1952

WHENEVER I read dispatches from Egypt about student riots and mobs surging through the streets, I remember the fantastic climax to such a scene of danger some years ago.

The debonair hero of the occasion was a gentleman I met in Cairo, one of the great detectives of our time, Russell Pasha. He was the Britisher who was Cairo's chief of police for many years. His full name was Sir Thomas Russell, but he was awarded also the local government's high and noble title of Pasha, which he wore along with the tarboosh cap and dangling tassel of the Near East. He tells of this adventure in his memorable autobiography, *Egyptian Service*.

For more than two months, in the spring of 1919, anti-British rioting had been tearing Egypt apart. Cairo mobs, spurred on by students from the great Moslem seminary of Azhar, were bent on trouble. Russell Pasha had spent a harried sixty days moving his undermanned police force about the city to maintain law and order.

One morning at breakfast Russell was told that a mob of 10,000 men was planning to attack the Continental Hotel, home of many British officers and their wives.

Quickly, Russell ordered a police squad of fifty men to hurry to the front of the hotel; presently, immaculately uniformed, he himself stood on the veranda. Before him was a frightful scene: a swaying mob was screaming, waving arms and literally foaming at the mouth:

"Death to the English! Long live the Revolution!"

Borne aloft over the heads of the marchers was an open bier on which lay a pale-faced corpse, with one arm flopping over the side.

These mobsters had planned well: this was a funeral service, and to interfere with it would be sacrilege. Sheltered behind a religious façade, the students would be able to inflame the mob to incalculable violence.

But Russell Pasha had an idea. With mild insouciance, as if he did not have a trouble in the world, he lit a cigarette. Then he walked down to the curb just as the mob leaders brought the corpse within reach.

Unnoticed, he coolly reached out his right hand with the lighted cigarette hidden inside his curved palm, and pressed the glowing end against the down-hanging hand of the corpse.

The corpse screamed with pain!

With a yell to awaken the truly dead, the prostrate figure leaped a full foot off his bier, and fell to the ground! A death-like coating of flour dropped from his face. The fake funeral was over, and the whole squirming mob, seeing the trick Russell Pasha had played, began to chuckle. The chuckle grew to a chortle and soon the whole vast assemblage was screaming, not with hatred but with laughter.

By alertness and audacity, one brave man had overcome a multitude.

F. O. had three slightly feverish hero-worshipping friendships with men who dealt with crime. Major Girard, the top British policeman of the world, a power in Shanghai; Russell Pasha, of whom he writes here, and J. Edgar Hoover, for whom he had an almost filial devotion. London's Scotland Yard and Paris' Sûreté were most gracious to him and he corresponded on occasion with all of them. He had visited with the police departments of Port Said, Alexandria, Naples and Marseilles, and considered the problems of the French port the most frightful—at least before World War II. One of his favorite phrases was* Brigade Mondaine, *which is the name of the corps policing what might be considered the French red-light district.*

*Sir Thomas retired in 1946 and died in London April 10, 1954, at the age of seventy-four. He was the last high British official to leave the Egyptian police force.

THE VISION OF THE ISLAND

LONDON, 1947

ONE foggy night in deep November, the Rev. George P. MacLeod stood on a soapbox at a Glasgow crossing and faced a huddle of shivering spectators. A tall, bony man swayed forward; the lightning-bug glow from a corner lamp fell on his moist, agitated face.

"Hey, Doc! Why is it you have to preach out-of-doors? Won't nobody come inside your church?"

"Some do come," expostulated MacLeod. "But I am looking for more."

Muffling his collar against the dark air, the stranger snorted:

"Three out of four never go inside any church any more; official statistics!" He flaunted a pamphlet over his head. "Second question: Wasn't your Leader once a workingman?"

"You know He was a carpenter."

"Well then, why don't He help the workingman? The union's our friend—but He don't belong. And I'll tell you why! Because men like you lock Him up in the church!"

MacLeod was aware of lowering eyes in the sullen

little crowd. This heckler was their spokesman; the minister felt like a man caught in an ambush.

"I came here to preach His message."

"The hell you did," the other lashed out. "All you talk about is prayer and patience. Never had to live like I do, did you?"

"I'm afraid not."

"Tell your Carpenter," the gaunt man said bitterly, "we need full meals in *this* world; not the next."

Beholding the hurt, contemptuous face, MacLeod rejected any glib reply; this man's brutal simplicity made the pastor feel guilty. He was man enough to say so.

"All right," he yielded. "It's your evening! You take my place; I'm going home to pray this thing out——"

But the minister remained in the dark about how his faith could be of help in those squalid streets until a message came from a hospital; one Archie Grey was calling for him. In a ward of hopeless cases, he found the street-corner cynic; fingers automatically plucking at the bedclothes and on the emaciated face the wraith of a courteous smile.

"I had to make my peace," Archie Grey whispered. "I shouldn't have mortified you——"

"But Archie—you were right!"

"Doc! For God's sweet sake, find the workingman's Jesus again—the Carpenter, the Builder——"

He gasped in a spasm of pain; one violent twist contorted his body. MacLeod heard the slam of a door and the hurrying footsteps of an interne, come too late.

"What did this man die of?" MacLeod demanded.

"Malnutrition; he literally starved to death. He was on the dole for a pound a week and sent a third of that regularly to a sister in Australia."

The last words of Archie Grey echoed in MacLeod's

conscience like the charge of a district attorney. That a man could die for want of food in wealthy Glasgow was a hideous indictment, a mockery of all that he believed. That night the minister made a new prayer:

"God of Archie Grey and me, don't let his death be in vain."

This prayer was answered, Sir George F. MacLeod believes; from his turmoil emerged a purpose at once blueprint and poet's dream; a design to purge cruelty and class hatred, greed and lust for power out of capitalists and laborers, hirers and the hired. Since then, all his energies have been given to the plan.

Holder since 1915 of the Military Cross and the Croix de Guerre, MacLeod finds himself gratefully astonished at his altered middle life. For he was trained at Winchester and Oxford; behind him marches a long cavalcade of aristocratic "meenister" ancestors, sticklers for theology, more concerned with the definition of compunction than with the feel of it.

Right after graduation, MacLeod was assigned to the richest church in Edinburgh. Four years later he told himself: "I can't stand another day in this pampered pulpit," and promptly transferred to Govan Old Parish, in the misery flats of Glasgow. But eight more years had passed when Archie Grey challenged him and he admitted: "My ministry has been a blunder, a flop."

Like the man in Pilgrim's Progress, MacLeod had not reached the Gate called Beautiful, but he thought he saw a light. Unaccountably, he found himself remembering a historic but neglected island off the west coast of Scotland, place of ravaged cathedral ruins, with the musical name of Iona.

Once upon a time, in the sixth century, the Irish St.

Columba and 12 henchmen had sailed to Iona in a frail boat made of hides stretched over ribs of wood. From headquarters on the island, their missionaries went tramping all over Europe, as far east as Vienna. To this day, simple folk believe the legend that if ever the world tries to destroy Christianity, it will be renewed on this beautiful island.

"Isn't now the time," MacLeod taxed himself, "that Christianity is in greatest danger?"

From the rails-end port of Oban, he made the three-hour voyage to those sequestered four green miles in the sea. On the deck of the ferry steamer stood the pilgrim, staring at the frothing shell beach, dunes of yellow sand and green meadows rising to craggy hills lost in veils of silvery mist. At this fair sight MacLeod was aware in himself of an inexplicable elation.

On the day he arrived, the island was inhabited by 234 people—farmers, fishermen and marble quarrymen and their families; dour folk, suspicious of strangers. Alone, with a pocket of peanuts to nibble on, MacLeod went stamping across the fields to the great monastery, once the seat of European Christianity, but now fallen to pieces.

For hours he brooded among desolate heaps; broken monolith and buttress, tumbled chancel and shattered tower and walls that date back into the twelfth century. Beyond the chapel stretched a charnel line of royal tombs; last resting place of Macbeth and Duncan and whole dynasties of Scottish kings and chiefs, sovereigns of Ireland and France, and ten Norwegian kings.

Leaping the pious epigraphs and other carved inscriptions, MacLeod fixed his gaze on a red-stone cross cut from a single block 14 feet high, the only perfect one remaining out of 365 scattered around. Was not this granite symbol his answer? Under its inspiration, old Christians had come here to dig and build. They had lived not merely in trances of fasting and contemplation, but toiling in the sweat of the quarry and tool shop, farm and garden; they, too, had been workingmen.

In the solitude of the lengthening afternoon, MacLeod began to feel a kinship with those long-dead friars and monks; a sense of majesty and mystery in the combination of labor and faith. As he traced the foundation outline of the fallen cathedral, the contour of a spiritual plan began also to take shape. Why not rebuild the old abbey and the old faith at the same time?

The lonely man was seized with sudden, eager ambition. These mossy ruins were his to work with if he wanted them; years before, the eighth Duke of Argyll had made them a gift to the Church of Scotland to be "the first building in Christendom that any denomination can call home."

MacLeod saw his opportunity; aglow with his project, he appeared before the elders of Govan church and asked to be released. Asked why, MacLeod told a row of puzzled faces that industrial good will had to be achieved or the church would pass away. If he could entice union leaders and Christian clergymen to spend a summer on Iona, rebuilding the old monastery, they would have a working laboratory for community problems; they could examine at first hand the discords in human relations and seek principles of harmony.

"Today's workingman," he reminded the elders, "is haunted by fear of personal disaster, and he is getting only infidel consolation and advice; he is being deliberately envenomed with class hatred. In the midst of a bitter, prolonged industrial struggle, Marxists are convincing him that science has proved God a myth and religion a superstitious swindle. So Communism and left-wing Socialism are winning Scotland. To meet that danger, the church must return to everyday life. The tragic blunder of the nineteenth century was the separation of the material from the spiritual. Religion was boxed up in Sunday and couldn't get out. God must be related to every activity if a man is to feel a moral responsibility to his fellow man."

And then he drove home his final point:

"We have almost forgotten the essential and unique fact of the Christian faith—that God Himself became a workingman to redeem the people."

Scurrying around the hinterland, MacLeod pleaded for recruits. Among church workers there was some skeptical derision; workingmen also smiled, sure that well-fed men of God would never last through a summer of hard labor and even harder debate. Some unionists agreed to join just to see the fun. The following June, a pioneer company of 50 workingmen, preachers and young seminarians sailed for Iona.

Their immediate job was to clear away thickets and underbrush, and to make a livable dormitory, but at once they ran headlong into human cantankerousness. Natives, resenting the intrusion, refused all help; forbade the visitors even to tap their springs. But plumbers among the colonists turned up church ground; without hazel stick or divining rod they sank their own wells. When they could not buy lumber for joists, crossbeams and ceiling, they salvaged what they needed from driftwood on the shore. Within a few days they had sheltered themselves and started the formal program.

At cockcrow every morning, after prayers before a newly-erected altar, they set to work swinging sledges and toting mortar buckets, hoisting, heaving, shoving into place ashlars and finished stones. The mechanics were the bosses;

the dominies were breathless, sweating apprentices; some even waddled with difficulty, due to stoutness, but before autumn they had slimmed down; not one quit.

After breakfast, in the second half of the morning, they held thrilling bull sessions on current problems. No one pulled punches; some veterans of union wrangles made not the slightest pretense of harboring in their hairy bosoms love for either God or man. But religion raised some staggering questions. A bricklayer, for instance:

"I want to apply Christian principles in my daily work. So a load of bricks arrives on the job. Just enough for three days' honest work—and no more coming till next week. If I work as hard as I should, I can be finished in half a week—but I will draw only half a week's wages. If I slow down and stretch it out, I can make the load last and collect the whole week's wages. In a case like that, where does Christian principle begin and my wife and kids finish?"

At once the scope must broaden. Who is to blame for the shortage of bricks? Is there a housing problem in the community, a real need for haste? What about a guaranteed annual wage? Is freedom in the long run worth more than security?

Someone demands to know what will be the incentive for hard work when men finally have complete protection. Another brings his answer down to a simple and awesome choice; either a dictatorship to *force* hard work or a new spiritual conviction to *induce* it.

MacLeod is grinning; no matter what track they start on, they always come back to religion. Day after day, all the arguments seem to wind up in a discussion about bread and how all can get enough. At this point, MacLeod closes the discussion; it is time for holy communion; bread and wine renewing an old poignancy of feeling.

For part of the summer afternoons the colonists labor again on broken walls; before supper all are convoked to read aloud. From hand to hand the books are passed; the rasping voice of a journeyman mason is heard declaiming Thomas a Kempis:

"But now God hath thus ordered it that we may learn to bear one another's burdens; for no one is without a fault, no one but hath a burden; no one is sufficient for himself; no one is wise enough for himself; but we have to support one another, comfort one another, help, instruct and admonish one another."

After dinner, evensong around an outdoor fire; and so to bed. . . .

When the white frost came, and the first season was over, nearly all had come to believe devoutly in the value of their strange emprise. Symbolic of the results was one dramatic move; labor and clergy pledged themselves for the next nine months, until they were reunited on Iona, to live within the income which—government statistics said—was the national average earning. Today that income is $720 a year for a single man and $320 more for a married man.

MacLeod was discreetly jubilant. In three months he had seen strong characters in his company change their attitudes. Clergymen who had piously believed that men should remain content "where God had seen fit to place them" became excited at the prospect of improving the lot of all. Unionists who distrusted a reactionary pulpit also changed; three members of the Communist party tore up their cards.

Only a caretaker was left behind. Traveling by twos and twos, the Iona preachers and seminarians went up and down Scotland urging a permanent crusade for peace in industry. Labor delegates began to startle union locals with the same doctrine. Eventually these reconverted unionists formed the Christian Workers League whose members frankly imitate the Communists; they come early to meetings, outstay everyone else and promote good will by subversive tactics. They tell you:

"The Reds bore from within for Stalin the dictator; we do the same for Jesus, the Carpenter."

Soon two mainland laboratories were going full blast, Acheson Home in Edinburgh and Mission House in Glasgow. Basic purposes are to discover, by trial and error, helpful solutions, especially for young people, and by training volunteers to extend the work widely in local communities. Before many years, the young people will be members of labor unions or wives of members; the time to win their enthusiasm is now.

In Glasgow the gray-faced Mission House looks down on the confusion of river and docks, but behind the red front doors is a rare symbol of order and peace—a whole first floor without partition or division. No dining-room walls hide the kitchen; no screen shuts off the chapel; those who come here by noon and night to eat and sing and play and study are never out of sight of kitchen fire or silver cross.

Between 400 and 500 are constantly enrolled; railroad porters, fishmongers, union apprentices, sons of employers, psychotherapists, active church members. One course seeks answers to Archie Grey's first question: why three-quarters of the people don't go to church. Iona's conclusion is that what the church has been saying had little to do with the realities of the needy. Here students are taught that the new universe revealed by science is still God's world and man's home, and he must make it a place of peace.

Another course deals with faith and the social order; housing, education and international relations, and the history of the labor movement.

"All these," MacLeod declares, "are inescapable spheres of religious concern. There is a political program for every Christian. Nothing to do with parties; only with principles. A voter must learn to weigh the issues of the smallest municipal election from a moral point of view."

Naturally, some officials object to mixing politics with religion, but MacLeod replies:

"More and more, your platforms are being shaped as if there were no God. Some parties, based on materialistic philosophy, claim as their sphere the total interests of a human being. When political theory invades the department of the soul, the church cannot stand off. That is why our job is to teach about the church and the social order; we become a rendezvous for people who are interested in the free and Christian way of life."

Meanwhile, the Ionians explore in even stranger directions. Suspicious of the mystical, these Presbyterians nevertheless know that healings by faith form a stirring chapter of the Island history. Five hundred years before Bernadette reported the apparitions at Lourdes, Iona was a shrine. From all over Europe, multitudes of invalids were brought on stretchers, hoping to be restored by prayer. Now on summer Wednesday nights, healing services are held by these moderns.

Have there been cures? MacLeod and his associates are not yet ready to announce their results—Lourdes waits three years—but they candidly admit that they are feeling their way back to a dynamic relationship between body and soul. In spite of what they have learned about psychosomatic medicine, they pursue their own search across the border of pain and prayer.

Another restoration is the venerable practice of meditation; the attempt of the soul to reach, in contemplation, a union with the divine. By nine o'clock it is dark; one walks into the abbey to find a single candle burning, with colonists clustered together, waiting for the coming of a sense of relaxation and elevation of spirit. This has become a favorite form of worship. Churchmen go home to institute the cultivation of silence in worship.

Skeptics say it will take a long time to rebuild the abbey; MacLeod himself once called that part of the enterprise "a blazing fraud." Actually, the reconstruction of the monastery will probably be finished in another six years, thanks to many gifts. Wood for the refectory roof has been sent by Norwegian timber merchants, descendants of Norse corsairs who once laid waste to the island. From far countries come other donations, to restore the kitchen, St. Michael's chapel, the library, the dormitories.

After ten years, MacLeod and his fellows have reached one clear assurance; the sovereign remedy for radicalism in the most radical program ever known; a purer Christianity. By it, man can solve problems that now seem immeasurable; that is the way to relume the hope of embittered people.

"The problem of the future," MacLeod declares, "is how to plan a society that will insure a fair deal to all, and at the same time preserve the freedoms of the individual. That can be done only through the wisdom of Calvary. It is in countries where they care nothing for Christ's death that they soon care nothing for any man's life!"

This experiment excited Fulton Oursler deeply. He welcomed each of the like movements of today; the many and spreading attempts to counteract evil and re-establish the living good. He loved to count the many names of those he considered contemporary saints, from George Washington Carver to Mother Cabrini, from Ghandi and Brother Bryon of Birmingham to Rose Hawthorne, Therese Neuman, Kagawa, Father Pio and Father Pro, Schweitzer, and the Four Chaplains. Matt Talbott, Brother André of Montreal. Even Theresa, The Little Flower who marked the turn of our century. Many of us have met and talked with a few of these—perhaps we passed them on the street, rode with them in a bus, and never dreamed we were within the circle of sanctity.

He cherished the realization, too, of great globe-covering chains for goodness and mercy begun here and there by one or two laymen, self-appointed workers in the Lord's vineyards; the painfully undaunted three lonely American salesmen who managed to place the Bible in every hotel room for other lonely ones, and the other lonely British worker who started the YMCA; the founders of the Boy Scouts; the Salvation Army, the Big Brothers, the Travellers Aid, SPCC and the SPCA.

Too much of our attention and thought fasten each day on the bullet and blood headlines, the criminals and the law-and-commandment-breakers, the fear and hate and grief breeders who absorb our attention and service. We ignore our saints who beg and beg for help. Some day, he felt, when laymen had more true fervor of faith and love, it would not be so.

ON THE SPOT

NEW YORK, 1952

SEVERAL years ago I sailed for Capetown in the good ship *African Enterprise,* and on land and sea I collected many interesting stories. One of them concerned a fellow passenger, the Reverend John Astrup, who had lived among the Zulus almost continuously since 1883.

When he was a young child John Astrup had been taken to Zululand by his father, who was a missionary. As he grew up near the kraals of the tribesmen, his father instructed him in Latin, Greek and Hebrew. When he was about 18 years old he was sent to the United States where he finished his education at Luther College in Decorah, Iowa. In 1896 he went back to Africa to take up missionary work in the footsteps of his father, and it was there, in the midst of great discouragement, that he had a remarkable experience.

His settlement was on the Tugela River, boundary line between Natal proper and the adjoining province of Zululand. For all his zeal, the young missionary seemed to make no impression on the neighboring tribesmen. The old king, who put his trust in the tribal witch doctors, did not conceal his contempt, as he refused Astrup's repeated pleas to be allowed to set up a church and school for Zulu children.

Then came disaster—the drought of 1904. The heat in the Tugela valleys was terrific, frequently registering 145° F., the luxuriant vegetation of grass and shrubs and trees burning to a crisp. The farm fields of the natives lay dead. The witch doctors were prancing and shaking their rattles day and night, but the drought did not end.

Then one day a delegation called on the Reverend John Astrup. Tall warriors, with the beautiful ceremonious compliments of the Zulus, announced that their king was turning to the missionary in desperation since the tribal gods seemed deaf to all pleas for rain. Would the white man pray to his God? Astrup replied that he would come next day to the king's kraal. He asked that the whole tribe be assembled for mass prayer.

Before dawn the pastor descended 2,500 feet to the valleys, walking through snake-infested bush and wading the Tugela River full of crocodiles. Soon he faced more than 2000 Zulus, gathering silently together; the faces of men and women and children haggard with hunger. As he announced the prayer, Astrup was startled to see 2,000 men, women and children fling themselves face downward in the dust. The missionary implored God to help the people in their distress, and finished slowly with The Lord's Prayer. And from the ground there was the muffled voices of Zulus repeating that prayer.

Then Astrup said good-bye and started on to another destination. With a Zulu boy to attend him, he climbed up and down two mountain ridges before pausing for a rest. It was then Pastor John Astrup heard the miraculous sound of thunder. Turning around he beheld an awesome phenomenon. There in the distance, above the king's kraal and the Zulu settlement, dark clouds were gathering. Lightning flashed and a silvery sheet of rain began to fall. A tremendous rainfall poured down—and on that district alone.

About three months later another deputation called on Astrup. The old king was dead. His young son headed the delegation. The Zulus all wanted to know one thing: how could they give thanks to God for that marvelous rain? Pastor Astrup conducted a service of thanksgiving in the kraal where grass was now growing four to five feet in height; shrubs everywhere green and full of flowers and the trees raising their leafy branches like arms lifted in thanksgiving for the abundant harvests in the valleys. The school and the church were started the following week.

"You may call it what you please," Pastor Astrup said to me as we stood at the ship's rail and watched the Southern Cross high in the heavens. "For more than 50 years I have been a Christian minister and I know that God's Providence is sure."

Taller than most men, stronger than most, in his 80's, Dr. Astrup still labors on. He is a member of the committee which is translating the Scriptures into Zulu directly from Greek, Hebrew and Aramaic. Besides this, he is translating a commentary of the Gospels into Zulu and is revising hymns to be used in their church services.

I salute a warrior for the Lord.

The dear giant of a man in his eighties, Dr. Astrup, is fighting time while he strains to finish his native transla-

tions before he goes completely blind. Twice, threatened operations (which would call for American experts and money) have been averted. By that same Providence.

Friends often read John the newspapers and magazines. Recently he wrote the Oursler family asking if a woman he had read about could be located, and if so, could his enclosed letter be forwarded to her. He had taken his precious strength to congratulate and admire the woman in Ypsilanti, Michigan, for naming her thirteenth child "Amen." Informed that his request had been successfully fulfilled, it impressed him that the mother was a Negro.

"To me it's a beautiful, beautiful name," he wrote, "with imagination and majesty and spiritual simplicity. These are the three qualities of the black man I have come to honor and recognize. I told you the Negro's faith puts our own in the shadow. They are 'as a little child'—even their strongest warrior types."

THE REAL MEANING OF EASTER

NEW YORK, 1952

THE saddest sound in the world, I think, is the crying of a child on Christmas morning. It was, therefore, a shock when my goddaughter, Jean Grace, merriest of five-year-olds, turned her back on her new doll and carriage and her illuminated tree, and screamed woefully and loud while she glared at something that gleamed in her hand.

Someone had given Jean Grace a crucifix. And someone else had explained to her about the silver figure on the cross.

"Is that really Jesus?" she wailed. "Is that really what happened to the little baby when He grew up?"

She knelt by the miniature manger; lifted and hugged the tiny child against her heart:

"That's an awful story, Mama, to end like that."

Mother told her that was not the end. There was a glorious new beginning to the story of Bethlehem; a happy ending at Easter. Jean Grace could remember Easter: chocolate bunnies, painted eggs and a pretty new bonnet. But Mother said Easter meant much more than that for everybody in the world. And then came my godchild's question that was to haunt me through the long winter that has just passed away:

"What is the real meaning of Easter?"

Not for my goddaughter, I knew, was the troublesome account of where the word came from, nor the fact that Easter is the first Sunday after the full moon, following the vernal equinox, which, of course, varies in different longitudes.

Nor would Jean Grace care about the uncertainty by which the Christian feast falls always somewhere between March 22 and April 25, with no one ever being sure of the original date of what, to the true believer, must seem the greatest event in history. The origin of the Feast of the Passover in the days of Moses, or its celebration a thousand years later, when Jesus sat at the Last Supper with His chosen Twelve, one a traitor—none of all this would clear up the mystery in the child mind.

She could rejoice that Jesus rose from the tomb, triumphant over death. Yet the dark blue eyes were still unsatisfied, baffled: why did He have to die at all? He chose to do that? Why?

The answer I found for my goddaughter came in thinking about two places at a wide distance from each other, yet united in the same universal truth.

One was at the top of a mountain, overlooking the Hudson River; the other in the heart of the ancient city of Jerusalem.

The first is a group of gray stone and white buildings on the heights of Garrison, down the river from West Point but on the opposite shore. The men who live in those solemn cloisters wear coarse brown robes, belted with white ropes, tied in curious knots. On their chests, they wear two stars—

the six-pointed Star of David, and the five-pointed symbol of charity and faith. The men are monks; Franciscan friars of the Monastery of Graymoor; men who have renounced the pleasures of the world, vowing themselves to prayer and to the service of their fellow men.

They have given up family life, the love of man for woman, money, personal ambition, even their own names, to work and pray that all people may be unified under one Shepherd.

Once the men of this order belonged to another faith; they were Episcopalians who later asked to unite themselves with Rome. They called their group the Society of the Atonement, because it was for atonement that their Master died on Calvary.

Surely, I thought as I pondered Graymoor, I am coming closer to the answer of a little girl's riddle. And then a ghost came walking down the corridors of memory. I recalled a long-ago friend of mine who had fled to Graymoor when he was hungry and without home or job. I call this man Everett, but that is only a part of his name. Once Everett was a writer of best-selling novels; a fellow with a deft trick of depicting men and women and sexual passion and a conflict between light and darkness that for a while found a ready market. Everett squandered his profits on liquor and philandering, until at last he lost the power to write, either of good or evil, and he could earn no more.

Sooner than he thought, he could borrow no more, either; he was evicted from his room and had to sleep in Bowery flea-joints, until someone told him about a certain inn.

"It is called St. Christopher's," a Chinatown hobo told him. Looking for something and not knowing what it was, Everett hitchhiked to Graymoor, for St. Christopher's Inn is there, one of those white buildings. Everett knocked on the door and when it was opened, he could see the lamps, feel the warmth of fire at the hearth, and inhale the smell of new-baked bread.

"Come in, Brother Christopher," said a voice.

"I am not a Brother. My name's not——"

"Every man who knocks at the door bears Christ somewhere within him. He is a Brother Christopher."

A year later, Everett dined with me in a New York club. He was literally a new man, risen from his dead past, already back at work. And from him I learned how hundreds of other men had found the miracle of resurrection in body, mind and soul—found it for themselves in the quiet white building known as St. Christopher's Inn; a part—and only a part—of the work of these brown-robed friars.

Forty-one years ago, when Father Paul James Francis founded Graymoor, "gentlemen of the road," as tramps were called in vaudeville jokes, would sometimes stop at the first little wooden friary to beg food and shelter. Today the homeless and helpless journey to the Inn from all over the country.

Not once in 41 years has any wanderer been turned away.

Let any traveler knock at the door of St. Christopher's Inn, and he can have a bed, food, cigarettes, even shoes, just for the asking. No questions. No pledges to take. No preaching at him. No head-shaking over him. And he can stay there as long as he wishes. Small things, the monks say—tobacco, a plate of stew from their own table, a smile of friendship.

Is the Inn, then, a racket, a free-loader's heaven, to be taken advantage of? What does it matter if the tramps think they are getting the best of these naive, brown-robed priests? The men of Graymoor are glad for every comer. Jesus, they remind you, shortly before He was crucified, declared that even a glass of water given to the least of men, is given also to Him.

Not a rehabilitation center, the Inn is simply a shelter for anyone who asks help. Yet under its mild influence hundreds of men have found new lives to live. Only heaven has kept count of the number of souls renewed in the peace of that white building. But now and then the friars see startling proof of their harvest.

There was that desperate time, in 1924, when Father Paul was trying haplessly to raise funds for building a new Inn to replace the first crude log hut, already outgrown. But not nearly enough money was coming in, and no one seemed interested in Graymoor, its friars or its vagabonds. The public was apathetic. Newspaper editors seemed indifferent, until, one hot Sunday morning, the break came.

In the New York *World* there appeared, to Father Paul's astonishment, a long article on Graymoor. And it was authentic! The author had once been a guest in the hostelry; one of a motley parade, a drunken reporter, adrift from his moorings, shattered by alcoholism. For two years he had floundered about, before stumbling into Graymoor. Like so many others, the newspaperman had stayed only a few days. But on the mountain he had found peace; he left, only to look for a job.

Now that he had written the article as his own thank-you-note, people who read it began to send contributions. Their gifts built the big white Inn that stands on the mountain today.

The monks wish they could tell the outsider what they get out of all this for themselves.

"But how," one has asked, "can you describe Beethoven's Fifth Symphony to a man who was born deaf, who has never heard a noise?"

With the Franciscans, every day is a New Easter. In an alchemy of service they are themselves born again each time they master themselves, enduring patiently the blasphemy of a derelict's despairing curses, or humbling themselves to wash up after a tramp's filthy hang-over.

At Graymoor men are also studying for mission work which they will carry on in far places and near. Where a man is sick in soul or in body, where a child needs milk or a boy needs shoes, there monks and nuns will go. In the dairy, the sandal factory, or on the farm at Graymoor, the brown-robed figures are toiling for love of a Carpenter's Son who exalted the dignity of labor. In seventeen chapels on the Mount of the Atonement, friars are praying.

Another friend of mine came back from a visit to the Graymoor Monastery and exclaimed in disgust: "That is a living death!"

He could not have phrased it better. These men have, indeed, died, to the world. But look at the faces in this Society of Atonement! Even the old men seem young, compared to some middle-aged businessmen, such as that disgusted friend. Peace is in their gaze—contentment, certainty. Theirs is the true fountain of youth, because they cherish the open secret of the Resurrection.

When my friend Everett revisited me, so truly a man back from the grave, he told me much of the mystery and meaning of the spiritual powerhouse of Graymoor.

"Do you mean that we should all put on robes and nurse bums?" I asked sarcastically. In those days, I called myself a contented agnostic and I knew even less then than

I do now about that secret of true happiness, which is the real meaning of Easter.

"No," said Everett. "But it does mean that we all have to crucify our own faults—especially hatred, envy, our feeling of superiority, resentments and grudges, the spitefulness of gossip; our utterly destructive selfishness; all the sins."

Each of us, he argued, could be a little like the men of Graymoor. At least, each of us could realize that God is our Father, so that all men and women are our brothers and sisters—and we can treat them as such.

"Today," Everett swept on, "doctors and psychologists talk about psychosomatic medicine. They tell us that often the arthritis that cramps our legs and backs, the ulcers, even the colds in our heads, may be self-inflicted; in the bitterness of our thoughts we give ourselves such things. Get them out of your system, says the scientist, and you may cure yourself.

"Well, what's new about that? Christ reminded His followers to love God with all their hearts, and their neighbors as themselves. After nearly 2000 years, the men of Graymoor obey the commandment."

Everett had found for himself "the way, the truth and the life," which is the Resurrection. Thinking of him, and of what St. Christopher's Inn at Graymoor had done for him, my mind sped in flight across the seas to the very holiest place in Christendom, the birthplace of Easter. And I remembered the shock I felt, the first time I stood at the place where Jesus arose from the tomb.

I stood in the tottering Church of the Holy Sepulchre in Jerusalem. Within its shaky walls lies what visible evidence remains of the first Easter—Calvary where three crosses stood, and the tomb that Joseph of Arimathea had ordered to be hewed out for himself, and then gave for the burial of Jesus. Why did it have to be that He who came to redeem a world by love, must be born in a stable, be crucified like any common criminal, and find burial in another man's grave?

Here at the borrowed grave I found, not peace, but discord. For in the dimmish light of the crumbling church five Christian groups worshiped in strictly chalked-off chapels and shrines. What was worse, Moslem guards with naked bayonets sprawled on shelves just inside the church vestibule, ready to intervene in squabbles and brawls between rival Christians.

What a travesty on the greatest event in history, here in this holiest of holy places! Turk and Roman and Saracen, Jew and Gentile, Arab and Christian, all had brought hatred to the spot where His love had conquered death.

This church was where it had all happened; where the angel had said to the bewildered followers of the Master, staring into the empty tomb:

"Why seek you the living among the dead? He is not here, but is risen. . . . And these words seemed to them as idle tales, and they did not believe them."

Ah, my little godchild, seeing these Moslem guards, I, too, ask a question: How many of us believe those "idle tales" even now? How many of us keep close to the real meaning of Easter?

For the real significance is not a casual matter. It is never simple to die, especially to our faults. There was anguish on the cross; nails in hands and feet, bloody sweat, sop of vinegar for the thirsty throat.

When I was last there in Jerusalem, I crossed the chapel, and stooping low entered the tomb of rock. Over in the corner I could see the stone burial couch where they had laid Him in death. The angel was right. He was not here. He was gone.

But once He *was* in this tomb! Wrapped in linen cloths, sealed into this tiny space as if forever.

The fact of His dying, of death, is what all comfort-minded persons like myself find it easy to forget about Easter! We rush glibly over the words: "He died and was buried," to hear that "He rose again, and ascended into heaven."

And that is the grim blunder that makes for Moslem guards here, and for violence and dissension everywhere!

Only one road led to the Resurrection and that was the way of the Cross. Jesus could not turn back from the Via Dolorosa. Nor can we, in our own personal troubles, skip from Christmas to Easter, and leave out Calvary.

Only by sacrifice can we be born again.

There is a cold, hard word. Not one sensible person relishes the idea of sacrifice. To our complacent minds it sounds pagan, melodramatic, even neurotic. We squirm at the thought of pain. But the business of dying to an unhappy life and rising to happiness, the business of being a Christian is not only a joyous experience; it is also bound to be, sooner or later, a painful sacrifice.

To anticipate how difficult sacrifice can be, try giving up something you love, like coffee or cigarettes or cocktails. Of course, there is nothing wrong with simple pleasures, used in moderation, but even when we use them wisely, it is a wrench to give them up.

It is a thousand times harder to give up our real sins.

We *love* those sins. Although a better part of us may deny that we do so, we enjoy them. We get pleasure out of being greedy. We relish our one-sided code of morals. We wallow in gossip, enjoying every tale we tell out of school.

And as a drunkard grips his glass, so we clutch our resentments to us for the vicious satisfaction of balefully rehearsing our hatred over and over, as one rolls a sweet under the tongue. It is not easy to bury these faults. But it is the way of all life.

Suppose a man had never seen a seed. You show him one, and say: "This will keep, just as it is, for a long time. However, if I bury it in the ground, it will soon stop being a seed, and instead, will become a plant with leaves and color and fragrance. And from one seed will come a hundred more."

The un-gardened man would call you a fool, a daydreamer.

Yet every seed carries within itself the promise of larger growth and utter transformation. As long as the seed remains a prisoner of its shell, the promise is suspended. The seed must die, it must be buried, and in the ground must sacrifice everything that makes it what it is, if it is to be born again.

We are all seeds. A man must sacrifice, and die within himself, shedding the shell of hate and fear and selfishness. Then he can rise to new life, as the seed finds its soul in a flower. That is when Easter comes to the heart of a man. From then on, he lives every day not only as if it might be his last one on earth, but as if it were also the last day for every person he meets. From his soul falls the burden of hatred, the heaviest cross any man can carry.

It always hurts to hear a child weeping. But I am glad now that my goddaughter wept over Jesus on Christmas morning. I envy Jean Grace her tears, and the simple love behind them. At five she asked a question that I had not asked myself in half a lifetime.

But on this Easter morning Jean Grace will have her answer in a happy ending. I shall know what to tell her. Not in any halting words of mine; three words by Jesus, spoken in farewell, tell it all.

"Love one another," He said, just before He died.

"Love one another!" In love we bury our old selves with all the lies and hatreds and fears. "Love one another" and we shall rise again in hope, all bitterness gone, all weeping over.

What a change in the face of the world if it would take to heart those words!

"Love one another——"

Nowhere in the universe would there be anything to frighten, for in God's love we would be unafraid and free. No wars. No famine. No pestilence. No one hungry or naked or homeless. No one in prison. No one lonely any more.

And nowhere in the world a voice raised in anger. Peace everywhere. God in His Heaven, and at last all right with the world.

DO WE NEED THE TEN COMMANDMENTS TODAY?

CAPE COD, 1951

ON the peak of Mount Sinai, amidst flame and thunder, God gave to Moses the tablets of the Law. That was more than three thousand years ago, and yet today, in a nightmare world, the Ten Commandments speak with dumfounding precision.

I do not pretend to be even an amateur scholar in the Scriptures. Merely as one average man, I read the Decalogue, searching for guidance, and in the immortal "Ten Words" I find a blue print for the good life.

The first Commandment begins:

> *I am the Lord your God, which have brought you out of the land of Egypt, out of the house of bondage. You shall have no other gods before Me.*

Perhaps this seems an idle requirement in an educated and progressive world, but we are, in fact, hemmed in all around, overshadowed and oppressed by false gods. And as long as some of us are their devotees, all of us may be their victims.

Just for glory and cash, a certain type of politician will make any sacrifice, resort to any skulduggery to keep himself in office, his whole career an oblation to power. His greedy neighbor may offer his prayers to a bank; another is ruled by vanity or lust. But chief among a whole herd of golden calves is that falsest of all false gods which we call Self.

Yet some plausible intellectuals are priests at the altars of self-sufficiency. They see no absurdity in teaching men to take their stand among starry systems in a fathomless universe, and worship themselves.

"Man must learn to stand alone. In fact, he *is* alone," is the substance of the teaching.

But discerning scientists of the age—Millikan, Jeans, Carrel, de Nuoys, Einstein—agree that design is visible in the universe. And design must have a Designer.

In the hearts and minds of thoughtful people there continues to echo the good sense of the first Commandment; no false and strange gods must stand between us and the one God of Truth, for He alone is real and all the rest is trash.

Following, comes a related injunction:

> *You shall not make unto you any graven image or any likeness of anything there is in heaven above or that is in the earth beneath or that is in the water under the earth. You shall not bow down yourself to them, nor serve them; for I the Lord your God am a Jealous God, visiting the iniquity of the fathers upon the children unto the third and fourth generation of them that hate Me. And showing mercy unto thousands of them that love Me and keep My commandments.*

We have many graven images. The speed demon adores his fast new car, an idol which in his hands may be a bloodthirsty thing on the highways, a new Moloch devouring children. Some women will give their immortal souls for diamonds and rubies, for the furs of animals and the feathers of birds, or for glittering electric light bulbs flashing their names on the marquees of Vanity Fair. Hapless little men sit at desks, hating the job, never sharing the homely excitements of work-a-day life, but stealthily waiting for 5 P.M. and deliverance from bondage. They worship a time clock.

Who can count the lifeless images we look to for the satisfactions of life?

And would not all existence improve if we took this Commandment to heart, using objects made by hands as tools of wisdom—the speed demon slowing down in consideration of others, and giving a fresh-air outing to poor kids that never get a ride? All things can be used constructively.

The next Commandment tells us:

> *You shall not take the name of the Lord your God in vain.*

Here is condemnation for today's most sordid phenomenon—a hard and bitter cynicism, a discourteous unbelief that holds nothing whatever in reverence or even respect.

Like a disease in populations, there is disillusion in a multitude of disenchanted men and women who have lost all faith. Their spiritual impotence is a consequence of the crass materialism in modern life. The carnival of debunking began with a blasphemous loss of reverence for God, symbolized in the use of the holy name as a curse. Having lost faith in God, we soon lost confidence in our fellow men and now in ourselves.

Will the world not be a happier place when we return to the lost values of olden times? The earth is wonderful enough to fill us with awe.

Another Commandment tells us that we must:

Remember the Sabbath day to keep it holy. But on the seventh day is the Sabbath of the Lord your God; You shall do no work on it, you nor your son, nor your daughter, nor your manservant, nor your maid-servant, nor your beast, nor the stranger that is within your gates. For in the six days the Lord made heaven and earth, and the sea, and all things that are in them, and rested on the seventh day; therefore the Lord blessed the seventh day and sanctified it.

Sabbath, of course, means Saturday the seventh day of the week, but early Christians changed the observance to Sunday, honoring the day on which Christ rose from the dead.

For the sake of prayer and devotion, could a sweeping paralysis of human activity be maintained for 24 hours in the complex rush of the twentieth century? Such a rest from high pressure might prove a most welcome blessing. Even now, some people continue to obey the command with literal rigidity. Others, equally devout, hold that the purpose is to give all men ample time to worship, and time for rest from servile or unnecessary work. Many Christians permit innocent amusements on Sunday, if people first attend a service of worship, the core of the Commandment.

Certainly, if all of us started going to church again every Sunday, we could then go on to play and work, feeling uplifted. To go to church is to set a potent example; it is any man's simplest and best chance to obey the Commandment, helping to turn back the tide of cynicism and despair.

The next Commandment, often surprisingly and scornfully abused, reads:

> *Honor your father and your mother that your days may be long upon the land which the Lord your God gives you.*

A young man has been having trouble with his wife, his boss and his friends, so he seeks help from a psychoanalyst. Lying on a couch, he murmurs the story of his life, paying perhaps a dollar a minute for the privilege. When the last session is over, he is dismissed with a new outlook:

"My mother has been the worst influence in my life. She has robbed me of the power to make my own decisions. I must emancipate myself."

"Mom-ism" and "Pop-ism" are prime villains of psychiatry. We are advised not to worry even about supporting parents; what are old-age pensions for? Let the state look to the feeble and infirm, and remove love and tenderness from the transaction. Any old-fashioned notion of duty, the joy of helping those we love, gratitude to old folks who once forgave us our trespasses, turned the other cheek to our impudence, and nursed us through diarrheas and vomitings and innate orneriness—such attitudes, according to the materialists, are a hash of sentimentalism. But the ancient Commandment still thunders from Sinai, telling honorable men to honor parents, even if, sometimes, they seem unreasonable.

But parents are admonished by the same Commandment. Newspapers print horror stories of bad mothers and fathers who abandon or slay their young. Even among so-called better families, children often drift from one household to another in the mazes of divorce. Busy with skis and rackets, cocktails and flirtations, a job to obtain a few more dollars, or perhaps prestige, some smartly styled mothers leave to nursemaids the training of their children in morals and manners, and later to boarding-school teachers and camp counselors. Such mothers—and fathers, too—"have their own lives to live."

If parents are to be honored, they should prove themselves worthy of honor. The Commandment has to do with all just authority; a man must respect his lawful superiors and obey their orders, and, like parents, the superiors have a reciprocal duty. Actually we are being commanded by God to live together, at home, at office, and wherever human beings associate, in good will and mutual regard.

Who can doubt that we will be better off when we do so?

We are also told: "You shall not kill."

A humanitarian objects: "There are times when if you don't kill, you'll get killed. How do you reconcile war with the Commandment?"

Rabbis, priests and ministers constantly remind conscientious objectors that the Scriptures hold that wars can be just. Under God's manifest protection, the Israelites fought many campaigns and killed many enemies, soon after the Ten Commandments were given to them. War is not necessarily a contradiction of the Ten Commandments; often it is the penalty of their neglect.

Another kind of humanitarian protests:

"Suppose your wife is afflicted with lingering, incurable cancer, and has already been so saturated with pain-killing drugs that they are no longer effective. You know she is going to die soon anyway—and she implores you to end her agony. Is it wrong to release her?"

Like prohibition, euthanasia is a remedy far worse than the disease. It does not take human nature into account. From the evil consequences of prohibition the nation has still to recover; much worse would come to pass, if mercy killings were made legal. Even now, men and women do secret murder to gain inheritance or insurance money, to free themselves for a new partner, or for other squalid motives, risking death in the electric chair for ignoble gains. Just as prohibition corrupted men in high places and low, euthanasia would open the door of temptation to doctors and officials—the stakes would be high. No legal safeguards would ever eliminate conspiracies of greed.

Moreover, any lessening of respect for life is a danger to free people. In a republic the right to life is inviolable but under dictatorships, the old and the ill are exterminated, and anyone can be liquidated.

More than assassination is included in the law which makes life sacred. It is every man's duty to take proper care of his own spiritual and bodily well-being, and he must look also to the health of those under his care. The implications of the Commandment forbid quarrels and fighting, anger, hatred, revenge, drunkenness, and bad example. Jesus, Whose purpose was not to destroy but to fulfill these same laws, made the larger meaning quite clear:

> *You have heard that it was said to the ancients: "You shall not kill" . . . but I say to you that everyone who is angry with his brother shall be liable to judgment.*

Even excessive eating and drinking are included in the anti-murder command; has not many a man digged his own grave with his teeth?

And "You shall not commit adultery."

The dictionary says adultery is "the sexual intercourse of two persons, either of whom is married to a third person," but immediately afterward it broadens the meaning to include all unchastity and unfaithfulness; any lewdness of act or *thought*. Here Funk and Wagnalls follow Jesus Who used these words:

> *But I say to you that anyone who so much as looks with lust at a woman has already committed adultery with her in his heart.*

So we are asked to be pure and modest in our behavior and our thoughts. Does anyone doubt that this Commandment is needed today?

There is no need to rehearse the current licentiousness. It is aided and abetted by erotic books, plays and pictures in various ways. Against codes of morals and manners and of good taste also, raised by society to protect itself, there are countless little men who use their energies to invent innuendoes, slipping foul and covert inferences, references and associations into radio and television jokes, cartoons and popular songs. They work for the delectation of dirty minds. When out of work, some of them no doubt, write words on walls. Even in the embraces of lawful marriages, such persons can commit adultery by their lascivious cheapness and brutishness, as many a wife has confided to her doctor.

But the answer to concupiscence is not to change our code, even by a majority vote, making violations lawful because there are more sinners than saints, but instead to go back to the old concepts of love and family life that lift passion above the tawdry and the vulgar. In the human heart there remains a deathless ideal of chastity—one man, one woman, one love under one God. This world can do with a little purifying through that wise and beautiful Commandment.

And "You shall not steal."

At a time when many people want to abolish private property—especially those who have none to abolish—this Commandment seethes with meaning.

Some conservatives hold that the prohibition of theft is, of itself, an endorsement of property rights. But the Commandment goes much further than simple or compound thievery. By those four strong and simple words we are held to a strict code of personal conduct—to pay our bills; to live up to our business agreements; to avoid debts beyond our ability to pay. We are not to live beyond our means, hoping that God will sometime, somehow pull us out of a hole. That is not reliance on God's abundance; it is presumption, in itself a great transgression.

"Better a little with justice than great revenues with iniquity," is one of the Bible's Proverbs.

Among the offenders of the law against stealing are the black-marketeers and those who patronize them; smugglers, bribers and takers of bribes; game-fixers, and workers who pad expense accounts. Equally thievish are the employee who loafs on the job and the big shot who arrives half an hour late for an appointment—both steal time, which is irreplaceable. Salesmen who misrepresent their merchandise are robbing us, as are peddlers of dubious stocks, any and all who take advantage of ignorance or necessity; greedy employers as well as crooked agents of honest workingmen.

Would not we be better off if the Commandment against stealing were obeyed; if no merchant ever used false measures, and the butcher's hand never weighted down the balance of the scales—and Pop did not rejoice and pocket money that did not belong to him when the gas company made a mistake in the bill?

"You shall not bear false witness against your neighbor."

It must be clear that society must break down and fall apart, if men cannot trust the words of other men.

By the form of this divine law, we are asked to speak the truth in all things, but most especially in what concerns the good name and honor of others—this in today's world, where the big lie has been exalted into a political weapon, chief tool of the current code of expediency.

The truth-telling Commandment forbids us to write libel, or to utter slander, detraction, calumny, or even the telling of secrets which we ought to keep. A student lies when he cheats at an examination; we lie, if we believe something harmful to another person's character without sufficient reason; all gossip is a violation, and even to listen with pleasure to tattling is morally wrong.

Can anyone doubt that this Commandment is still needed in every community?

Finally we read:

You shall not covet your neighbor's house; neither shall you desire his wife;
Nor his servant, nor his hand-maid, nor his ox, nor his ass, nor anything that is his.

Wife-coveting today is a national pastime in the forty-eight states. A woman is not a chattel, a kind of property, to be desired as a man envies another man's television set, yet often she is coveted just as ignobly, as something to be used. This Commandment affirms human dignity, and protects the sanctity and decency of marriage. It is the exaltation of domestic felicity and a condemnation of lust.

But the coveting of another man's material possessions is also forbidden. It is not wrong to desire material prosperity—only sophists deride decent human ambition and enterprise—but one must succeed only by honest and just practices. We are forbidden to be envious of the success of others, which is one of the principal sins of today's revolutionists who raise up envy to be a virtue, along with hatred and contempt for those more prosperous.

Men who do achieve wealth by conspiratorial devices are mortal enemies of our free way of life; they sow the seeds of communism, sinning doubly by arousing hatred and envy in others, and in endangering freedom. "Some in their eagerness to get rich have strayed from the faith, and have involved themselves in many troubles," said St. Paul in his letter to Timothy.

Would we not all be better off if men obeyed not only this Commandment but every one of the Ten?

Most certainly the Commandments are needed today; perhaps more than ever before. Their divine message confronts us with a profound moral challenge in an epidemic of evil; a unifying message acceptable alike to Jew, Moslem and Christian. Who, reading the Ten in the light of history and of current events, can doubt their identity with the eternal law of nature?

They begin by telling a man how he must conduct

himself toward his Maker, and then give him the pattern of behavior toward his fellow man—as affirmed by Jesus when He said that we should love God with all our heart and our neighbors as ourselves.

What Moses said of old, he would now declare to us again:

> *These words, which I command you this day, shall be in your heart, and you shall tell them to your children; and you shall meditate upon them, sitting in your house and walking on your journey, sleeping and rising.*

This was written at editor John J. O'Connell's pressing request and brought wide and enthusiastic comments. The statistics of various surveys showing (a) how many in our Armed Forces never heard of the Ten Commandments or thought they were some Jewish code; (b) how few citizens can recite them; (c) the number of children under ten who drew a blank on the subject, had shaken Fulton Oursler. Even if no prayer be permitted in our schools, it seemed incredible that the Ten Commandments could not be taught as urgently as the salute to the flag.

Mr. Oursler's mail from this piece so moved him that he started outlining ten stories for a possible series of television plays based on the Ten Commandments. Before his death one had already been finished, done with Henry Denker, who has been script writer of The Greattest Story Ever Told *radio program from its start.*

THE GREATEST MOTHER OF ALL

NEW YORK, 1952

THE jury had found the prisoner guilty. The court had condemned him. The higher court had affirmed the sentence. So he was put to death and one of the front row witnesses of the execution was his mother.

It is hard to repress a shudder at the thought of such a nightmare.

Yet so it happened. For three hours, Mary, the mother of Jesus, stood at the foot of the cross, watching her Son die.

Even the toughest Roman guard must have wondered why she was there. Friends surely had tried to lead her away. But nothing could move her from her purpose; in the memory of her vigil, unborn generations would find courage and hope.

Mother's Day began at Calvary.

Coleridge calls a mother "the holiest thing alive," because she shares with God the miracle of creation. And she keeps near to perfection afterward, in the completeness of a love which finds no test too hard. Sacrifice is the splendid commonplace of mothers.

From the beginning, Mary of Nazareth knew sacrifice. Not for her the calm and natural life of a Nazareth girl, engaged to be married. Instead, she was to see a vision and to hear a voice, bringing a supernatural assignment; Mary was to bear a child who would be the Son of God; she who had not known Joseph, her betrothed, nor any man.

Her answer was instantaneous obedience; she would do the will of God and that is the first virtue of motherhood.

"Behold," she whispered, "the handmaid of the Lord."

Never did her obedience falter through the wonders and terrors that followed. Her promised Son was born in a Bethlehem stable, the cattle's feeding box His only crib. She saw kings from afar come kneeling at the manger. She heard shepherds at the barn door, telling of choirs singing in the stars: peace on earth to men of good will.

But then, as now, there roamed the earth men of ill will and they were coming close to her Child.

Joseph was warned of the danger in a dream. Herod the King, hearing prophecies about the Infant born in the stable, feared He would grow up to seize the throne. So he decided to slaughter all the babies in Bethlehem just to make sure that Mary's Baby should not escape.

In the middle of the night, she had to mount a donkey and go off with Joseph, through the darkness into the desert, carrying the Child to safety beyond the wastes of sand. In Egypt, Mary and Joseph and the Infant Jesus had to settle as displaced persons; Jewish refugees in a land poisoned with anti-Semitism.

But when Herod the King was dead at last, the exiled three could go back to Nazareth. It was a peaceful, happy childhood, except for one domestic crisis—Passover time in Jerusalem—when Jesus could not be found.

What is more fearsome to a mother than the thought of a lost child? Is my little Boy in your house, my friend? No, Mary, not here. In the courtyard of the inn? No, Mary; no one has seen Him there.

At last she found Him in an alcove of the Temple, and standing silent for a moment, she watched and listened. Her little Boy was the central figure of a circle; around Him loomed gray-bearded philosophers and teachers; legalists, hairsplitters, disputationists—all of them haggard now, outfaced and confounded by a Child of twelve. His innocent eyes had pierced the tangles of their lifeless logic; He admonished them beyond contradiction, returning them to issues that matter in life, to mercy and repentance; to the spirit, not the letter of the law.

What was Mary to say?

"Son, why have you done this to us? Behold, your father and I have been looking for you, sorrowing."

In every mother's life there comes a time when a child's mind seems beyond comprehension. As now to Mary:

"How is it that you were looking for Me? Do you not know that I must be about my Father's business?"

She took her Lad by the hand and led Him homeward. But:

". . . His mother kept all these words in her heart."

That is how all mysteries are to be solved; in the heart, where truth, beyond the mind's grasp, can be fathomed. By patient, waiting, understanding hearts our mothers feed our souls.

Long years afterward—when Joseph had died, and Jesus had fasted in the desert, had been tempted on a mountain, and baptized in the Jordan—He returned to Galilee and performed His first miracle for Mary.

It happened at a modest wedding feast in the Palestinian village of Cana. Today travelers to the ancient town are shown tall stone jars; once, so guides solemnly avouch, they held the water that Jesus turned into wine. The hapless father of the bride had more guests than he counted on, and the vessels all ran dry. Mary said to Jesus:

"They have no wine."

"Woman! What is that to me and to you?"

In our phrases His reply sounds harsh, but not so to Mary's ears. "Woman" was the respectful salutation of the day, as if He had addressed her: "Lady!" And the question He put to her meant infinitely more, as if He were implying:

What is it to us, this little social mishap? Your kind heart is saddened for the embarrassed bride and groom and you want to mother them; you ask that I should call upon the omnipotent power of heaven to fill up their empty glasses. But have you forgotten, oh, lady? By my first miracle, I set myself apart from all other men. I call attention to who I am and to what I am. For us, then, things will never again be the same. It is still not yet quite time. Will you hasten it; hasten the journey that in the end will lead to a cross on a hill—for both of us?

But mother told the waiters:

"Whatever He shall say to you, you do."

For His mother's sake, Jesus changed water into wine, and the world forever remembers the transformation as a symbol of the larger miracle by which grace can turn the drabbest life into a noble experience.

She had to loose Him and let Him go; cheer Him on His dangerous way. But everywhere and from everyone she was to hear of Him, preaching and healing. Not all who talked to Mary praised her Son's words or deeds. Some even tried to tell her that now, having become famous, He had disowned her. There was the time when the town of Capernaum was jammed with His followers, and Mary made the journey down from Nazareth with a party of relatives. Someone got word to Jesus that His mother was standing near, and He returned a startling question:

"Who is my mother?"

He looked around Him at all the crowd until he searched her out. Fond eyes fixed upon her, He said:

"Whosoever shall do the will of my Father that is in heaven, he is my brother and sister and mother."

And her heart rejoiced in the precious secret they had always shared: the truth that the love of God must come first in every heart; otherwise, men make breathing idols of mothers, sweethearts, wives or children forgetting God in false worship.

Year by year, she watched His skies darken. She was in Jerusalem the night of the Passover when one of His own twelve friends sold Him to His enemies with a kiss. At dawn, she was standing in the street as He came struggling down the Via Dolorosa, dragging the cross.

Just before He died, He spoke to her, and the great reason for her anguished presence at the Crucifixion at last became clear:

"Woman, behold your son."

She saw Him turn His head, then, and seek out a young man standing close by, the beloved of His twelve apostles, John. And to John, He said:

"Son, behold your mother."

But not to John alone He spoke; His message was to those unborn generations; even to me and to you. When her Son was born, there had been no room in the inn for her or for Him. Now at the finish she held His Body again in her arms, and there was no place for her to lay Him except in a borrowed grave.

Mary had suffered everything.

Yet even at that most bitter hour her faith did not falter. She never knew despair for she was sure of the Resurrection.

In our frightened times, the figure of mother at the foot of the cross remains a blessing and a light. As we share Mary's faith and courage, and take heart from her, we, too, can be sure of God's wisdom and mercy no matter how deep the darkness all around.

Son, behold your mother.

In the last baker's dozen years of his life, Fulton Oursler found the Lady Chapel in St. Patrick's Cathedral an island of peace. He once wrote touchingly of it as being the final cause of his conversion. He made it his spiritual home. It became the goal of his daily walk and he would drop in for a visit after almost every appointment in town. When deeply troubled or angered, he would go there to sit and "not think."

Frequently, on leaving, he would pause at the great figure of the Pietà to the south side.

Surely the Lord might have spared His Mother all that heartbreak?

But if He had we could not feel so close to the Mother He bequeathed us.

This article was written at a time of a special and deeply wounding sorrow. He did it in what was almost a brief retreat from the world around him. He emerged with a great peace, and never discussed the article or his grief.

IN EVERY LIFE—
THE RESURRECTION

NEW YORK, 1949

WE moderns can move faster than sound but we are still going around in circles. At the heart of things this Easter, changed and different as outwardly it appears, the world is strangely as it was, nearly 2000 years ago, when Jesus of Nazareth was put to a shameful death as a common criminal.

For then, as now, imperialism and force ruled enslaved and hapless millions. In the days of our Lord, Palestine was occupied by a foreign power, just as France and Belgium and Sweden and many other lands were held by invading aggressors within our recollection. In those lands there were rich collaborators who played palm to palm with the conquerors. Those quislings betrayed their own flesh and blood for profit and power. So, in the days of Jesus, there were mighty leaders who were chummy with Caesar's agent, Pontius Pilate—and for the same greedy reasons.

There was, however, in the olden time, one great difference.

The people had heard a new voice and had seen a new light. It was a voice proclaiming freedom, a light revealing God as the Father of races, and all men, therefore, as brothers. This voice and this light frightened and enraged the ancient collaborationists, who tried to silence the voice and extinguish the light forever. But because of the miracle that followed their dark business, the world found also a new hope; the sting was drawn from death, the grave robbed of victory.

In the story of the Resurrection of Jesus Christ, there is today a persisting meaning, a hope for everyone, in our own bewildering and distracting time.

Let us, as if possessed of some scientific machine that can pierce both time and space, and bring the eternal into mortal view, look back across seas and deserts, and down through twenty centuries, to behold for ourselves what happened in Jerusalem that first Easter.

On that spring day, there were lodged just outside the Holy City a wayfarer from a northern province, and His twelve friends. One would have thought that a poor man such as He was, and His ragged band of followers, most of them fishermen, would have come into town unnoticed. Already the capital was thronged with hundreds of thousands of pilgrims from upper and lower Galilee, Transjordania, and even more remote places, arrived to celebrate the great Passover feast.

Yet this young Nazarene artisan of thirty-three, Who for most of His life had worked as a carpenter, supporting His mother, Mary, had become a sensation among the multitudes. More, He had so alarmed the political bosses of the town that their hearts were filled with fear and with hatred, which is the misshapen child of fear.

In the chill of that Thursday gloaming, the conspiracy was being hatched. Lord Annas, leader of the Temple aristocrats, and one of the oldest and richest men of his time, had retired to his private chamber. Standing before him was his son-in-law, Caiphas, here on a desperate errand; pleading with the old gentleman to connive with him at a murder. The crime he proposed was to be committed this very night, yet with all the aspects of legality, a whole courtful of judges to be hoodwinked and used, in the murder of that same young Carpenter from the north.

The only light in the chamber was a blood-red glow from a grate of burning coals, over which Annas, uncrowned ruler of the Jews, warmed small, stiff hands that were eighty years old. His glance at his daughter's husband was disapproving. Annas had always detested Caiphas, as a brainless fop with a perfumed beard. The only reason Annas had ever appointed the fellow High Priest of the Temple was because he had run out of his sons. Seven of his own had served in the great priestly office. But Caesar would not let any native ruler stay long in public office, fearing he would build up too powerful a political machine; every few years the Temple got a new High Priest. The latest considered himself the handsomest man in the province; gorgeous, mellow-toned Caiphas.

"Why do you fear a mere wandering Carpenter from Galilee?" the old man complained petulantly. Before the son-in-law could reply, he went on:

"I realize that He has gone all over the place for the last three years preaching to people. I understand that some believe He is the Messiah. Is there anything new in all that? Aren't the provinces always overrun with preachers, who appoint themselves Messiahs? They are a nuisance, yes—but 'menace'? No! Why is this one more dangerous in your eyes than the rest of such fanatics? Now, don't bother to tell me that He heals sick people. There's no magic in that, either, my dear Caiphas—they probably would get well by themselves. Anyway, it's an object lesson to our physicians—with their utterly abominable fees."

With fat white hand, the High Priest milked his black beard:

"Lord Annas, you are just back from the baths at Jericho, and they are, of course, expensive. But you have not heard what happened here in Jerusalem, not a week ago. Your so-called harmless fanatic made an entry into Jerusalem that can be called nothing less than triumphant. He came riding through the Gate Called Beautiful, on a milk-white ass. Need I remind you that such a beast is the traditional mount of a King of Jews? A million people greeted Jesus—shouting His name with joy, casting palm branches at His feet, and screaming hosannas. Be sure of this—the Jewish people love this Galilean! The whole world has gone after Him! He could lead them in any kind of movement; they would follow Him to the death."

Annas turned his head partly. Rubbing his back, which had begun to ache in the twilight frost, he walked slowly toward his golden, Roman-style easy chair, with its crimson cushions.

"I can see," he temporized, "that such a fellow might cause anxiety. I never underestimate the value of a fact; it may turn out some day to be the truth. Because what the multitude says is so—or soon will be, Caiphas! Perhaps we ought to get rid of Him, as you say. We might arrange to have Him sentenced to the galleys. That's sensible. But why are you proposing this emergency scheme of holding a hurried trial in the middle of the night—tonight, on the eve of the Passover—and sentencing Him to death? That looks like terror!"

"If we don't do it tonight," argued Caiphas solemnly, "we'll never be able to do it. The people will tear Him from us, rescue Him and force Him to start a revolution. That, Lord Annas, is why we must try Him while the town is asleep. Put Him to death before the people wake up. It is our only chance."

"I still fail to see," insisted Annas stubbornly, "that such extreme haste is necessary."

The blue stone on his ring gleamed like a six-pointed star, while the High Priest's teeth shone like white lightning through the black storm of his beard. He prepared to play his winning card.

"You have still to learn what happened in the Temple only this morning," he resumed suavely. "This harmless provincial created an uproar. Can you fancy what He said? He told the people who were buying sacrificial birds and lambs—that He was the Lamb of God and would take away the sins of the world. In other words, He was all the sacrifice they needed. Even that wasn't enough. With a whip in His hand He walked up to the banking tables and scourged the money-changers, overturning the tables and driving our tellers into the streets, crying, 'Make not My Father's House a place of merchandise.' There I think we have Him, hip and thigh. He dares to call God His Father. That means He calls Himself the Son of God. Blasphemy, Lord Annas. Under our laws, as you well know, punishable by death. The people believe this man, and if something is not done, you and I and all the first families of Jerusalem will be ruined."

For nearly sixty years old Annas had held the political

power in his thin aristocratic hands. Now he sat in his golden chair with its red cushions and stared into space—a wisp of a man, no more than five feet of him, nor a hundred pounds of him, with a long, narrow face, and black eyes that still sparkled with antic energy. The blankness of his expression concealed a turmoil in his brain.

Indeed, those last clinching words of his popinjay son-in-law had deeply disturbed him. Though he well knew that his grave was waiting for him, yet he could not contemplate yielding up his possessions and his power. In season and out he had labored to acquire and to hold on to his gains. While the masses of people thirsted for liberty, he had made secret bargains with officials from the Tiber. When Pilate, the latest Roman procurator had arrived, Annas had promptly broken bread with him. Before the meal was over, they had come to a perfect understanding. What, he had asked, did Pontius Pilate want from Judea? The answer:

"Taxes! And tranquillity."

"Ah, then Lord Pilate! We guarantee you both—I and my followers of the Temple leadership. You have only to let *us* collect the taxes. We promise cash and quiet."

So the tax-gatherers of Annas and his corporate friends fell upon their own people. They taxed twice as much as Rome required and kept one half to line their own pockets of silk and velvet. They had a multiplicity of other rackets, too, the richest of which was the business of exchanging money at the Temple banks. Under the laws of Caesar only Roman money could be used in Judea—with the simple exception of one notable area, the domain of the Temple. Within those walls, a worshipper must carry the old Jewish money in his pouch. But how could he get that kind of money? Why, how else but by changing his Roman denarii for Jewish shekels in the only place he could do so, in the outer court of the Temple, at the tables of the banking house of Annas and company. Of course, there had to be a fee for this transaction; the charge was 50%; and those transactions in simony and extortion went on by thousands day after day and year after year. At Passover time, with hundreds of thousands of visitors, the money-changers of Annas, Caiphas, and the rest, would take in more than a ship's cargo of treasure.

Well, then! Was Annas to permit some mendicant preacher who, unlike the foxes of the field, had not even a hole in the ground to shelter Him, to break up a business like that?

Especially since Jesus had also told the people His own life was their perfect sacrifice and they did not have to spend any more money at all on lambs and doves! It was Annas and his gang who sold those lambs and doves, charging three times more than they were worth. For once in his life, Annas groaned to himself, his coxcomb son-in-law was right.

"Where can we lay our hands on this Jesus?" he demanded.

"He seems to have a way of avoiding pursuers," replied Caiphas uneasily. "Once when a mob tried to kill Him in His home town, He vanished while in the very midst of them. No one ever found out how. But you and I know human nature, Lord Annas—it is frail. I have ten fingers and I am perfectly sure at least one of them cannot be trusted. Waiting outside right now is a follower of Jesus, one of His twelve best friends—and for a slight fee, *he* will tell us where we can nab his Master at any moment we choose. Excuse me."

With stately tread, Caiphas walked to the doorway, pulled back the curtains of Tyrian purple and called:

"You may come in now—Judas!"

Thus the conspiracy was set in motion while Jerusalem slumbered; while there lay dreaming peacefully in the golden city a million Jews who loved Jesus, some of them men and women whose blind eyes He had opened, whose lame legs He had straightened, palsy stilled, dumb tongues made to speak—and whose heartache He had healed with compassion and tender understanding.

In the stillness of the night, soldiers of the collaborationists followed the red-bearded Judas; let that man, whose very dog would not come near him except at mealtimes, lead them through dark streets to the postern gate, and down the steep eastern slope. After crossing the brook of Kedron, they climbed the side of Mt. Olivet. Straight to the Garden of Gethsemane they marched. And there, pausing undetected at the gate, they saw and heard strange things.

They beheld faithful friends of Jesus, the very disciples whom He had asked to stand guard for Him, lying on the ground fast asleep. They heard the lonely voice of Jesus lifted in a prayer that, after this night, was to strengthen the resolution of frightened and bewildered souls to the end of time—the prayer of one pleading to be let off!

This same Jesus, who had defied the mighty in the Temple, and who knew better than anyone else that they sought His death, was now on His knees before a great white rock in the moonlit orchard of olive trees, and He was entreating His Father in Heaven to spare Him from agony and execution. Socrates, the great philosophical hero of Athens, had not weakened as his end drew near. He had even refused a chance to escape. He had died without a cry. That grim example of fortitude aroused the admiration of posterity—but never could it arouse love, or trust, or the faith which possesses men so that they will become martyrs in its service. Jesus once had wept before a grave. Now He prayed before His own fate—and ever since this weakness has endeared Him to frightened hearts. Remembering that He was afraid, they could also remember that He went on straightway to add, "Nevertheless, Thy will, not mine be done."

Then it was that Judas crept up to Him and kissed Him on the cheek. That was for a sign to the arresting squad; now they knew which one to seize. All the other awakening disciples ran away, all fled, friends leaving their Master deserted, to face torches, spears and armored men; to be marched back into the city.

In the Hall of Great Stones, Jesus faced the tribunal junto, to answer a charge that was punishable by death—the accusation of blasphemy. Annas and Caiphas brought in their hired and perjured witnesses who, even so, contradicted themselves and that made matters difficult. And meanwhile there was also a hired and motley mob of tavern cutthroats and bullies outside the Hall, to scream at the judges as if they were the voices of the people, whose will was that the prisoner be convicted.

The same mob of hired goons followed Him from the trial court to the palace of Pontius Pilate. That old Spanish soldier, whose wife had been dreaming of Jesus and urged her husband to acquit Him, tried to dodge the issue. On a jurisdictional theory, he sent Jesus on to Herod, ruler of Galilee, who was visiting in the Capital. After all, Jesus was a Galilean. Then let Herod deal with Him. But the mob dogged the captive's heels and roared at the little drunken tetrarch, who called himself King Herod. Jesus was mocked by the intoxicated king, who dressed the prisoner in Herod's own robes and sent Him back to Pilate.

By now the hireling mob was calling for blood. So, by order of Pilate, Jesus was beaten within an inch of His life. So weak He could barely stand up, He was made to rise while they put a crown of thorns upon His head. They spat on Him. They reviled Him. And when Pilate pleaded that surely now He was punished enough, they put fear of Rome in Pilate's heart with their shouts:

"This man called Himself the King of the Jews. We have no King but Caesar. If you let Him go, you are not Caesar's friend."

That was enough to scare any employee of Caesar!

Promptly Pilate washed his hands of the whole matter. Roman soldiers lugged out a giant cross and commanded Jesus to carry it on His back, a mile to the Hill of Execution, called Golgotha, which means place of the skull. Jesus stumbled forward the long, sad way to Calvary.

Between two thieves they nailed Him to the cross, while Mary, His mother, stood and watched. But others watched the long agony with different eyes. Caiphas was there to see that the job was thoroughly done. Annas was with him, at the very moment when Jesus cried from the cross:

"My God, My God, Why Hast Thou Forsaken Me!"

The High Priest turned to his father-in-law, with a mocking smile.

"I guess that settles it, Lord Annas. He wanted the people to believe that He was a god. Now He wants to know why God has abandoned Him. That seems to settle everything very nicely; the people must hear of this . . ."

He would have gone on to show his erudition by talking about many dying gods of history—Tammuz of Babylon, Dionysus the Great, Osiris the Egyptian, and Attis, the Phoenician, but for the ferocity that suddenly covered the older man's face.

"You helpless ignoramus, you," whispered Annas. "You incomparable fool. I made you High Priest—and you don't even remember the words of King David. In the twenty-second* psalm, prophesying the Messiah, he wrote those words: 'My God, My God, Why Hast Thou Forsaken Me!' Perhaps that figure on the cross spoke them with a purpose. I want to go home," finished old Annas with a shiver.

Forty days later, Annas and Caiphas sat in the warm sunshine that came through the open window of the old man's private room.

"Caiphas," he said, "you are in a bad box. You crucified Jesus and the body disappeared from the tomb. How was that?"

"His followers must have stolen the body."

Annas gave a cackling laugh.

"After you, yourself, had Pilate put Roman soldiers on guard? You know it would be death for them if anything went wrong. His followers say He rose from the dead. They say they have seen Him, talked with Him, broken bread with Him. How about that?"

"Lies."

"It would be most unreasonable for those men to lie. When we arrested their Leader they ran away. They knew He would be put to death and they wanted to escape this same fate. But now they have all come back. They are braving crucifixion for themselves, preaching on the streets of

*Douay Bible—Twenty-first Psalm.

Jerusalem that He arose from the dead. What gave them the courage to come back?"

Caiphas shrugged. "They must be fools."

"But there has to be some reason for such folly. When they ran away they were acting like sensible people. Something must have happened to change them. Could it be that while they had followed Him for three years they still, in their innermost hearts, did not really believe in Him at the crucial hour? If so, something terrifically important must have convinced them, Caiphas, so that now He is dead they really do believe. Perhaps they did see Him alive again—eh?"

Caiphas reached for his staff, preparing to go.

"It's too late now," said Annas. "I don't know what to believe about it. But one thing I am convinced of; this Man whom we put to death was not the kind of revolutionist you and I made His judges believe Him to be. He taught mercy and forgiveness and tenderness and compassion and a way of life on this earth which would make the world itself a heaven. He preached a revolution, not of arms and bloodshed but a social and moral revolution in the mind and soul of man. That sort of revolution cannot be ended by crucifixion. It was truth itself that we nailed to the cross —and truth will always rise from the grave. Even on the cross He prayed for you and me—'Forgive them, Father,' He said. 'For they know not what they do.' I think He would say now that even you and I, if we were to turn from falsehood to truth, could rise from our own dead lives into a new birth. The meaning of that prisoner's death was that in *every* life there can be a resurrection. Some day the world will have to listen to Him—and when that happens, there will be Heaven on earth, and not before."

Without replying, Caiphas strode to the doorway.

One fat white hand was on the purple curtain, when he heard once more the crabbed old voice:

"If you go to the Temple at sunset, I hope you will pray for the future—pray that history will see clearly your guilt and mine. Otherwise, untold generations to come may blame our people, who really loved Jesus. May they not be blamed for what we did to protect our wealth. Oh Caiphas, may the world understand the difference between our innocent people and our guilty selves."

And the old man turned his face to the open window; his lips moved in prayer.

THE BOOK WITH ALL THE ANSWERS

(America's Eight Great Problems)

NEW YORK, 1952

IN the town of Nablus there once lived a woman whose reputation was so bad that decent people would have nothing to do with her. Seven times she had been divorced and between times she had not been idle. No one remembers any of her seven names, yet this outcast has a place in history; she will never be forgotten.

It happened one day when she found a stranger at a well outside the town, a man who had no jug to draw up water. He asked her if she would give Him to drink.

"You ask . . . of me?"

Her voice was shocked, full of her feeling of degradation. For she was not only a town derelict; she belonged to the despised community of Samaritans and this unknown was dressed as a Jew.

Yet He had hope to give her; his gaze was kind. Perhaps, He suggested, it would have been better if she had asked Him to give her to drink; His words rang with promise for this outsider:

"Whoever drinks of this water shall thirst again. But he that shall drink of the water that I will give him shall not thirst forever. The water that I will give him shall become in him a fountain of water springing up with life everlasting."

Jesus of Nazareth began His ministry by counseling the bad woman of Nablus, in the country of an untouchable race, and His first promise was of relief in mind and heart to any person who would ask for it—a resource that would never fail.

The secret of life that He was offering consisted of the law of the Lord, the wisdom of the prophets, and His own enlargements of these teachings, all contained in the book we call the Holy Bible. The thirst He slaked was of the soul; the restlessness every man of conscience knows in a guilty time; the need to feel secure in an incomprehensible cosmos; a reason for living, a goal worth achieving, a faith that rests on universal truth.

To all bewildered and frightened souls, the Bible is now, as it was then, the water of life. It has the answer to America's eight great problems—war, immorality, dishonor, crime, juvenile delinquency, racial and religious prejudice, atheism and despair.

Far from what its enemies call it—a collection of folklore, garbled history and outmoded dogma—the Bible is the most modern of books; for the people of today it stands, as it stood for the ancients, like "the shadow of a great rock in a weary land, and as a pool of water in a thirsty place." With aptness and precision, it offers solutions for the problems of individuals and for distracted governments; for both it is a practical handbook of peace, a legacy for the downhearted, and an invincible protection against the madness of the times.

Speaking of the very laws and prophecies which Jesus offered the woman at the well, Dr. Toynbee, in his *Civilization on Trial,* remarks: "In the vision seen by the Prophets of Israel, Judah, and Iran, history is . . . the masterful and progressive execution, on the narrow stage of this world, of a divine play. . . ." And Frank Glenn Lankard, author of *The Bible Speaks to Our Generation,* declares: "Any age may look into the Bible and behold as in a mirror its doubts and perplexities. . . . If we come to the Bible honestly seeking for a philosophy of life, we might find that the writers of the Bible are strangely up-to-date and thrillingly modern when they insist as they do that 'The fear of the Lord is the beginning of wisdom.'"

To any thinking person, it must be clear that the world did not make itself, nor was it created by chance. It was conceived by a Poet, designed by an Engineer, and made subject to order by a Law-Giver. Finally it was endowed with life and with love by a Heavenly Father. Of the origin, the purpose and the destiny of man, the Bible speaks with authority. But can we believe it?

There was a time when nearly everybody accepted the Bible uncritically, but in our scientific age, skepticism spread like a plague. Geology, archeology, anthropology become the latter-day scriptures. Some lovers of the ancient text held onto it, explaining away the wonder tales as no more than parables; the incredible becoming merely the symbolic. Others swallowed the new materialism whole, satisfied that the universe had neither brain nor plan, soul nor meaning.

But true scientists kept steadily at work, and soon Jeans, Millikan and Einstein were finding design in creation; the evidence of law, of pattern, of mind. Alexis Carrel affirmed the healing power of prayer, as real now as when Naaman the leper went to bathe in the Jordan. But the Bible's uncontradictable message is addressed to the heart and conscience, and its purpose is to show life as a part of eternity.

You are worried? But not by worrying can you change or help anything. "Which of you, by taking thought, can add one cubit unto his stature?" Jesus asked, and he also said: "Let not your heart be troubled: ye believe in God, believe also in me. . . . Perfect love casteth out fear."

A few years after the Crucifixion, St. Paul repeated the admonition: "In nothing be anxious." A thousand years before him, David the psalmist, had rejoiced: "The Lord is my light and my salvation; whom shall I fear? The Lord is the strength of my life. Of whom shall I be afraid?"

Danger of war, treachery of nations, were hazards familiar to Bible writers; those who talk peace and practice war were no novelty: "The words of his mouth were smoother than butter but war was in his heart; his words were softer than oil, yet were they drawn swords."

Our protection? We must love God, serve Him, and the promise is reaffirmed over and over: "He shall give his angels charge over thee, to keep thee in all thy ways. . . ."

"Thou shalt not be afraid for the terror by night; nor for the arrow that flieth by day; nor for the pestilence that walketh in darkness; nor for the destruction that wasteth at noonday. A thousand shall fall at thy side, and ten thousand at thy right hand; but it shall not come nigh thee."

"God is our refuge and strength, a very present help in trouble."

St. Paul's words trumpet down the years:

"For I am persuaded, that neither death, nor life, nor angels, nor principalities, nor powers, nor things present, nor things to come, nor height, nor depth, nor any other creature, shall be able to separate us from the love of God."

Now, as always, in peace and in war: "The eternal God is thy refuge and underneath are the everlasting arms."

All that we dread today has long been familiar: "And when ye shall hear of wars and rumors of wars, be ye not troubled: for such things must needs be; but the end shall not be yet."

The end, however, is certain: "And he shall judge among the nations, and shall rebuke many people: and they shall beat their swords into plowshares, and their spears into pruning hooks; nation shall not lift up sword against nation, neither shall they learn war any more."

"I will break the bow and the sword and the battle out of the earth, and will make them to lie down safely."

But many will object: "I know people who believed and trusted in God—and war took their fathers, or sweethearts, or sons. Other troubles ruined my friends. How can I believe such promises?"

This much is certain—that no one can feel sure, by serving God and living a conscientious life, that he will escape pain and trouble. There is no insurance in the Bible against pain or failure or betrayal; we cannot count, no matter what we do, on health or wealth, though we can hope for it. "He chasteneth those that He loveth," is a part of the meaning of the way of the Cross; we have to trust in the goodness of God, even when we are suffering and feel we do not deserve it. This does not mean that "the will of

God" is always tragedy and suffering. It does mean that God is a loving Father whose will is always good, even when it seems to bring sorrow.

Something else is also certain; the Bible can show any honest man or woman how to meet wisely and serenely whatever fate may bring. This ability to meet the worst that may happen is one of the Bible's greatest gifts: a secret beyond price.

"Though he slay me, yet will I love him"—that cry of Job illustrates the completeness of trust the Bible calls for. And Jesus, praying in Gethsemane, said, "Thy will, not mine, be done." In acceptance lies the peace that passeth understanding. Only thus can we adjust sanely and contentedly to the confusion of the world; only by forsaking the arrogant attitude of wanting to stand alone. A man must see himself as the servant of a power in which he puts complete confidence.

One of the richest of present-day Americans never knew quietude until he came to the discovery that the reason he worried about his money was that he thought it belonged to him. Once he realized it was not his, but God's wealth, and that he was the steward and trustee, given the opportunity to make good use of it, he became a benefactor of his fellow man, and a serenely joyous person.

There was also the poor shoemaker who announced to his friends: "Tomorrow I'm going to be completely happy!"

"How do you know that? Maybe you will break your leg tomorrow."

"Maybe I shall find a fortune, too. Whatever happens is the will of God. And the will of God is my only true happiness—so I'm going to be happy, broken leg, fortune, or whatever comes."

It is, of course, hard not to envy the prosperity of

crooks and swindlers and evaders of the law, but it was always so:

"Behold," goes one of the Psalms, "these are the ungodly who prosper in the world; they increase in riches." But Jesus made it clear that "a man's life consisteth not in the abundance of the things which he possesseth." There are a hundred promises that the wicked shall be overtaken in their wickedness; income tax collectors take graft and are found out; "For they have sown the wind and they shall reap the whirlwind."

Even so, we must feel no hatred. Vengeance is God's, not man's; and we must forgive the trespasses of others if we want our own trespasses to be forgiven; we all share in imperfection:

"Why beholdest thou the mote that is in thy brother's eye, but considerest not the beam that is in thine own eye?" Only he that is without sin among us can "cast the first stone."

Many today fear the world is going to hell in a Cadillac because of widespread indecency and immorality. But there is nothing new in displays of nudity, or of lasciviousness in song and dance and gesture. Isaiah was quite familiar with exhibitionism and incitation to lust.

"Because," said he, "the daughters of Zion are haughty, and walk with stretched forth necks and wanton eyes, walking and mincing as they go, and making a tinkling with their feet. . . ."

Even the pledged servants of God yielded to the fleshpots, notably David. His lust and murder were the subject of a recent Hollywood eructation nearly two hours long; the Bible tells it very simply:

"From the roof he saw a woman washing herself; and

the woman was very beautiful to look upon . . . And David sent messengers and took her . . . And the woman conceived. . . ."

But Joseph, pursued by a licentious woman, was steadfast:

"His master's wife cast her eyes upon Joseph; and she said, Lie with me . . . But he refused . . . How then can I do this great wickedness, and sin against God?"

The grand prophet Jeremiah said of those who corrupt morals and manners: "Were they ashamed when they had committed abominations? Nay, they were not at all ashamed, neither could they blush; therefore they shall fall among them that fall."

But David, king and sinner, was ashamed; he learned to pray: "Renew in me a clean heart, O God; and renew a right spirit within me."

Many are appalled at today's increasing lack of integrity in public life; at the scandals of the last few years, dishonorable behavior seemingly rampant. But the Bible tells us: "Fret not thyself because of evildoers."

Nothing is happening in Washington that did not happen in Judea and Israel. Men took bribes then as now: "Gather not thy soul with sinners . . . In whose hand is mischief, and their right hand is full of bribes." And: "A wicked man taketh a gift out of the bosom to prevent the ways of judgment."

Amos, the prophet, thundered: "For I knew your manifold transgressions and your mighty sins: they afflict the just, they take a bribe, they turn aside the poor in the gate from their right . . . Seek good and not evil, that ye may live."

The stern command of the New Testament against

divorce, "What, therefore, God has joined together, let no man put asunder," is an unwelcome idea to many ears; outmoded and ignored. But the evils of divorce are manifest in increasing juvenile delinquency, and in children growing up without the security of home and the love of father and mother. While the spirit of compromise with moral authority is in the air, the Bible offers comfort but no compromise.

What is the chief reason for juvenile delinquency, for teen-age drug addiction? Is it not that not one child with a bad home background can learn a single word of God's love and wisdom in public school? On this point, the Bible is explicit:

"Suffer little children to come unto me, and forbid them not, for of such is the Kingdom of Heaven."

Jesus might have been speaking directly to those who sell drugs to children, when he said: "It were better for him that a millstone were hanged about his neck, and he be cast into the sea, than that he should offend one of these little ones."

As for labor-management strife, the Bible flatly declares the laborer to be worthy of his hire, but it also reminds laborers, managers, everybody, to be diligent: "Whatsoever your hand finds to do, do it with all your might," and "Seest thou a man diligent in his business? He shall stand before kings." Hundreds of texts celebrate the rewards of hard and faithful work—"the sleep of a laboring man is sweet."

Racial and religious intolerance are very ancient evils: "The Egyptians might not eat bread with the Hebrews, for that is an abomination unto the Egyptians."

The wrongness of that was made clear in the Proverbs: "He that is void of wisdom, despiseth his neighbor." And

Malachi said: "Have we not all one father? Hath God not created us? Why do we deal treacherously every man against his brother?" St. Peter, after a vision, cried out: "God hath shown me that I should not call any man common or unclean."

Greatest of modern villains are indifference, atheism, cynicism and despair, all leading up to the grim question: "Is life worth living?" and sometimes to the final ruin of suicide.

Of indifference, Isaiah complained: "They regard not the work of the Lord, neither consider the operation of his hands." But Paul held up a higher ideal: "Whatsoever things are true, whatsoever things are honest, whatsoever things are just, whatsoever things are pure, whatsoever things are lovely, whatsoever things are of good report; if there be any virtue, if there be any praise, think on these things."

Atheism itself is as old as the Bible. In earliest days, men were saying, "Who is the Lord that I should obey His Voice, and what profit should we have if we pray to Him?"

"Lo," said Jeremiah, "they have rejected the word of the Lord and what wisdom is in them?" The same question is provoked by the state of the world today. For the fool still says "in his heart there is no God." Against such folly and despair, words spring like lightning from the ancient text:

"What doth the Lord require of thee but to do justly, and to love mercy, and walk humbly with thy God." And: "If ye had faith as a grain of mustard seed, ye might say unto the sycamore tree, Be thou plucked up by the root, and be thou planted in the sea; and it should obey you."

But what if you have not faith? What if you can't make yourself believe?

A man in St. Mark gave the answer when he prayed in the midst of doubts: "Lord, I believe; help Thou mine unbelief." His example has been for many a man since the way to find faith, instead of jumping out of the window.

It is still true, as Isaiah told us: "Thou wilt keep him in perfect peace, whose mind is stayed on Thee." And: "They that wait upon the Lord shall renew their strength; they shall mount up with wings as eagles; they shall run and not be weary; they shall walk, and not faint."

Fears of disease, of death, disturb many. But every day we are learning anew that the miraculous healings performed by Jesus during his ministry and reported in the New Testament (the very shadow of St. Peter made people well) are being repeated not only at the shrines of the devout, such as Lourdes, but in modern hospitals, where psychosomatic medicine is opening the minds of materialists to forces deeper than they know, forces reached only through faith. The world of today is coming to realize what David knew in his wonderful 103rd Psalm: "Bless the Lord, O my soul, and forget not all His benefits. Who forgiveth all thine iniquities, who healeth all thy diseases."

And David answered the deeper fear: "Yea, though I walk through the valley of the shadow of death, I will fear no evil; for thou art with me; thy rod and thy staff, they comfort me."

More than merely giving comfort, the Old and the New Testaments call upon man for a positive dynamism; they urge him to lead a life that is hopeful and constructive.

St. Paul, writing to the Ephesians, said: "Brethren, be strengthened in the Lord and in the might of His power. Put on the armor of God, that you may be able to stand against the wiles of the devil. For our wrestling is not against flesh and blood, but against the Principalities and the Powers, against the world-rulers of this darkness, against the spiritual forces of wickedness on high. Therefore, take up the armor of God, that you may be able to resist in the evil day, and stand in all things perfect. Stand, therefore, having girded your loins with truth, and having put on the breastplate of justice, and having your feet shod with the readiness of the gospel of peace, in all things taking up the shield of faith, with which you may be able to quench all the fiery darts of the most wicked one. And take unto you the helmet of salvation, and the sword of the spirit, that is, the word of God."

More and more thinking people are beginning to read the Bible. The experience will bring wisdom to any life and bless it. The entire Bible can be finished in a year, simply by reading three chapters every weekday, and five every Sunday—a devout practice of many persons in my boyhood.

Its origins are vague and lost in the mists of ages. It has been pieced together from fragments of clay cylinders found in the rubble of cities lying under the ruins of other cities, dead towns piled on dead towns, precious fragments plucked from debris. Some of the noblest prose of literature comes down to us imprinted on the dried inner skins of beasts, or on old papyrus leaves, or chiseled in marble from vanished quarries. It is made up of the works of many men, of many kinds and of many times, spanning 5,000 years. Some of those authors were kings and others slaves; they were shepherds and prophets, some learned in the lore of various civilizations from Egypt to Babylon; others poor and unlettered, yet chosen somehow, mysteriously, to utter the divine purpose.

Although they lived hundreds of years apart, there is a consistency in their message, a central and unvarying teaching which, from the closing gates of Egypt to the fallen wall of Jerusalem, proclaims the hope for the redemption and perfection of man. No philosophers since those days have been able to improve on that.

In the midst of human troubles, man, woman, and child can go to the Bible and read such words as those spoken by Jesus before he left the world:

"I will not leave you comfortless."

"Peace I leave with you, my peace I give unto you; not as the world giveth, give I unto you. Let not your heart be troubled, neither let it be afraid."

"Lo, I am with you always, even unto the consummation, the end of the world."

Once, on Fulton Oursler's last voyage, a long idyllic sail to South Africa, a man walked up to him and asked abruptly: "What's your favorite Bible verse?" Without an instant's hesitation the answer came softly: "Matthew 25:40."

It is a verse he never quoted, never wrote about.

The man came back after dinner—he and a number of others had looked up the text. "Why in all those pages of beauty and wisdom would you pick that?" he demanded. "Just as a guarantee of a good last Judgment and Heaven?"

"Partly," nodded F. O. with a grin. "I know a bargain when I see one. But because it makes charity glori-

ous. To think I'm doing something for Him. Giving Him something. Helping or encouraging Him. That's staggering. Then again, it's one way of never wanting human gratitude. You've had a noble privilege. And finally, but most important, it makes me sharply aware that the most hopeless person is identifiable with God Himself, a point that's shockingly easy to forget."

THIS I BELIEVE

NEW YORK, 1952

I BELIEVE in the power of faith, and in the power of love. As I see it, all the achievements of man flow from these two great rivers of strength.

I am often asked how faith took command of my life. It is a simple story. For years I had lived as a contented agnostic. Then, on a tour of Palestine, I was suddenly overwhelmed by two thoughts. First, I saw that we could never make the world safe for democracy unless and until we had a citizenship of high integrity and character, worthy of the freedoms of democracy. Second, that Jesus Christ was at once the teacher and the Exemplar of the life of integrity. I decided then to write a life of Christ in popular language to reach the masses. I studied hundreds, perhaps a thousand books. All my studies brought me nearer to the Master. Soon my heart was on fire with faith and now the flame is brighter every day.

The various dictionary definitions of faith confuse me. But I have always known, instinctively perhaps, what faith means to me: not a credo but a blessed assurance; neither belief, nor hope, but knowledge. When I was a child, I knew that father and mother were good and kind. I did not have to believe that they were; my faith in them was complete, because of my experience with them every day.

So it is with my faith in God. The assurance is complete and, for me, there is no doubt, because of daily experience.

The logician will demand to have the matter proved —with evidence of the laboratory and slide rule. But I am content with Saint Paul's definition of faith: the substance of things hoped for, the evidence of things not seen.

Still, how can I know what I have not seen? There was a man in the Bible who wanted to believe, who almost believed, but was beset by reservations. He made an honest prayer: "Oh Lord, I believe; help Thou mine unbelief."

Theologians tell me Faith is a gift. I think it is a gift that can be asked for, as this earnest old Biblical character asked for it. It can be worked for.

As for love, it is for me the open door to faith, the only approach to truth. The practice of love brings me the awakening knowledge and conviction of faith.

How do I practice love? It is so easy for one to give a coin or write a check against people's misery. But love is not giving money. It is giving myself. I must minister with my own hands, reach out and give some personal help to someone, not just occasionally but every day. And I must go out of my way to do it, not in the mood of a Lord Bountiful, but with tenderness. Such love begins with the person who is nearest to me at this moment; it knows no end, anywhere. All living responds to tenderness.

The potency of love and faith has transformed my life. In them lies my only true security. Embracing them,

I confront the universe unafraid. I know, then, it is a good universe, and friendly. I know this even when disaster overtakes me and sorrow overwhelms me and I feel I have deserved neither sorrow nor disaster. Nevertheless, because my faith in God is a sure knowledge, I trust in Him even in anguish, even without understanding.

So I am strengthened even by misfortune; my sympathy deepens, all of my forces quicken, and I become—or try to become—an even more ardent servant in the good cause, the value and meaning of my life raised to a new level of effectiveness.

This was broadcast, from a recording, and published for the syndicate and radio feature of the same name, two months after Fulton Oursler's death. It is, therefore, what, to his fellow man, were his last words.